In *Literature, Art and the Pursuit of Decay*, Timothy Mathews examines work by a range of writers and painters working in France in the twentieth century. The well-illustrated book engages with canonical figures – Guillaume Apollinaire, Marguerite Duras and Jean Genet, Roland Barthes, Pablo Picasso and René Magritte – as well as more neglected individuals including Robert Desnos and Jean Fautrier. Mathews draws on psychoanalysis, existentialism and poststructuralism to show how both literature and fine art promote the value of generosity in a culture of anxiety and intolerance. Decay emerges as a surprising ally in this quest because of its ability to undermine intellectual complacency and egoism. Integrating theoretical and material approaches to reading and viewing, Mathews engages with the distinctive features of different literary genres and different types of painting to develop an original history of artistic ambition in twentieth-century France.

TIMOTHY MATHEWS is Professor in the French Department at University College London. He is the author of *Reading Apollinaire: Theories of Poetic Language* (1987) and co-editor of *Violence, Théorie, Surréalisme* (1994). He is co-editor of Bloodaxe *Contemporary French Poets*.

CAMBRIDGE STUDIES IN FRENCH 66

Literature, Art and the Pursuit of Decay in Twentieth-Century France

Literature, Art and the Pursuit of Decay in Twentieth-Century France

TIMOTHY MATHEWS

CAMBRIDGE
UNIVERSITY PRESS

PUBLISHED BY THE PRESS SYNDICATE OF THE UNIVERSITY OF CAMBRIDGE
The Pitt Building, Trumpington Street, Cambridge, United Kingdom

CAMBRIDGE UNIVERSITY PRESS
The Edinburgh Building, Cambridge CB2 2RU, UK   www.cup.cam.ac.uk
40 West 20th Street, New York, NY 10011–4211, USA   www.cup.org
10 Stamford Road, Oakleigh, Melbourne 3166, Australia
Ruiz de Alarcón 13, 28014 Madrid, Spain

First published 2000

Printed in the United Kingdom at the University Press, Cambridge

Typeface Monotype Dante 11/13pt.   *System* QuarkXPress™ [SE]

A catalogue record for this book is available from the British Library

Library of Congress cataloguing in publication data
Mathews, Timothy.
Literature, art and the pursuit of decay in twentieth-century
France / by Timothy Mathews.
   p. cm. – (Cambridge studies in French)
Includes bibliographical references and index.
ISBN 0 521 41970 0 (hardback)
1. France – intellectual life – 20th century.   I. Series.
DC33.6.M33 2000
944.081 – dc21   00-029262

ISBN 0 521 41970 0 hardback

Contents

Illustrations

Acknowledgements

Translations of quotations in French are given in the notes. The majority of these are taken from the English versions detailed in the notes. In some cases, I have adapted these translations. Where no details are given, the translation is my own.

Versions of chapters 1 and 3 have appeared respectively in the *Journal of the Institute of Romance Studies* 1 (1992), and in *Jeu surréaliste et humour noir*, edited by Jacqueline Chénieux-Gendron and Marie-Claire Dumas (Paris, 1993). I am indebted to Jacqueline Chénieux-Gendron for inviting me to the CNRS, Paris, as *chargé de recherches* in 1992, during which time much of the early thought that has gone into this book was developed.

Jenefer Gross has been an invaluable assistant to me in all the aspects of getting the manuscript of this book ready for publication. Jonathan Carr-West has supported me with enormous energy in the final stages of preparing the typescript. Only they will know how indebted I am to them both.

I would like warmly to thank Patrick ffrench, Sarah Kay, Michael Moriarty, Morag Shiach and Michael Worton for reading versions of the essays that make up the intellectual journey of this book; and especially Michael Worton for his generous support during the concluding stages of this writing. Malcolm Bowie has been not only an exceptionally patient editor, but a uniquely responsive one as well.

In nameless ways, once again, this book goes out towards Patti, Sonny and Guy.

Prologue: form and decay

I

One of my earliest impressions of reading is of listening to books I do not understand. Whether of *Alice in Wonderland* or *Winnie the Pooh*, the reading in this memory is addressed principally by my father at my brother; the books are not of my age though I am being lovingly or indulgently included in the event. The words have an odd resonance which I imagine has remained with me since, word and sound wrap me in a security blanket made largely of my own silence; an uncomfortable cocoon nurturing the language that I am given to speak.

I realise now, with all the clarity of hindsight, that many of the issues raised by this anecdote are pursued in these essays: reading; generosity and exclusion; intimacy and coercion; the revolt and determinism acted out in reading. But why France? I suppose that given an ear for the word such as I have just described, it is easy to chart the journey of my interest in both literature and images not drawn from my native culture, my pursuit of the places and stories lying behind my parents and from there, paradoxically, to some striving for a thinking and a speaking place of my own. But in any case, a fascination with France hardly needs any explanation of that kind, though the indeterminacy of living in English and working with French has given me much to think about in writing the essays that are my chosen form of expression in this book. To be immersed in the arts and the intellectual life generally of France is to be exposed to many of the dominant cultural developments in Europe: the Renaissance; Cartesianism and deconstruction; the Enlightenment and the Romantic counter-charge; Cubist brutalisation of appearance and Surrealist contempt for it; postmodernist downgrading of vatic empires. At the same time, paradox and lack of direction seem to proliferate and make a mockery of any definite trajectory or the attempt to impose one – any education we might glean from France can only be characterised, it seems, by the notorious 'défaut de ligne droite' that Frédéric suffers from in *L'Education sentimentale*. Montaigne writes the authentic self only to add to the tower of Babel he abhors and adores; Corneille seeks heroism and discovers the bureaucrat; Baudelaire frankly pursues beauty in decay; and Proust, at the very moment of synthesis and resolution, reminds us of what the mind can never capture of its own flights, and enjoins us to read his enormous work over again, or even to imagine a wholly different one in tracking down the secrets of our souls.

This combination of discovery and hazard, fanfare and disharmony is a dominant feature of the new Renaissance that is twentieth-century modernism in France. I still find it striking to think of the chance encounters that mark the lives of so many of the participants in this polymorphous innovative mesh. Having introduced Picasso to Braque, triggering in that way the great Cubist upheaval of mimesis, Apollinaire, now invalided out of the Great War, meets Philippe Soupault in the Café de Flore and says to him of Breton: 'Vous êtes faits pour vous connaître.' The unpretentious spontaneity with which two such major investigations of perception and unconscious impulse are set in motion is a constant reminder of the confidence and the idealism characteristic of art not only in France but in Europe from the turn of the century to the outbreak of World War II. But the stakes are high, the ambitions elusive, the prospects of failure as troubling to artists as they may be disappointing to viewers and readers.

Impatience with the old and pursuit of the new in French art has taken its place in the diaspora of such approaches not only in Europe but in North America, not only in the arts themselves but in critical debate. Many would still argue that promises of innovation have flattered only to deceive. Much disappointment has emerged with the hopeless and hapless ambition to change the world through art; and with the disintegration of that ambition into formalism on the one hand and relativism on the other. Distinctions between the modern and the avant-garde and even the postmodern seem to tumble into so many ruins faced with what has developed into a barrage of disappointment in the apparent incapacity of any self-consciously contemporary art to deal adequately with the dominant cultural and political issues of its time.

In *The Waste Land*, T. S. Eliot seems to have handed on to us not only a canonical moment in modernist innovation, but also a focal point in the disaffection it triggers. The poem offers a freedom of poetic expression unparalleled in 1926, the year of its publication, a breadth of focus powerful enough in itself, perhaps, to reorientate the mind and the heart. But *The Waste Land* is also a testimony to a sense of woeful and wilful isolationism at the heart of its own practice and artistic practice at large. The plurality and the cultural diversity of the voices involved in the poem is but a performance, it might seem, of Poetry's disintegration into the nomadic and the monadic. The intertextual relations between these bits would seem but another sign of confusion, of the futility of Poetry's attempts to sustain some language with which to speak history and the unfolding of a sense of self. Tiresias the sooth-sayer is now definitively blind and the 'dugs' Eliot gives him appear to signal yet another phase in this *Götterdämmerung*, and not some androgynous power to redraw the boundaries of knowledge and of the imagination.

At another extreme, the collapse of the epic embrace staged by *The Waste Land* triggers a corresponding, equally disaffected, response to the 'modern'. Berated for its obsession with the fragmented and the contingent, conversely it is suspected of insidious, translucent attachments to some 'Grand Narrative'. Symptoms seem to abound of a yearning for the recovery of some synthesis or synthetic form. For a moment, works of art might have seemed able to bring together endings and their beginnings, experiences and their places, voices and the bodies they might call their own. Instead, the poetic grand embrace of our experience seems only to feed us on timorous, insidiously static accounts of history and the psyche.

So the modernist text both in France and in Europe is both criticised for its failure to put bodies in places and martyrised for its efforts to do that. A purely aesthetic or formal investigation of the social and economic relation would seem to affirm nothing but its own impotence faced, say, with two world wars and the vested interests of class and state that drive them. And a formalist investigation of the unconscious emerges all but empty-handed, perhaps, in its fabricated attempts to come to terms with the Holocaust. Oedipus and Julien Sorel seem equally hollow. Furthermore, the alternative prospect of a space free of contamination by myth and narrative, a micro-identity responding impulsively to psychic and informational environments seems to offer that lack of direction which favours only market forces, their emblems and their magnetism. At such a point, postmodernism seems antici-pated by that breathless but immobile energy of Flaubert's sentimental 'edu-cation'.

Brecht's alienation effects have had much to say about the capacity of individuals, either sitting in theatres or faced with the wider spectacle, to break their attachments, to reform their perceptions and reconstruct their identifications. But perhaps these effects' most important lesson is still the one coming at its loudest from *Galileo Galilei* – a message that is the most con-sistently denied. Why should we expect to have heroes able to solve the intractable and dynamic problems of life? Why should artistic expression of any kind perform the heroic task of resolving the contradictions of our social, cultural and psychic experience? If relativity and formalism are in fact to be the life-blood of aesthetic expression in a modernist mode, why should those features be laid exclusively at the door of art? Why should art be solely responsible for provoking these spectres or, ultimately, for laying them aside? On the contrary, might not a new partnership of the relative and the formal allow new and different constructions of place, space and self?

Aesthetic experience is an experience of forms; it is driven by an attempt to reach beyond form, beyond that complacent formalism that is the disappointing legacy of Marcel Duchamp's Dada-ist anti-art. Richard Wollheim, writing on R. B. Kitaj, argues that modernism – and its self-questioning, self-exceeding incarnations as the avant-garde – can be divided into an investigation of art and an investigation of sensation. To distinguish Duchamp from Kitaj in that way allows Wollheim to speculate in highly fruitful ways on the Romantic element in the ambitions of twentieth-century art in Europe. But this continuing face-off of figurative and abstract expression suggests interplay and interaction just as much as opposition and difference. Sensation is sensed as form; not abstracted into form, but breathing in forms that range in their appeal from the bodily, to the perceptual, to the mnemonic, to the psychic . . . To deny this action of form would be merely to elevate sensation to the status of redeemer, to purify it of its vitality, its slipperiness, its ever-presence and its transience – in fact, to formalise it. Equally, to overestimate the power of forms would be to give in without much struggle to the tendency of the mind to deal in certainties, in the different kinds of immobility which, while greasing the wheels of enlightenment, also lower the foundations of entrenchment and authority.

Form and authority are as inextricably linked to one another as subversion and relativity. Blinkered relativity may leave us rudderless and exploitable, with no comment to make beyond the contingent; and yet to fragment is an analytical and rhetorical procedure that allows for new beginnings, new platforms in our self-awareness and its temporality. But fragmentation also signals loudly the hubris of its own ambition not only to make new beginnings but to create, and to assert that God-like independence we mourn so consistently and on which we nevertheless depend to function at all in the real world of the relative. Much French writing has thrived on the lessons to be learnt and unlearnt from this range of ambivalences. From the investigative essay writing of Montaigne, to the dilettantish essayism that one of Nerval's narrators is accused of indulging in, to the enormous continuity of memory and its interruptions that is the writing of Proust, and up to the erotic pull of the broken up that is put on display in Barthes, the unfinished and the dispelling of endings have made possible a sense that experience may be laid bare, or at least come to terms with on unfamiliar grounds, elucidated beyond the coercions of expectation and habit.

Such aspiration in French writing and art depends on a specifically textured practice of reading or looking, a hermeneutics of textual place, an open-ended but involved encounter between text and those to whom it is offered. To insist, as I shall be doing in these essays, that the text can act as an arena for engagement with questions of identity and its representation, is neither to seclude texts in a retrogressive delusion of their own autonomy, nor to extend their spheres of influence beyond measure, beyond the compass of any temporal or social context or conflict. The amorphousness of the textual approach does make it resistant to the particular qualities of any one reading or analysis, and also to the limits of context; but resistant also to appropriation and censorship. And that same amorphousness makes the text the site of its own invasion, its own dispelling or vaporisation at the hands of those moments in history and discourse, those moments in subjective and affective life that it seeks to engage with. To designate as 'text' is to dissolve the authority needed to designate. Looked at in this way, a text is able to perform its own protest against formalist and formalised complacency, if not necessarily its own immunity to that; and its own protest against the smooth passage from such complacency to fantasies of autocracy and the incitement to pursue them.

Imagining texts involves an economy of some kind, then. An all-too-familiar experience of exchange, perhaps, of trying at so many levels – symbolic, egoistic, amorous, imaginary – to get some return on the investments of energy and pain demanded in the social domain. But this economy stretches over a terrain which, though still a terrain with boundaries, is continually shifting and changing shape. Creativity is a crucial part of that economy, demystified from the Freudian analysis of the ego and its incurable discontents to the postmodernist dismay at the vicissitudes of individualism, in the light of which notions of creativity seem to serve merely as a set of nostalgic bulwarks. But the ego will not let go, it does not recover from those discontents but clings to them, even in the Lacanian manhandling of its misreadings and acquisitive cognitions. This working insight forms the basis of the Lacanian theory of the Imaginary, under whose spell Barthes thinks and writes so consistently, and which he develops through his reading of Sartre among others. This book will also fall under that spell to the extent that it will seek to examine some of its qualities and effects, and the shrouds it envelops us in. But the essays that follow also endeavour to remain alert to hope as it is rekindled, the spectacular hope reigniting in French art and thought that these mantels of imaginary response might fray or blow off or decay, or be given new life.

And yet the impulse to drive the many through the channels of the one seems indomitable; it is that same indispensable impulse which seeks out ways of dealing with the diffuse, the incomprehensible or the yet-to-be-understood, as well as the traumatic. Such impulse has no source, but thrives on traces of projects and failures. Well-known as such traces are to the procedures of deconstruction and structural psychoanalysis, they are just as active in the multitudes of encounters, in the specks of image, dialogue and solitude that make up experience at its most transitory; and just as active again in the insidious magnitude of the dominant idea or model. These traces and imprints are what I mean by form; and it is for that reason that responses to form will have such a leading role to play in the essays that follow.

The plastic adaptability and malleability of form seem inexhaustible, especially but by no means exclusively in French art: the exuberant inconsistency of Balzac's narrative voices; the mobile narrative silences with which Flaubert sketches in the air affective responses of all kinds from adoration to revulsion; let me mention as well the magnificent stagings of impassioned commitment married to inconsequence orchestrated by Puccini; and the simultaneous joy and despair displayed by Barthes at the fragment, at the incompletion it offers as well as the resumption of rhetorical and imaginary power it warns against. George Santayana has written that knowledge is not an embrace but a salutation; form, like knowledge, is both. Alternately tyrannical and generous in the impulses it stages, form gives voice and place to the passion, the malice, the collaboration and the abdication . . . that make up the relations of an 'I'.

If art consists in formal play, then it meets non-art at every corner. Such is the mark left in the mind by André Gide and Marcel Proust amongst so many other French writers. Formal awareness need not involve withdrawal from the issues of the day and the sensations of the body. It may also signal the efforts of the mind to draw on experience and the range of projects and memories that each one of us carries forward through time: a process that produces mobility rather than stability, prompts further readings, further platforms of foresight and hindsight and their collapse. Form consists in the form taken by an idea – any idea, even the idea of a word or a sensation; and art is then a balletic mimesis, a dance in the dark with the brilliant shadows of our identifications, their power as well as their hollowness. The death of the author proposed by Barthes at the beginning of the postwar textual revolution emanating from France has not involved the death of the subject. Neither postmodern euphoria nor the systematic suspicion that illuminates thinking on gender have displaced the subject as a privileged focus of speculation and fascination, of speculation about fascination. Rather than dismembering the subject, dispelling the spectres of intentionality has re-immersed subjectivity in an indefinite range of symptoms and signifiers. For practitioners and critics to espouse anti-art in any antagonistic way is to tilt at windmills, to imagine a beyond to discourse that few would claim it has the capacity to produce, and which in any case would be as illusory as the power of knowledge generally to embrace and to hold.

Marcel Duchamp and Francis Picabia perhaps still more brutally know how to distinguish between the clockwork and the enigma of their art; but this is juxtaposition rather than burial, a broken or suspended dialogue rather than an escorting from the stage. This face-off involving fabrication and detritus has the capacity to lay identifications bare, or if not those, then the idea of them, if not that then the appeal of them, or the horror of them, or the tyrannies and even the disappearance of them. Art does not evaporate when it is invaded by the arbitrary, nor when anything and everything can be designated as art at a Dadaist stroke. Art does not have that utopia in its gift. On the contrary, the malleable quality of aesthetic forms is itself a performance of an indomitable imaginary power to adapt to the novel and to the unknown, a power woven out of both shedding and assimilation, a power that absorbs the new and the vital exactly to the extent that it gives it form, which mobilises, but also recognition, which stabilises.

Such concerns, specific to much French art and thought of the last century, link up that art with parallel developments in the rest of Europe. Take Damien Hirst's *Shark*. It clings to the notions of art by its place in the gallery and in the columns of art criticism. But such a place has been eliminated from the work itself, which constructs a dynamic exclusion zone for itself out of shark carcass suspended in formaldehyde. But if only through the refractions of the glass box that houses this chemical sarcophagus, as well the striking cleanliness of its surfaces that also signal a green knot of depth, Hirst's object probes its way into some of the dominant crisis points of its day: the urge to imprison, environmental pollution, the technological and philosophical violence with which humanity establishes its domain.

This piece as well as others by Hirst continues the project initiated by Duchamp's *The Bride Stripped Bare* of having the surface tension of an external form picture the internal, behind-the-scenes mechanisms that produce such a surface and hold it in place. In *Shark* that surface is displayed for the appearance of a surface it projects, a surface appearance which covers not only that range of issues I have just mentioned (it is not just a thematic surface), but the capacity to think them, and to think them all in the same intellectual sweep. The vitality and appeal of this formal, imaginary breadth and breath comes from the spontaneous mobility it gives to the eye and the mind.

But on the other hand, this mobility is also formed in a codifiable context, one that begins in that way to show its seams and to disintegrate – despairingly perhaps, or insouciantly – into its constituent elements, to lose its range and deftness, and even glamour and to *show that loss*. Like innumerable, magnificent, courageous works from the past, Hirst's piece is addressed at what is not known or what apparently cannot be known. Picturings, forms and surfaces, whether inside out or eyes front, have that power to extend beyond their own textual properties without abandoning them or succeeding remotely in any attempt to abandon them. Textual properties continue to abound uncannily even in the uneasy space of their disappearance. This capacity to invent an inside out, an evaporation of its own terms of reference, provides formal play with the basis of a decay, and of a generosity emerging from that which this book has as its mission to explore.

II

To suggest that there is any one dominant concern in French twentieth-century art might turn out to be a precise example of some of the problems I have just been evoking: the fascinations and silences, the fantasies and despair, the promised land and the exiles, the bold affirmations and stark decay of the image.

Notions of the image seem to invite their own collapse and simultaneously to resist it. Psychoanalysts as well as phenomenologists and poets have thought that in some senses the image acts like a synthesis. Let me take the perspective of psychoanalysis for a moment. In *Civilisation and its Discontents*, Freud acknowledges that synthesis is an integral part of the capacity to think and learn, to grasp the basic principles of body and society. But he goes on to argue that the need to synthesise provokes resentment of the steps in the ladders of authority that learning leaves us no option but to climb. Will this orthodoxy survive and impress, or be dismissed and made to crumble? If the latter, would we then be left in a utopia of pure self-expression, or without any way of intervening in the arbitrariness of experience? Put in these terms of a pursuit of synthesis, the image seems at once appropriative and timorous.

Many poets and artists subscribe to this synthetic quality of the image and all its ambivalences. But what of the stunning exuberance, admired by Picasso and many others, in Velázquez's visualisations of the body in its circumstantial moment? Or Baudelaire's dramatisations of sense, sex and mortality? Or Magritte's silent witness to psychic invasion? Or Picasso's own magnificent account of the endless possible marriages of form and body? In these terms, the image seems adventurous, taboo-breaking, with the power not only to transcend category but to brutalise it: the stuff of invention itself, the springboard of an ability to juggle with the dimensions of life.

As I suggested earlier, notions of *l'imaginaire* in postwar French thought confirm this ambivalent type of response to the image. Put simply, at both the conscious and the unconscious levels, a sense of completion and the pursuit of dominance loses out to messages of exchange, of community, of the Word at large. But competition of this kind easily gives way to coming together; competing against involves not so much competing with but within. To say I is not necessarily to espouse the bitty plurality of social exchange; it is far more, perhaps, to reignite the impulse to singularity, the drive to re-anoint the only true narcissistic One, centre stage, free to name without the interference of others. Knowledge, after all, is built on synthesis renewed, not just shattered; the unconscious is built on repression and not in some dialogue of equals with that process. To be unconscious of the unconscious, to be blind to symptom and codes of all kinds is certainly to exist in an imaginary seclusion and delusion; but is it not also simply to *function* in symbolic exchange and in the jostling for a dominant point of view that makes up any cultural moment?

And if the imaginary – where word is matched to body, or to objects, or to memory – and symbolic – where words breed in the mouths of others – compete only to meet, then this is more than a theoretical nicety. It is a further chapter in the narratives of violence and discontent announced in the Freudian logic and traced in the formal revolts of the French twentieth-century avant-garde that this book deals with. Narcissism is not set aside in such stories, but takes ever new forms, finds ever different places, hide-outs and positions within discourse from which to resume its operations. This narcissism is at the heart of the discontent that Freud diagnoses in civilisation, and which is his bleak answer to the bleak question 'why war?'

Issues of power and dominance and the unrelenting pursuit of them will abound in what I will have to say in these essays. But this is not a book of political philosophy or of cultural theory. I leave to others the rewards of engaging with, say, Althusser's work on a Marxist imaginary, or with a post-colonial imaginary, to take that other example. This book returns to the intellectual tradition in France stretching back from the *nouveau roman* and its vicissitudes in the postwar period, through Breton to Baudelaire and beyond. My revisiting takes on, and takes at face value the belief evident in that tradition that in various ways and with various degrees of confidence, an investigation of the formal properties of aesthetic practice has the power to point the way, at least, to some mobility, to some slack in the constraints of bodily and psychic place. Art may not change the world, but it may give us the power to imagine new beginnings and endings, different stories of exchange and coercion, of bankruptcy or generosity.

Such investment in form reaches beyond formalism, and beyond those critical distinctions I mentioned earlier that have divided modernism from avant-gardism. The twentieth-century French texts, visual and verbal, that this book deals with also reach beyond such divides in their formal examinations of the relation of word to image, image to body, body to sign, sign to authority, authority to exchange. The essays here offer their own kind of history of that formal, textual engagement in France with the psychosocial dramas of the time.

I am not troubled, or have ceased to be, by opening the book with a return to Cubism, that canonical starting-point in the history of the European avant-garde. The focus of my attention has moved to the model. I have become involved here in the tentacles of emulation and the ways in which they manoeuvre, with Mephistophelean vitality, amidst the prospect of some all-pervasive deconstruction of authority that Cubist practice insistently holds out some hope of.

The issue of the model is taken up in chapter 2 through a discussion of the particular fascination of Roland Barthes with things imaginary which is evident from his early writing onwards. The chapter charts a navigation from Barthes's early Structuralist optimism to his later writerly fascination with the volatile, rather wild and unlikely dreams of autonomy and impermeability that for him seem to characterise the tendencies of mind and psyche in response to culture. Each of Barthes's own accounts of these tendencies signals a further pursuit of some resistance to the coercions but also the allures of sense.

It is in that retrospective light that my discussion of prewar French avant-garde practice draws to a close with the two following chapters on Surrealism. In my presentation of Robert Desnos's verbal games as well as of René Magritte's visual ones, the emphasis is shifted away from ludic anarchism in the signifier, away from utopian visions of a mind without repression and a society with no police, and towards the imaginary dimension of that very ambition. At once desperate and inventive, these investigations of the sign feed and fuel the pursuit of a beyond to sense-making, rather than dispelling such an idea and escorting it from the stage. And even if that pursuit were in the end to meet with some kind of success, subverting the conformity of making sense might still leave untroubled the adaptable conservatism of the orthodox and the known.

In its investigation of imaginary, happily intact awarenesses of mentality, sensuality and their boundaries, Barthes's writing is itself made of an intertextual space involving Sartre and Lacan. Perhaps the maleness of this panoply advertises in advance the problems and the impasses encountered in this book: that endless oscillation between the twin mirages of phallic autocracy and a social relation free of the ego. Certainly the poeticised theorising of Irigaray, to take that one salient example from feminist philosophical inventiveness, has opened up the dynamic possibilities of an aroused, sexualised living space of difference, of exchange promoting separation rather than assimilation, of a separateness in dialogue with coming together, but not bound or destined to bring together; an ability to think genders and sexualities, the range of other places of thinking and sensing, without also thinking their antagonism. Barthes's own strategic silence on the subject of his own sexuality signals that same desire for a non-antagonistic mode of thought – 'y-a-t-il une transgression de la transgression?'; and signals also a strategic humility that acts as an antidote to the empire building of his own and of any other discourse. His as well as Irigaray's approach or *Weltanshauung* or rhetoric is a concerted attempt to extricate itself from Antony's heuristic 'I have come to bury Caesar not praise him.' Burial at one level serves only the battle over boundary and the need for it; it resists decay quite as much as bearing witness to it. Ways of accepting decay, or working, writing and imagining with it rather than against it are what the final three chapters of this book are devoted to exploring; and it is a commitment to that idea of decay that I am proposing as a defining feature of postwar development in French avant-gardism.

The idea of decay may be troubling; but it need not be morbid. There is still no more troubling, nauseating, speech-defying occurrence than Nazi atrocity. Jean Fautrier's *Les Otages* deals with that face on. Without blaming the victim or espousing its position, these paintings work in the most starkly material and bodily dimension of that experience and make it over into a platform for undercutting the undeniable, unstoppable, voracious pursuit of a power to asphyxiate. With Fautrier's art, the stage is set in this book for seeking out generosity in discursive, sexual and social relations – a generosity that seeks to set aside even the hubristic ambition to do away with violence; a generosity that seeks instead to work with the existential violences of mortality on the one hand and the demands of socialisation on the other. Duras seeks a way beyond incomprehension and resentment in the sexual relation. Genet seeks passages past the image-fortresses of racialism and colonialism. But these are not purely wilful affirmations; this is not thinking or imagining modelled on the edifice or the secured alternative. A beyond comes from a within; the within of the reader's experience and its scope, but also its passing and its scattering.

Earlier in this Prologue, I set out in polemical terms the ambition for reading that my engagement with French modernism of the last century has committed me to. That polemic develops into a plea in the rest of this book: a plea for reading as translation and transport; for the silent subjectivity discovered every time the eye absorbs word or image; for the imagining of an other 'I' within 'I'; and for the imagining, if nothing more, of a community and a music of collapsing defence.

CHAPTER ONE

Looking and loving: Harlequins in Apollinaire and Picasso

L'amour est nu
Ainsi que tout
Sauf les humains

Et revenu
Se tient debout
Sur ton chemin

Guillaume Apollinaire[1]

Harlequin has exercised a magnetic symbolic power on artists as diverse as Watteau and Verlaine, the performers of the *commedia dell'arte* and Daumier. His suit and his movements give forms to erotic adventure and betrayal, imaginative mobility and thieving, the effects of both money and modernity among many other experiences of life and art, high or low. His catwalking and cat-burglary in amongst the alternately bursting and depleted treasure-chests of mimesis are both seductive and troubling. At one level, both within and external to the canon, the Harlequin is an incarnation of intertextual acquisitiveness and creativity: an enviable position, perhaps, if the Harlequin's scriptwriters can give sight of the strings that hold up their character and make him dance. But an awareness of intertext can induce panic as well as complacency. On the one hand, it encourages a deluded and deluding embrace of all the outposts of our reception in the eyes of others and their memories. But it also pushes us into an infantilising position in relation to language as a labyrinth of effects, systems and associations we will never finish learning about, and in which we will never find a coherent voice. Harold Bloom's anxiety about influence puts readers and writers in the position of seeking to recapture discursive freedom, and diagnoses in that way a fantasy of solipsism born of 'the dread of threatened autonomy'.[2] For Bloom, Poetry has the capacity both to comfort and dispel this fantasy; it is the realm of neither/nor, neither within nor beyond solipsism.[3] Poetry is not secluded in the fantasy that responses come from the inner minds of readers and writers alone; nor are poets at ease with the awareness that their voice comes over in what they and their readers have read, canonised or forgotten.

But this unease, this exile beyond solipsism, at least offers intellectual mobility and not just acquisitiveness. Apollinaire's texts are famous for inventing networks binding Order to Adventure, and for poetic narrators and presenters who act as Apollonian magicians within the dimensions of discourse. And yet these texts cast ubiquity as so many expressions of a rudderless self. This failure of poetic omnipotence is one which brooks no forgiveness. At a moment in Apollinaire's 'Les Fiançailles' of 1908, the male narrator finds memory fructifying autonomously, from the outside, and in that way he is dispossessed of his inheritance in the perception of it.[4] Remembering is present as an invasion here, and this is the price it pays for resisting being transformed into a commodity and having its destiny fixed. In seeking to internalize this unforgivable overrunning of his own uniqueness, the narrator addresses his poetic predecessors and pleads for forgiveness himself:

> Pardonnez-moi mon ignorance
> Pardonnez-moi de ne plus connaître l'ancien jeu des vers
> Je ne sais plus rien et j'aime uniquement[5]

In a neat figuration of repression, Apollinaire's narrator here turns a wiping out of his own power of intervention into a nothingness by which his voice and his affectivity can claim the stage for themselves. Ignorance and the decay of understanding create the possibility of this unique loving that Apollinaire names here – 'J'aime uniquement' – a loving that can meet diversity without being swamped, and which keeps at bay the threat to its own autonomy posed by diversity and difference.

Such uniqueness imagined from within diversity and antecedence is claimed still more aggressively by Rimbaud some thirty years earlier in *Une Saison en enfer* – a text dealing head-on with the structuring of the sense of self at the hands of rhetorical blueprints. 'Mauvais Sang' begins with an obsessive and ironic tracing of imagined inherited features:

> J'ai de mes ancêtres gaulois l'oeil bleu blanc, la
> cervelle étroite, et la maladresse dans la lutte [. . .]
> D'eux, j'ai l'idolâtrie et l'amour du sacrilège.[6]

By developing this perception of cultural inheritance into a hatred of the social organisation in the present, the narrator ironically asserts his independence from the inherited, asserts a self-isolating completeness and intactness: 'Moi, je suis intact, ça m'est égal'.[7] As Nathaniel Wing points out in *The Limits of Narrative*, this statement of indifference is an attempt to withdraw from all difference and to stand outside Oedipal structuring.[8] This sealing over of castration, of the scars of being unwanted and unheard, of the marks on the psyche and manner of the societal implant seems to result only in an alienated disengagement.

> Si j'avais des antécédents à un point quelconque de l'histoire de France!
> Mais non, rien.[9]

The narcissistic rejection of all voices past and present deprives Rimbaud's narrator of any model through which to represent impulses or desires and to intervene in them; the need for dialogue with such a model has all but disappeared and left – 'rien'. But in 'Mauvais Sang' and in *Une Saison en enfer* generally, attitudising at moral decay or at the absence of any stomach or back bone combines with a rhetoric that milks that sense of decay in a futile clinging to a monadic and nomadic linguistic I; both emerge as a defining element of the creativity that Rimbaud constructs for his narrator, and for himself through him. In 'Mauvais Sang' the narrator presents his slovenly complicity with the mythological and ideological given as a product of his *involvement* in his linguistic heritage rather than a rejection of it. Language is thus not simply presented as a dead and alienating weight, but as a construction of identity cemented in the loss of voice. Rimbaud's notorious exhortation to be 'absolument moderne'[10] is an acceptance of the body and the mobile, temporal, futuristic, decaying, ambitious, alienating otherness it immerses us in. And in 'Les Fiançailles', Apollinaire's manufactured, willed uniqueness is also formed in opening out to the diverse and unpredictable: 'je souris des êtres que je n'ai pas créés'.[11] But this smiling acceptance of an 'I' pouring in from without is not an uncomplicated embrace of Rimbaud's 'la réalité rugueuse'.[12] The image of Narcissus in the pool is a mirage, but all its representations foster that mirage; attempts to let it go fuel only resistance and seem to offer only grief.

Such are some of the experiences engaged with in Apollinaire's and Picasso's responses to the *topos* in art of Harlequins, street performers and circus performers, 'saltimbanques'. Insecurity about creative autonomy; a compensation in a kind of desperate seclusion; appeals to an imaginary audience and to a power to predict its reactions. Many of these concerns are manifest in Picasso's *Young Acrobat on a Ball*, completed in 1904/5. It is an instance of Picasso's treatment of the circus-performer motif, but also of the 'blue period' style which dominates his painting at the time. The very idea of circus acrobats suggests audience, though here a paying audience and a definite

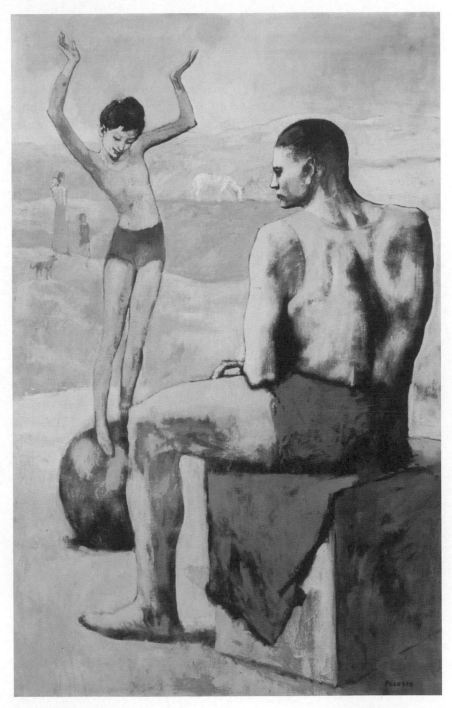

Figure 1 Pablo Picasso, *Young Acrobat on a Ball* (1905). Oil on canvas, 80 × 60 cm.

theatre are absent. The spectator's position is taken up by the large figure in the foreground, who seems to adopt the role of the Master watching the pupil perform his exercises. But the Master averts his eyes, as though unable to bear the grace of his pupil, and the anxiety of influence begins again as the pupil's rehearsal seems to embody canonic knowledge.[13] Moreover, this sense in the Master-figure of his own image, his own embrace of his past and future being under threat of decay, is further expressed in the minimal presence accorded, from his point of view, to the other figures in the picture. The young acrobat has his back to them and is unconcerned. But the Master's gaze, on the other hand, has an indeterminate focus, simultaneously admitting others to the scene and banishing them from it. Moreover, these other figures are those of a mother and children. The combination of these figures with the domesticated horse and dog, and with the Master/pupil duo or the father/son one, adds up to an emblematic family unit which the massive male form in the front of the picture alternately dominates, excludes and is overridden by.

'Will there ever be a relation between the sexes?'[14] Does the Oedipal family allow dialogue or resist it continually? If the acrobat is a boy, the Master's admiration might project an only ever imagined assumption of the boy's maleness, a simultaneous acceptance and an appropriative, imaginary grabbing of sexual difference. But this incorporation by the Master is also corporeal, now he feels his mortality and the mortality of his age as he both watches and refuses to watch the young acrobat, who mimes a magisterial position of his own and improvises the coming of a new generation. But we can also imagine the Master accepting the androgyny of his one-time pupil, responding with averted stare to the surging of an unknown grace able to confuse and reconfigure the available sexual flow. Will this hermaphrodite agility have the power to re-weave a narrative profusion of sex? Or will this very imagining reproduce a sabotaged dialogue, a hallucination of difference caught in the immediate destiny of any image: immobility and silence?

In *Portrait de l'artiste en saltimbanque* Jean Starobinski provides a fascinating account of the poetics developed in treatments of the circus-performer motif: an overview made of the same mobile, self-fragmenting stuff as Harlequin's suit.[15] I would like briefly to take my own refracted look at one of the ways this motif builds up into a figure of poetic influence. Baudelaire's treatment of this topos concentrates a number of its defining elements in ways which anticipate Apollinaire's and Picasso's work. Many of Baudelaire's prose poems, in fact his approach to the prose poem as form, prompt questions of voice, its coherence and dissolution. Barbara Johnson's starting point in her *Défigurations du langage poétique* is the way that, in dialogue with his verse, Baudelaire's prose poems set about ironically disempowering symbolic representations of transcendental fantasy.[16] In 'Le Vieux Saltimbanque', first published in 1861, the *saltimbanque,* the acrobat or trickster, is compared to the artist who has lost both his powers and his audience – a situation which the large figure in Picasso's *Young Acrobat on a Ball* also seems to find himself in and to muse on. In 'Une Mort héroïque', first published in 1863, the mime-actor Fancioulle is dramatically interrupted in his trance-like performance, made aware of his hostile audience, of the limits of his stage and of his art, and is killed by this act of hostility.[17]

But the collapse of the artist's performance in the poem stretches to the performance of the poem itself, which not only sets out the decay of poetic prowess but supports it, implants it in the fabric of prose-poetic voice. The rhetoric of address in these texts fragments the fantasy of lyrical fulfilment. On a purely allegorical level, 'Le Vieux Saltimbanque' might be taken as an expression of an impotent Satanic revolt: the outcast angel lapses into a simplistic aggression that does no more than to invert the categories of the existing moral order. Furthermore, the outcast, the poet/acrobat, claims the status of artistic master simply by virtue of being rejected by the audience. But in Baudelaire's poem, the mobility of the narrative perspective complicates the position of the performer in relation to his audience. The narrator is both part of the crowd enjoying the fair, and separated from the crowd by his own discourse of observer, disengaged 'flâneur', 'raconteur' of 'faits divers' and 'choses vues'. But at the same time, in identifying his own superfluity with that of the decrepit acrobat, the narrator is situating his gaze *within* the crowd and its hostile indifference, and within the amorphous mobility that pushes him along:

> un grand reflux de peuple, causé par je ne sais quel trouble, m'entraîna loin du saltimbanque.[18]

What kind of 'trouble' is this that the narrator refuses to comment on? Is he terrified by the sadism of the crowd, or by his own participation in it? What is his position with regard to authority and orthodoxy? Certainly the backward look directed at the victim suggests an attempt to cast him as a receptacle or a mould into which to stuff creative anxiety. If the narrator identifies with the 'vieux saltimbanque', his position is a masochistic one with regard to antecedence and sequence. On the other hand, if he is swallowed up in the dominating gestures of the crowd, his position is sadistic. Either way, the 'vieux saltimbanque', the model of the poet's pursuit of dialogue, is imprisoned in the networks of address that make up the text.

The sadism and masochism in Baudelaire's poems highlight what is at stake once looking and telling are made to focus on position and positioning. Picasso's *Young Acrobat on a Ball* might still seem to have little to do with the violence, implicit and explicit, in Baudelaire's 'Le Vieux Saltimbanque' or in

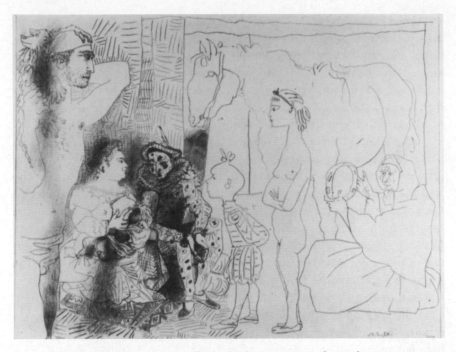

Figure 2 Pablo Picasso, *La Famille du saltimbanque* (1954). Lithograph, 50 × 65 cm.

'Une Mort héroïque', or with the aggressivity characteristic of sadism and masochism. Clearly, some of the most striking features of Picasso's painting are the passive mourning of the heavy seated figure in the foreground, and the grace of the boy, neither of which seem violent. But in *La Famille du saltimbanque*, a lithograph composed in 1954 that is one of many returns by Picasso to the same motif and which focuses particularly on the image of the family, the relations between looking and loving and looking and hating are made apparent.[19] The picture is dominated by looks and by gazing rather than glancing. Here I am picking up on the ways in which Norman Bryson develops this distinction in *Vision and Painting*. Painting of the glance, Bryson suggests, directs itself at the viewer's activity of viewing, comprising perusal, perceptual construction, and the sense of time involved in these. Painting of the gaze, on the other hand, involves a suppression of dialogue, and the pursuit of a moment where the eye can view the world alone, 'severed from the material and from labour'.[20] This picture is permeated by the embattled gaze, and within the dynamic of the text it rediscovers some dominance. The young boy in the centre looks not only questioningly, but aggressively into the eyes of his mother – or of motherhood generally, you might imagine, as the seated figure suckles a child apparently of a different race. She meets the boy's gaze with an aggression he might feel to be still greater than his own.

But in her case, it is an aggression born of the confidence, the contentment that comes with an integration, however figural, of the psychic and the physical, the indefinite and the shaped, the liquid and the contained. The boy's stare seeks to take possession of such integration, he seeks a place in the sexual relation. But the mother's look is a glance, it is a gesture emphatically situated among others, it enacts relation and sexual relation. Preservation of her body and the procreation of others improvise their own harmony. Her glance is predicated on dialogue; it is this performance of life and not death which seems to attract the fascination of the Pierrot to her left, whose look seems to embrace mother *and* child – rather than one or the other – and in particular the meeting of the mother's breast and the baby's mouth. Though at rest here, on stage the clown's act embraces tragedy and comedy, alienation and facility, so that his acting as well as his fascination here in the picture seem to free him from the tyranny of anxieties about origin and completion.

Not so for others in the picture who are not given the positions of clown or motherhood. Father and daughter figures come face to face with each other in an outer circle of the picture. In the pose of artist and Christ simultaneously, the fatherly figure, sequestered in his own gaze and its attempt to suppress temporality, physically dominates and incorporates the mother and child duo which he does not glance at, thus fixing it in an image, even the eclectic one we look at now. The male gaze would wish to keep the daughter and womanhood at large at bay – a necessary part, we would then believe, of male sexual identity. This aggression, however, is met with a look from the daughter that is fixed without being fixated, that accepts dialogue even in giving the appearance of waiting for it perpetually. This mixture of waiting and accepting make up the strands of her grace. Since the figure stands and waits, her sexuality is also presented as given rather than immanent or integrated. The divisions of public and private remain mobile. The face of this figure looks dressed, it seems moulded to the emulation of invisible models; this is also the mark of the young woman's openness and her readiness for dialogue. In contrast, the undressed body waits, momentarily outside fixing and fixation, huddled as well in the sensual mnemonics of self and loss.

What about *Young Acrobat on a Ball*, its own forms of grace and mourning? In Freud's account of it, mourning is not a period of withdrawal from the theatre of human activity, or from difference and sexual difference. It expresses a withdrawal of another kind: the loss of a loved object is experienced as a loss with regard to the ego. The ego withdraws its libidinal attachment to an object now lost, and instead of desiring it, the ego identifies with this lost object. Loss is not itself the source of grief, since for Freud, loss is itself one of the goals in terms of which the ego is structured. The ego is defined in terms of an ideal intention to keep off stimuli. In his *Instincts and their*

Vicissitudes (1915) as well as in the paper *On Narcissism* (1914), Freud argues that in this respect the ego is in conflict with the instincts. The ego's ability to process instincts is much more problematic than its capacity to deal with external stimuli and to dismiss them. Freud writes that 'external stimuli impose only the task of withdrawing from them'.[21] But the fundamental instinct for Freud is to procreate and maintain the species, and this involves the human subject in impulses which cannot be kept at bay. The sexual drive itself is thus a source of conflict with the ego, since it frustrates the ego's drive to individuation.[22] Because of this conflict, the ego is drawn towards a banishment-loving, as Kristeva might say.[23] In mourning and in melancholia, the ego, in identifying with the lost object and ceasing to love it, identifies with loss itself. When identified with rather than desired, loss seems undifferentiated. It seems to demonstrate the possibility that the history of procreation, as well as the grammar of cultural antecedence, might decay into a one-ness to which the ego would be equal and by which it would not be threatened. There is a primary drive in the ego to abolish desire, to recapture libido, to keep it for itself and to turn it on itself. This aggressive self-preservation of the ego, this ego self-love, is the legacy of Freud's narcissism or narcissistic loving.

It is tempting to read *Young Acrobat on a Ball* with this in mind. The grace of the 'boy' owes much of its appeal to the sense that the melancholia of the male audience and the indifference of the female one are both signs of the boy's own autonomy and of his own indifference to external stimuli. Moreover, much of the melancholia of the male figure that dominates the foreground derives from the fact that he averts his gaze from his pupil who, according to the logic of the anxiety of influence, is now the elusive object of his desire. The melancholia of this figure is the price he pays for his refusal to love the boy, for his defensive exclusion of the image of autonomous fulfilment that he and the viewer with him, at this point, grants the boy the power to manufacture.

But the picture does not reveal but figure narcissistic desire. There are no narcissistic references, only positions – just as sadism and masochism are functions of the positions of narrating and being narrated in Baudelaire's 'Le Vieux Saltimbanque'. This dynamic of position provides the 'saltimbanque' topos with much of its drama. This notion of position, and its effects, emerge from Freud's distinction between primary and secondary narcissism. In *On Narcissism*, Freud argues that the primariness of any tendency in the unconscious means that it cannot be 'discovered', only 'recognised'.[24] In the case of narcissism, this means that the primary narcissism of the subject only makes its appearance in the subject's attempt to recover that lost, blissful state of narcissistic wholeness. This lost narcissistic fulfilment is the ideal ego, and to compensate for its loss, the ego constructs a substitute which Freud calls the ego-ideal.[25] As Jacques Lacan underlines in his own seminar on

Freud's *On Narcissism*, this neat play of signifiers – ideal ego and ego-ideal – encapsulates Freud's account of the ego's relation to eroticism.[26] Instead of turning all love on itself and thus destroying it, the ego constructs a new model of wholeness – the ego-ideal – built from those very social and socializing elements that have made impossible our original love – a love that takes two forms, for Freud: the love of ourselves, and the love of the woman who nurses us.[27]

These elements making up the ego-ideal derive from the 'critical influence of [. . .] those who trained him and taught him and the innumerable and indefinable host of all the other people in his environment – his fellow-men – and public opinion'.[28] This indefinite eclecticism of the other removes us from the singular gaze of adoration coming to us as infants from both our parents individually and collectively.[29] These elements make up what we know as our conscience, and it is from this that Freud is able to 'recognise' the secondary narcissism of the ego. For the purpose of the conscience is to return the ego-ideal to the state it enjoyed as ideal ego. 'The ego experiences a kind of estrangement, passing via a middle term, which is the ideal, and returns later to its primitive position.'[30] The ego tolerates the conscience and the blows it inflicts to the extent that conscience casts external stimuli in the form of a gaze directed back at the ego. Structurally, the ego is vulnerable to paranoid delusions of 'being watched' – the ego masochistically espouses paranoia, the weight of the others made other, in that this seems to allow the ego to transform its love of objects into love of itself once more.[31] The infinite range of voices in the mind are translated and transformed into a first person perpetually on the brink of both opening dialogue and suppressing it.

As Lacan stresses in his seminar, the very idea of a return to the primitive or the primary is a form of imaginary illusion. But this illusion is volatile as well as fixating. The imaginary dimension of our psyche allows a sense of completion to be continually manufactured, to be displaced in and as any number of new forms. Thus the ego-ideal, while belonging in the secondary psychic realm dealing with society and the enforced exchanges on which society depends, is also the product of imaginary (re)grouping since it deals in forms, its own formation, its own capacity to adapt its forms and suppress any other that might signal difference or incommensurability or mismatch.

This unresolvable ambivalence of form – adaptable and reductive, generous and aggressive – is acted out in the versified and visualised theatres of Apollinaire's and Picasso's 'saltimbanque' texts.[32] Working with Freud, in his *Painting as an Art* of 1987, Richard Wollheim develops with regard to painting his own distinction between the primary and the secondary. For Wollheim, the primary meaning of painting is its expressive meaning, defined either textually, or historically, or in combination. It is the secondary meaning which concerns me particularly here. The secondary meaning of a painting, Wollheim writes, 'derives from what the act of making a picture means to the artist'.[33] What task does the artist set himself or herself in the meeting of gaze and brushwork? Is she or he turning to the act of looking to fulfil fantasies of ego-omnipotence and autonomy? Is the indefinite variety of possible formal vocabularies forever harnessed to the combustible sterility of imaginary response? Or can we see, in the practice of imitating the material, elements of a resistance to this kind of psychic determinism, however formal or illusory? Must we accept the inevitability of an alternatively sadistic and masochistic entry into culture? Is creativity structurally aggressive, or can it heal? In describing the narcissistic trap, Freud quotes Heine in suggesting that creativity itself is what is needed to dissolve the stagnant networks of self-regard:

> Erschaffend konnte ich genesen
> Erschaffend wurde ich gesund[34]

Such a notion of creativity seems absent from the secondary meanings of Apollinaire's early treatment of the 'saltimbanque' *topos*. 'Crépuscule', included in *Alcools* of 1913, was published in 1909 and coincides with Apollinaire's critical response to Picasso's blue period of which *Young Acrobat on a Ball* is a part.[35] Two motifs predominate in the poem: death and languor on the one hand, mirror images and the subjugation of the audience on the other. In his critical comment subsequently included in *Les Peintres cubistes* of 1913 on these treatments by Picasso of the 'saltimbanque', Apollinaire also brings to bear expressions of death and languor in evoking the infirmity of many of Picasso's figures from the series:

> Ce sont des infirmes, des béquillards et des bélîtres.
> Ils s'étonnent d'avoir atteint leur but et qui n'est plus l'horizon.[36]

The performers are crippled and bedridden, alienated from their own achievements. This collapse of achievement and of expressive power that Apollinaire is fascinated by in Picasso's forms is also evoked in 'Crépuscule'. The female 'Arlequine' is

> Frôlée par les ombres des morts[37]

The other performers are pale, indistinguishable in the twilight, and, crucially, *charlatans*. This sense of performance irredeemably entangled in its own artifice is further emphasized by the characterization of the audience as a group of bored colleagues gathered to watch one of their own go through the tricks of the trade:

Sur les tréteaux l'arlequin blême
Salue d'abord les spectateurs
Des sorciers venus de bohème
Quelques fées et les enchanteurs[38]

The idea of a few fairies dropping in deprives fairies at large of mythological wonder and the enchanters seem merely a familiar and expected part of the routine.

But the Harlequin, with all the harmonies of his self-proclaimed virility, is more dramatic than expected:

Ayant décroché une étoile
Il la manie à bras tendu[39]

He displays a startling ability to manipulate the dimensions of space and time. But juxtaposed with this is an image, derived from Tarot cards, of a hanged man beating symbols with his feet in the last convulsions of death:

Tandis que des pieds un pendu
Sonne en mesure les cymbales[40]

Yet the poem seems to fight back: the Harlequin is magnified into a figuration of Hermes, the messenger of the gods. This reflects what Apollinaire in his comment on these pictures calls the 'agilité difficile' of the circus figures.[41] This difficulty suggests that the role of Hermes as conveyor of messages from gods to mortals has to do with the undermining of prohibition, with a drive to reveal the secrets buried in divine signs, and to make the language of the gods human. But this transgressive energy is met with an indifference which recasts it as a vast overestimation of creative power. The 'arlequin trismégiste'[42] is regarded with ungalvanized sadness by a dwarf-clown:

Le nain regarde d'un air triste
Grandir l'arlequin trismégiste[43]

The rest of the audience to this isolated moment consists of two family formations: the blind parent, sexually indeterminate and passive, nurses a child; the doe passes by with its fawns. Thrice-crowned Hermes is met with indifference, the human and the animal share no common code of reading. In effect, human transgressive myths of omnipotence are met here with an incarnation of everything that threatens this ambition. The blindness of the human parent in the poem

l'aveugle berce un bel enfant[44]

acts as an image of creative anxiety, or a projection of it. Rather than reading signs of his own visionary power in the attitudes of his audience, Hermes is met with a configuration of prohibited vision and a return to infancy. This infantilising prohibition of creativity and of mobility is both affirmed and transformed into a shroud by the way in which the blindness in the poem serves to efface the sex and the role of the parent ('l'aveugle'), obscuring still further our reading of the glances coming at us from the past and which we sense on our bodies.

This melancholia circulates indefinitely in the text. As I said a moment ago, the poem opens with the image of Colombine, the female Harlequin

Frôlée par les ombres des morts

touched by her sense of the dead, by what she has retained from them and by the power this exercises over her. This invasive and sensual touching suggests decay of her own sense of self at the hands of antecedence. But this is a fearful, defensive response, rather than a dynamic one: the Colombine's languor isolates her from stimuli coming at her from the present, allowing an imaginary, restricted integrity as she gazes narcissistically at her own reflection in the pool:

et dans l'étang mire son corps[45]

The appeal of this reflection suggests an idealization of Colombine's own image, a diminished pressure to sublimate trauma and grief. This suggestion is given force by Apollinaire's choice of a poetic form – five-line stanzas of octosyllabic lines – belonging explicitly to his predecessors, and to what in 'Les Fiançailles' he calls 'l'ancien jeu des vers'[46] of Symbolist expression. Paradoxically this choice has the effect of neutralizing the threat of antecedence, or at least of seeking to. The poem's formal immersion in the effects of tradition silences novelty and allows the antecedence carried by prosody to be ignored.

Such a response to models is a dominant feature of the melancholia that circulates amongst Apollinaire's and Picasso's circus figures and the 'secondary meaning' of these texts. The model comprises first theoretical or psychological constructions of an artist's own potency, along with the threat to this potency coming from creative predecessors; and secondly the physical model, object or person, which triggers the desire to capture, to emulate, to move beyond. Is there a way for the Harlequin model to produce some movement beyond the impasse of narcissistic trauma and withdrawal? Is the 'saltimbanque' topos a theatre of this withdrawal or of its passing?

The sense of models provided by predecessors is central to these

'saltimbanque' texts, in that each contains an element of rehearsal, the learning of a part, the adoption of a role, the emulation of the performances of
others. The pressure of antecedence is also reproduced by the intertextuality
of the 'saltimbanque' motif. This applies to the pictorial as well as the visual
texts in the cluster. Picasso's *Family of Saltimbanques* of 1905 is developed in an
intertextual relationship with Manet's *Le Vieux Musicien* of 1862. The
composition of the figures in both cases is organised on the basis of gazes and
glances they exchange, of the anticipated or suppressed dialogues that they
articulate. Picasso is equally vigorous in his intertextual response to Manet's
other more notorious treatment of artistic performance and of the models it
adopts or devours. *Le Déjeuner sur l'herbe*, scandalously received in 1863, is a
depiction of artists at rest with their models, who are cast in relaxed poses
having, we imagine, posed more formally during the artists' session of work.
The position of power granted the male artists could not be more blatant.
They are dressed, they are in conversation with each other, the man on the
right gestures to emphasize his point and underline the rhetorical dominance
of his own narrative. Just as emphatic, however, is the gaze of the female,
unclothed figure in the foreground. It seems unmediated by the frame, it
seems locked into and locked up by the gaze of the viewer. A mutual relationship of fixity and possession is set up between the viewer of the picture, and
the viewer of the viewer, that is, the female model herself.

In *Painting as an Art,* Wollheim discusses Picasso's aggressive attempts,
in his own *Déjeuner sur l'herbe* series, to disrupt this static relation of fascination, and equivalence is subverted in favour of the viewer, of the artist, of the
male artist.[47] In his four series of works devoted to treating the *Déjeuner sur
l'herbe* scene, Picasso, like Manet, emphatically includes representations of
the artist. As Wollheim suggests, in each of the two pairs, both completed in
1961, the artist is cast in the position of authority, a figure who directs. The
figured artists are not just present but engaged in their art. By introducing the
artists in this way, the pictures do more than indicate their own practice, they
give form to the nature of the particular artistic ambition that they seek to
fulfil. These figured artists are instigators of abstract art, that is, they point to
their own power to *rework space.*[48] This reworking not only wards off material
stimuli, it dominates the instinctual sexual drive as it is manifested and manip-
ulated in the forms of the model – the model, that is, of sexual desire. This
domination of the material and the instinctual takes place in the form of the
manipulation of style – and the replacement of one style with another. In the
first pair, the artist is cast in monumental and sculptural forms, and his model
reflects and projects this. But the artist is masked: Picasso seems to return to
his dramatic *Demoiselles d'Avignon* of 1907 and his use of African masks there.
But here, the mask is carried by the artist and not the model, turning him into
the kind of bovine figure that is the seated form in the foreground of *Young*

Figure 3 Pablo Picasso, *The Artist and his Model* (1970). Coloured pencil on cardboard, 22.1 × 31.1 cm.

Acrobat on a Ball. In each case, the massiveness of these figures undermines their assertiveness, complicates the direction of their gaze, obscures their cultural position. On the other hand in the second pair, produced in the following month in 1961, the style is overridingly classical or classicising, reminiscent once again of the grace of the acrobat on the ball as well as of the young woman in *La Famille du saltimbanque*. The figures' classical lines demonstrate the ease in which the artist casts his creative power in this picture. All eyes are fixed on him, and his own gaze escapes definition in relation to any particular object. The gesture of his hand seems to manipulate the poses and responses of others. It also manipulates with equal stylistic mastery its own intertextual infrastructure which takes the form of allusions to Rembrandt's *Woman Bathing* (1655) and to Cézanne's *Les Grandes Baigneuses* (1895–1906) as well as to *Le Déjeuner sur l'herbe*.

But this magnificent freedom with which the artist in this picture manipulates the impressions that come to him of his own make-up and his own ambition might still not take us that step beyond art as acquisitive and aggressive I promised a moment ago. But there is an element in the dialogue of artist and model, in the mediation that it gives form to, of moving beyond. The fifth in the series of pictures entitled *The Artist and his Model*, which Picasso produced in 1970 and which Wollheim also discusses, is characterised by the same classicising freedom of line as the second pair of

'Déjeuner' drawings and the earlier 'saltimbanque', acrobat pictures. But in the case of the artist represented here, the agility in which he is cast is in ironic tension with the expression it also projects of anxiety and depression. Moreover, the canvas on which he paints, seen from the side, represents a bar dividing the image of the female model we all see, from the signifiers the artist attempts to construct, and which we do not see. The painting in the painting, since its own status as signifier is emphasised, along with that of the picture as a whole, puts the model back in the public domain along with the artist's own private fascination with her. The bar of the side of the picture in the picture is a stark demonstration of sexual difference, and gives rise to an idea of art that declines a sadistic devouring of its models and their confusing allure.

Picasso further demonstrates or represents this mediated capacity to create in one of his last pictures; here, to paint is not just to model but to imagine a painting able to embrace without throttling the bodies and the eyes of others, their power and their decay. In *L'Etreinte*, painted in 1969, the phallus is formally presented in such a way as to be sourceless, as not belonging to one body and not to another; it is an object of desire *because* it is an object of exchange, an object of sourceless provenance and mobile, airy destination. And it is the manipulation of form in the picture as a whole which produces this mobility of the phallus.

Formal plasticity has acquired the power to take artist and viewer – or the imagining by each of the other – from idealisation of the self, from an over-estimation of the ego's creative potency, to a corporeal and psychic absorption of trauma, to an openness to the division, loss and decay germinating in the spasmodic, orgasmic embrace. The love of others is here not a prize but an offering, a gift the picture might educate both artist and viewer in accepting. The painting represents a *jouissance* of form, and through form, of a materiality in which form has drowned. The painting expresses an appetite for materiality, rather than the attempt to master it which Picasso dramatizes in his *Déjeuner sur l'herbe* series. Formal plasticity in this picture makes two bodies one, but this is a oneness fragmented in the evenness of emphasis of each plane making up the picture. Narcissistic wholeness is formally broken up. But at the same time, the forms which articulate this fragmentation are those which retrigger a formal, imaginary pursuit of a body sensed as intact and secure in its boundaries and outlines. The stunning ability of the picture to manipulate bodily forms itself suggests an obliteration of the distinction between two-dimensional painting and three-dimensional sex. In the mind and the image, paranoid delusion finally meets its elusive goal of omnipotence. But ultimately this matching up is not granted us by looking at the picture; looking is fragmented into any number of glances and in this we the viewers as a non-group and non-community recognize sexual desire

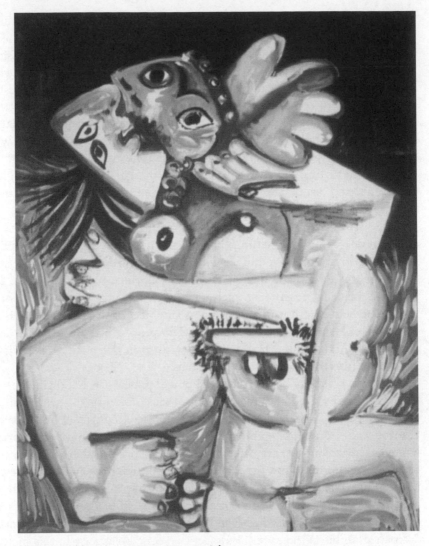

Figure 4 Pablo Picasso, *L'Etreinte* (1905). Oil on canvas, 162 × 130 cm.

without naming it or taking possession of it. The signifier alienates by implanting desires whose energy remains impenetrable; forms ensnare us in a hallucinatory flow of knowing and having. But within this economy of signifier and narcissistic nostalgia, this picture reinvents the love of others.

But of what kind? Any formal play has a provenance – intellectual, inter-textual, subjective – that specifies it, that enriches and diminishes its effects in equal measures. Part of the formal magnificence of Picasso's *L'Etreinte* is its ability to display its debts – particularly to what Picasso had kept from his Cubist inventions, which themselves mark a fundamental turning-point in his pursuit of painterly freedom. Apollinaire's pleasure in developing Cubist theory is equally apparent.[49] And Picasso uses Harlequin-like iconography in his development of Cubist expression and development beyond it. In *Circus Family* and *Harlequin* of 1909, the patterns in the Harlequin's costume are exploited in the creation of a series of fractured planes typical of the various Cubisms that Picasso developed subsequently, and in which he sought to display the processes by which the three dimensional and the bodily are figured in the two dimensional and its fields of vision.

Norman Bryson in *Vision and Painting* argues that Cubism, despite its stark fragmentation of the pictorial surface, traps and immobilizes the visual activity of both the painter and viewer. In this early work, Bryson acknowledges that a Cubist artefact involves an emphasis on transitional phases in the pictorial appropriation of objects, none of which is granted authority over the other. But he goes on to argue that within the Cubist artefact, each phase, that is each figuration of planes the viewer chooses to focus on, functions 'obliteratively' in relation to others.[50] The notion of the picture as sequence is banished, carrying us back into the myth of a founding position and a founding perception or perspective, and trapping viewers in a passive viewing attitude. Looked at in this way, Cubist artefacts would invite withdrawal from objects, a warding-off of the hand of friendship and engagement extended by objects and bodies. Cubist artefacts would in that case encourage egoistic seclusion and melancholia.

But by tracing the obliteration of successive planes of viewing, Cubist painters find as many ways to represent the experience of seeing, the sensations of seamless perusal. In looking, we select and group. There is no pure sequentiality, neither is there uncontaminated deferral. This is further explored in the practice of collage to which Picasso also brought the Harlequin motif to bear – in his *Harlequin* of 1915 and his *Harlequin with Violin* of 1918, for example. By making recognisable forms out of bits of paper and other bits acquired from different contexts, collage artefacts invite us to wonder about the decipherability of context at large. The diamond shapes on the Harlequin's suit offer a series of visual hinges that allow positions or moments in viewing to be explored, as well as the temporality of them and even their forgetting; one juxtaposition of visual elements succeeds another, each new one adding to the harmonics of viewing while displaying a further entanglement in the subjective associations that have built up in this way. The Harlequin hovers, implodes along the invisible border-line of shared and private vision. Conversely, the cultural cloak of the Harlequin floats from the recognisable, the culturally coded, into the intimate reverberations of looking and remembering. The mythological impact of the Harlequin – Hermes-figure, acrobat, puppeteer as well as puppet – is formally explored by Picasso for the fascination it solicits, but also for the power of his Cubist work

Figure 5 Pablo Picasso, *Harlequin avec violin ('Si tu veux')* (1918). Oil on canvas, 142.2 × 100.3 cm.

with Harlequin to renew its own models and to loosen its own compositional grip on them. An art develops around the Harlequin, carried on not only from Baudelaire but also from Daumier, of a creativity grounded in its own loss and its own dispersal, in an estrangement that is the price and the joyous prize of offering viewers the freedom of the visual space, and of Harlequin's balletic entwining of spontaneity and emulation.

Apollinaire's 'Un Fantôme de nuées', first published in 1913 and included in *Calligrammes* which appeared in 1918, is a kind of tribute to this modernism: any pretension to reinvent art has gone, narrators and spectators merely try and tell the stories of how they have been changed and affected. As opposed to the voiceless stasis of 'Crépuscule', this poem is narrative and also mobile in its narrative perspectives. The first-person male voice that guides us through seems to shed specificity as he moves in and out of the 14th of July crowd that has gathered, and he adopts a variety of different kinds of rhetorical distance. The wandering position of the narrator merges with the figure of the wandering artist and the wandering Jew. The narrative mobility of the text gradually focuses on a boy among a troupe of street performers that is attracting interest. But the boy's performance, as opposed to the narrator's, cannot begin until the bargaining for money is complete. The fact that less is paid than the performers hoped for saddens them, not because of any sense that their art is reduced to an unvalued commodity, but because it suggests a lack of audience involvement. Bargaining, here, not only involves the marketing of generosity, but the tacit acceptance that intimacy finds its voice in the community. When the boy finally appears, it is the effect of his performance on others that occupies the text. Just as the boy-performer seems to dissolve in his own grace, the audience and the other performers that look on lose their immediate sense of shape and definition which disappears both in ancestry and in procreation:

> Le petit saltimbanque fit la roue
> Avec tant d'harmonie
> Que l'orgue cessa de jouer
> Et l'organiste se cacha le visage dans les mains
> Aux doigts semblables aux descendants de son destin
> Foetus minuscules qui lui sortaient de la barbe[51]

Self, its physical generation and its temporal, smothering opaqueness meet here in a place where voice and the eye lose all desire for authority. The voraciousness inspired even by the performance of others is dissolved in their inventions, their grace and their scripts. An unfaithful self is a renewed one. The boy disappears suddenly, leaving the audience to seek in themselves those forms and those bodies that would make plain the enigma of their desire:

> Mais chaque spectateur cherchait en soi l'enfant miraculeux
> Siècle ô siècle des nuages[52]

Where the intimate decays, lyrical voice re-emerges, is re-born steeped in the placenta of its passing, the unheard voices within you and I. Beginnings and endings emerge in the poem from nowhere and are constructed in the air; the voyeur links hands with a community opened out to anonymity and made fearless. 'Chaque spectateur cherchait en soi . . .' – in this silent mourning, perhaps we read a self made from nothing in the imagining of another.

CHAPTER TWO

Signs and the imaginary: the pleasures of discontent in Roland Barthes

L'imaginaire, assomption globale de l'image; est-ce que ce n'est pas là, épistémologiquement, une catégorie d'avenir?[1]

I Sign and image

There is no beginning or end in Roland Barthes's writing. His later work in particular solicits the opprobrium of methodologists and sceptics alike for failing to formulate plots to unravel, refusing to specify goals achieved, positions established or systems enthroned. But the mobility of Barthes's approach nurtures a creative decay in his responses to thought and expression which in turn allows him not only to focus on what for him is an overriding anxiety, but also to offer a writer's resistance of his own to some of its effects. This overriding concern is the collusion of challenges to power with some of the most intimate attachments to it. And in response, Barthes presses time and the crumbling edifices it projects into divesting the unheard and the unknown of their codification, as well as divesting codes of their insidious and spontaneous familiarity.

This anxiety at the heart of Barthes's thinking emerges through a drift in his focus from structure to image and the imaginary. From instrument of cultural critique or at least of cultural transparency, the 'science of signs' projected by Saussure is seen to feed delusions of overview and dominance. Such delusions lurk in analysis at large, Barthes suggests, rather than any particular analysis. The mind feeds on synthesis to build the platforms of retrospection and projection that it needs to negotiate past and future, to exchange images of agreed common good or evil – of a society that can be accepted and worked within. Such synthetic platforms, whether cast in the concrete of vested interest or cast like a fly on the ephemeral waters of perception, are the stuff of that sense of integrity we rely on in saying 'I' and to move around within ourselves. They are also signs and symptoms of an impulse to hold on to what is already lost: some continuity in the self and its capacity to survive, some capacity to establish authority or at least to appeal to it with some security, however manufactured.

The mobility of Barthes's methods and writerly attitudes is a response to this dynamic, played out at the most intimate levels of mind and body where deconstruction and complicity go hand in hand. It is a response which seeks to match not only a theory with a practice of writing, but ultimately with an ethics of writing. Barthes sheds intellectual mantels continually, each under the sign of language, text, writing: as both analyst and practitioner, Barthes's critical gaze rests on myth, popular culture, ideology, methodology, image, voice, time, decay, the somewhere of the body. But this mobility is not simply an energised, or confident, or impatient movement forward or away. The discontents of future positions are anticipated in earlier ones; the response to future discontents is built on the remains of earlier ventures and disappointments. Barthes focuses on position itself and the strategies to produce it exactly for their capacity to evade focus – a capacity that is their most lethal weapon against any challenge to their authority.

Notions of image and the imaginary are as crucial to Barthes in the development of his theories of text and of subjectivity as they are to Lacan in developing structural psychoanalysis, or to Irigaray in developing a feminist psychoanalysis and a theory of the female subject in culture. This is a theoretical space with no beginning or conclusion. I want to start my revisiting of Barthes's contribution to this space and his itinerary through it at the polar opposite of its outcome – the notion of structure. Barthes's role during the 1960s in developing semiology as a 'science of signs' is particularly ambivalent. *Système de la mode*, published originally in 1967, functions as an application of this 'science' and thus as an apologia for it. It enacts the very purpose of semiology, it cannot but realise the critical grasping of the world proposed by semiology. But precisely in this way, the book draws this method to a close – in fact indicates its closure:

> le sémiologue est celui qui exprime sa mort future dans les termes mêmes où il a nommé et compris le monde.[2]

These are the final words of the book, concluding the particular exercise in semiology that is *Système de la mode*. Later, in accepting his chair of semiology at the Collège de France, Barthes again bids semiology farewell, and especially the way semiology presses linguistics into service as the grounding theory of its own practice. Semiology is constructed in its own failure to reinvent the linguistic sign, Barthes finds. A blindness ensues to a central issue in any critical or cultural theory – the issue of power:

> Cet objet en quoi s'inscrit le pouvoir, de toute éternité humaine, c'est: le langage – ou pour être plus précis, son expression obligée: la langue.[3]

In articulating this disaffection with the sign and with the sciences that support it and construct it, Barthes in the *Leçon* not only re-examines but also rediscovers with a certain amount of despair the appeal of the structuralist account of making sense.

> Parler, et à plus forte raison discourir, ce n'est pas communiquer, comme on le répète trop souvent, c'est assujettir.[4]

The instruments of this subjugation of the subject, the tying of the subjective to the discursive, are the sign and the codes that allow it to operate. Barthes seems always to have known that speech acts, even ones expressing doubt or the suspension of judgement, assert and affirm a linguistic mask based on recognition and repetition, on the perpetuation of a self-verifying authority. In any sign 'dort ce monstre: un stéréotype'.[5] In uttering, we emulate.

This anxiety, this devastating account of the sign, is signalled in Barthes's writing both before and after *Système de la mode*; even in that work of 'high' structuralism, Barthes grapples with the imaginary dimension of a scientific account of signification. Ever-present in this plural focus is Barthes's further textual grappling with his own conception of 'le sens', developed in response to Sartrean accounts of making sense as well as to structural linguistics. It is worth reiterating at this point that 'Qu'est ce-que l'écriture?', the opening essay of *Le Degré zéro de l'écriture*, is openly written in response to the challenge of Sartre's *Qu'est-ce que la littérature?*; each of these pieces attempts to map out the responsibility which the user of language, in particular the writer, can manufacture for his or her own expression. But coming back to the afterglow of structural linguistics, Barthes reminds us in *Leçon* that for Jakobson 'un idiome se définit moins par ce qu'il permet de dire, que par ce qu'il oblige à dire'.[6] Elsewhere, Barthes toys with but also brutalises visions of utopia prompted in resistance to this all-pervasive obligation:

> Visiblement, il [Barthes] songe à un monde qui serait *exempté de sens* (comme on l'est de service militaire). Cela a commencé avec *Le Degré zéro de l'écriture*, où est rêvé 'l'absence de tout signe'.[7]

Ever-present and boundless, the sign and the production of sense are part of a legal system which the language-user has no power to opt out of. A deconstructive approach to semiological accounts of the sign is as much a feature of Barthes seeking to establish a structuralist methodology as of Barthes seeking to undo its sphere of influence. Both *Système de la mode* and *S/Z* work with the grounding elements of what constitutes a structure in such different fields of enquiry as structural linguistics, structural anthropology and the structural analysis of narrative. But for Barthes, to work within a methodological attitude is itself an interrogation of such an attitude. I want to look in some detail at the mobility of Barthes's sense of the structure in two such different works as *Système de la mode* and in *S/Z*, two works apparently sharply divided over the issue of confidence in the structure itself. In revisiting these books, I shall try and follow delusions and mirages of discursive freedom that unfurl under Barthes's excited and horrified gaze.

II A critical image

Foucault's conception of Classical knowledge developed in *Les Mots et les choses* is an attempt to map out a metaphysical belief in the power of representation. This belief is not a valuing of mimesis or of the prestige of the image-maker. It is rather an epistemological assumption that it is in the nature of thought to be represented, and to advance itself in terms of the development of taxonomies.[8] The synchronic quality of a classification allows the thinker to affirm knowledge in the circumscription of it.

The focus on classification, and the synchronic approach to data which allows it, signal one of the fundamental properties of the structure as asserted or rather affirmed by the structuralist practitioner: its ability to account for the totality of the information it addresses. The ability of the structure to account for a defined body of phenomena allows not only the establishment of knowledge but also its deployment. The structure is aided in this by its two other fundamental properties. The first is the ability of the structure to transform its functioning in response to new information coming into the system, and the second is to regulate that transformation.[9] These three properties of the structure – its abilities to give totalising accounts, to transform its own functioning and to regulate this transformation – combine to grant the structuralist thinker the powers of critical distance, epistemological mastery, and ultimately, methodological impregnability; the speculative will have conspired with the specular. This is a far cry from the desired, idealised detachment required to redirect cultural and discursive coercion. A detachment that knows no bounds or that is too sure of them may be no detachment at all and may produce merely figments of its own ambitions and terrors. Such are the spectres that loom in Barthes's structuralism and which form the increasingly fascinated, horrified and scattered focus of his life as a writer.

Système de la mode and *S/Z* share a simultaneous enjoyment and investigation of the properties of the structure – the former in response to fashion, the latter to the procedures of realist narrative. At the outset of *S/Z*, Barthes announces that in his own reading of it, the realist narrative asserts its power to represent the world and to classify it. This classification functions in terms of five codes, five codified figurations of cultural and subjective experience. These codes are well known, and have served frequently in the past both to situate *S/Z* and to reduce it to a thumb-nail sketch of itself. The hermeneutic code encourages us to seek truth and to believe in it as a value outside all code. The semiotic code itemizes the elements in the signified which allow it mobility within the narrative system. It is supported by the effects of connotation. The symbolic code allows the articulation of unsayable but nonetheless dominant values and desires. The proairetic code, or code of action, systematises the devices which propel the plot. Finally, the code of cultural reference frames unimpeachable ideological values and *idées reçues*. The presentation and subsequent questioning of these codes is accompanied by Barthes's further divisions of Balzac's *Sarrasine* into 'lexies' or units of reading.

My point in going over this very familiar ground is to emphasise the extent to which the interactions set up by Barthes of unit and code, and of the codes themselves, testify dramatically to his fascination not only with the analytic properties of the structure but also with the folly of that. This is an enraptured engagement with the folly of enumeration, as Homi Bhabha might think of it – the enumeration, circumscription and corralling of all the elements in a particular pattern of behaviour or interpretation, or of the elements in the notion of pattern itself as an idea and as a pursuit.[10] The impact of the structure in *S/Z*, of the way its elements come together in that text, seems to shadow this folly and to mime it; images, perhaps sensations, are floated past the reader of an indefinite web of effects which anticipates mastery but foreshadows insecurity at the same time.

In relation to *S/Z*, the earlier *Système de la mode* advertises with much greater confidence the notion of structural organization as an invulnerable basis for the pursuit of knowledge and of closure. It is a study which bears many of the hallmarks of 'classical' structuralism. It establishes its kinship with structuralist methodology – be it structural linguistics or structural anthropology – by modelling its analytical practice on synchronic qualities in the functioning of the linguistic sign. This takes a particular form in *Système de la mode*. The analysis of fashion is presented at the outset as an analysis of *captions*, of linguistic descriptions of fashionable clothes in fashion magazines. Barthes further establishes the structuralism of his study by assigning definite synchronic boundaries to it: Barthes's data is to be drawn from fashion journalism of a single, arbitrarily chosen year: 1958–9.

But in spite of this affirmation of a methodology above suspicion, or rather by means of this, Barthes interrogates and refashions structuralist methodology. Boundaries, once established, become fascinating for the passages across them, to and fro, that are uncovered: 'qu'est-ce qui se passe lorsqu'un objet, réel ou imaginaire, est converti en langage?'[11] Synchrony, Barthes argues, is not simply the way to scientific soundness.

> Le vêtement 'imprimé' livre à l'analyste ce que les langues humaines refusent au linguiste: une synchronie pure; la synchronie de mode change tout d'un coup chaque année, mais durant cette année, elle est absolument stable.[12]

The 'pure' synchronicity manufactured by the fashion system offers practitioners and consumers the apparent freedom – the imaginary one – to invent forms of signification and even to ensure the desired reception of them. Moreover, this self-evident synchronicity offers the analyst of the fashion system an imaginary fulfilment of his or her own practice as analyst, as circumscriber of experience and purveyor of mastery over it. But this freedom, this fulfilment are limited ones – 'une liberté surveillée'[13] – controlled and monitored by the terms of the system's performance, now suddenly, in their very self-evidence, allowing no signs of critical intervention.

So much so that on one level of the written fashion system in Barthes's account of it, synchronicity produces an absolute coincidence of signifier – an item of clothing – and signified – fashion itself. 'Le vêtement décrit [. . .] est tout entier *sens*'.[14] The production of meaning – significance and signification – is nothing but perceptible, manifest, the sign nothing but transitive and readable. This utopian completion of the sign in its reception arises within a suppression of diachrony, which is now not purely the result of methodological assertion, nor even a defining feature of the fashion system, but a source of alarm arising both from the method and the object of its study. The matching or doubling of the performances of method, and the system submitted to the regime of that method; this synchronic completion of structural method and its application inspires an imaginary or form-bound, form-enhanced sense of power in relation to any set of cultural or contextual phenomena that it might turn its attention to. Method is steadily removed from the focus of attention as a result if its own increasingly manipulative and triumphalist independence. Rather than complacently presiding over what is a relatively simple-looking drift from rationalism to systemisation and back, Barthes is drawing the unwilling attention of his contemporary reader, as well as his own, to the imposing and restrictive narrowness of the structuralist range. Suddenly, far from promoting a serene encompassing of data, the tautology of method and data, or of affirmation and application, now seems not only to herald a new dawn of analytical beginning and cultural redirection, but to defy it. And this defiance is not a purely comfortable sign of liberal resistance to closure, but of an orthodox and terrified resistance to the new and the unknown. The excitement of matching method to data has produced nothing other than a return to the illusions of signifier matched to signified. Those monsters of stereotyping, emulation and cultural asphyxia that

Barthes warns us of in *Leçon* lurk not only in the sign but, even more surrep-
titiously, in the attempt to account for its effects.

The ambivalence of tautological matching of perceived and manipu-
lated structure is underlined in the way the synchronic is given use value.
Where diachrony cannot actually be excluded from the fashion system, it is
turned to its advantage and in that way made manageable. 'Le passé n'est plus
liquidé, il est utilisé',[15] Barthes writes. The system adapts to time – and rec-
onciles its users to temporal passage – through the micro-transformations it
is able to operate as a structure. The structuralist practitioner not only cir-
cumscribes system as structure but *enjoys* system to exactly that extent. 'Le
vêtement imprimé livre à l'analyste [. . .] une synchronie pure [. . .].'
Methodological tautology is appropriative, and relies for that on enmeshing
fulfilment in immobility.

I suggested a moment ago that it is at one particular level of the fashion
system Barthes puts on display that the suppression of diachrony is secure.
But Barthes's description of fashionable clothing, or of fashion-as-printed-
word, is meticulously isometric and divides the data into *two* related systems,
each further divided into their respective operating elements. Going into
these here a little will enable me to sketch in some of the history of another
of Barthes's calling cards and the part it plays in the drift from structure to the
imaginary as the focus of Barthes's thinking; and that calling card is the relation of connotation to denotation.

Barthes dryly terms these two systems of fashion-as-printed-word 'les
ensembles A' and 'les ensembles B'. 'Les ensembles A' are statements,
'énoncés' which refer the reader and the consumer to a social context that
assigns purpose and significance to a particular fashion accessory – e.g. 'les
imprimés triomphent aux courses'.[16] 'Les ensembles B' comprise those
'énoncés' I mentioned before in which the written garment, 'le vêtement
écrit', itself signals Fashion – i.e., it acts as signifier of the implicit signified
Fashion. An example Barthes gives is this: 'Que toute femme raccourcisse sa
jupe jusqu'au ras du genou, adopte les carreaux fondus et marche en
escarpins bicolores.'[17] Hence it is in 'les ensembles B' that the 'pure' synchronicity is affirmed and performed.

It is this isometric account of fashion that allows Barthes to introduce
the further oppositional interplay of connotation and denotation:

> la Mode est un valeur connotée dans les ensembles A et une valeur denotée
> dans les ensembles B.[18]

Barthes's interest in the interplay of connotation and denotation is a further
element in the well-known ambivalence of his response to linguistics that I
mentioned at the start, and to the work of Hjelmslev in particular; and it is
one of the most evident of the intellectual and procedural linchpins of *S/Z*.

There, denotation has the function of designating and fixing. Supported by the predicative structure of the sentence, denotation seems to reduce the known to what can be made intelligible in syntax, a system Barthes presents as essentially static. Diversity or mobility in the signified is restricted in procedures of denotation to association of ideas, which for Barthes simply 'renvoie à un système de sujet'.[19] In this way, the syntactic subject intermeshes with the notion of a thematic subject to produce self-repeating structures of 'sens'. Connotation, on the other hand, operating within the semantic codification of cultural experience, produces a plurality of signifying operation and effects. This works at least in a limited way against the orthodox functioning of classical narrative:

> la connotation assure une dissémination (limitée) des sens, répandue comme une poussière d'or sur la surface du texte'.[20]

Put differently, this gold-dust of semantic possibility intensifies the undermining I indicated earlier of the stability of the five cultural codes that ground realist narrative.

I shall come back later to this dynamic uncertainty. For the moment, I simply want to highlight that in *Système de la mode* it is denotation, and not connotation, that momentarily holds out the prospect or the image of a self-sufficient intervention in the cultural given.

> Cette différence tient essentiellement à ceci: que la Mode est une valeur connotée dans l'ensemble A et une valeur dénotée dans les ensembles B.[21]

'Les ensembles B' – where the signified is Fashion – have three levels to their functioning, each operating on the signifier / signified axis. 'Les ensembles A' – referring readers to the contextual function of a fashion accessory – have four. The level lacking in 'les ensembles B' and active in 'les ensembles A' is the level of connotation. In 'B', the signifier consists in what is noted about the correctness of printed clothes at the races, to use the example from before. Connotation therefore has no part to play, and it is this that ensures the self-affirming power of the system.

> Au niveau 2 B, le sens de Mode ne provient pas de la simple notation (acte de noter), mais des traits vestimentaires eux-mêmes; ou plus exactement, la notation est immédiatement absorbée dans le détails des traits, elle ne peut fonctionner comme signifiant, et la Mode ne peut échapper à sa situation de signifié immédiat.[22]

Code 2 of the B system comprises the written garment itself; neither the physical garment (code 1), nor the rhetoric distinguishing one description from another (code 3). Barthes's argument here is that the written garment paradoxically has no power as signifier. For the action of the signifier is absorbed in the detail of the characteristics described – which *are* fashion. In the B system, description is transformed into the performance of Fashion.

What all this self-aggrandising rhetoric of method and science ends up testifying to is the inescapable absorption of sensation in structure. The restrictive immediacy of the B system seems to Barthes the semiotician to act as a confident rather than estranging affirmation of the cultural.

> Or la Mode est une valeur *arbitraire*; dans le cas des ensembles B, le système général s'affiche par conséquent comme un système arbitraire, ou, si l'on préfère, ouvertement culturel. [23](My italics)

The grounding of this confident affirmation, of this alarming embracing of culture as formulation of human desire, is provided by the grounding principle of structural linguistics and semiotics: the arbitrariness of the sign.

A kind of managed and manageable arbitrariness, exposed subsequently by Derrida and many others, is one of the prizes claimed by Barthes in the mode of semiotician:

> Décrire; 'une veste-brassière toute boutonnée dans le dos', etc., c'est fonder un signe. [24]

I have already suggested that the ambition of the semiotician is to effect a passage from the descriptive to the critical – or even a dissolution of one in the other. The semiotician claims at least the rhetorical power to account for and potentially to reorganize the relations that make up culture. Culture is open to circumscription exactly in as much as the analysis of it performs that circumscription.

This is exactly what Barthes sends out warning signals about here – and not just in his later attitudes as epitomised in the *Leçon* – as he charts the surreptitious passage from describing a sign to founding one. As sensation signals its involvement in sense and in structure, Barthes observes cultural effects drift unstoppably to a sensation of nature: to sense culture would then be to sense it as immutable. And all the appeal at the heart of structuralist practice of an imaginary independence from cultural structuring is thereby exposed *from within that practice itself*:

> Décrire; 'une veste-brassière toute boutonnée dans le dos, etc.', c'est fonder un signe; affirmer que 'l'imprimé triomphe aux courses', c'est masquer le signe sous les apparences d'une affinité entre le monde et le vêtement, c'est-à-dire d'une nature. [25]

What glorious confusion under the guise of isomorphic certainty! Against all the odds, it would seem, Barthes argues here that to describe has the power to found, to initiate: description would otherwise be a purely passive mode of discourse. Whereas affirmation ('affirmer'), seemingly the more confident intervention in social context, is characterized as *masking* its own operation, as seeking to transcend its own power to signal and thus the requirement itself to do so.

This confusion is clearly heuristic. The effect is to cast nature again as relative rather than absolute – '*une* nature'; culturally specific, though *not* culturally specified here by Barthes, who thus seems to give up on one of the principal objectives of 'the science of signs' which is to describe cultural codification. 'Nature' is cast as an operational element in the structuralist attempt to circumscribe culture, not an element with a singular function or position. Indefinite, unplaced, a source of appeal and fascination no less powerful for being accounted for within structuralist critical methodology as an object of nostalgia, nature in Barthes's play here acts as a shifter in relation to which culture drifts from affirmations of a human power to intervene, to mapping with a semblance of novelty scenes of human alienation. This humble and fragile novelty consists in evoking an alienation that is not oppositional or exilic, not an alienation *from* a 'natural language'. Rather, Barthes invites us to share in his own acceptance of an alienation *in* the continuing, multiformed, multi-masked, energising *but still* futile desire for a natural language of forms – 'le masque d'une nature fatale'.[26]

The fashion system in Barthes's handling of it loses its limited and policed utopia and proceeds via alienation. Such is the consequence of Barthes's unresolved interplay in the book of nature and the arbitrary, terminology and rhetoric. The aspirations associated with any structure to give a total account of its material, to transform itself in contact with the data it analyses and thus to regulate itself, all come under intense pressure from connotation:

> Le système se défait lorsqu'il s'ouvre au monde par les voies de la connotation [ensembles A]. Le double système de la Mode (A et B) apparaît ainsi comme un miroir où se lit le dilemme *éthique* de l'homme moderne: tout système de signes est appelé à s'encombrer, se convertir et se corrompre dès que le monde le 'remplit': pour s'ouvrir au monde, il faut s'aliéner.[27] (My addition in square brackets, my italics)

If 'l'homme moderne' here signals a heightened awareness of system, a specific moment when cultural determinants seemed transparent, definitively responsive to representation and manipulation, then connotation is a reminder right here in the elaboration of it of the hubris of such ambition. Barthes's structuralist 'modernity' does not remain blind, in need of subsequent deconstructions of it including his own, to the complacency and autocracy of new, utopian signs impregnable to the old. His own 'structuralism' rubs the noses of his colleagues in the notion that the organised utopia of any structure might encourage only basking in discursive supremacy. Fashion is championed for its decay, which the structuralist practitioner that is Barthes in this book seeks to implant into his own method; such would be his resistance to the affirmation encouraged by that method, and specially the functioning of denotation there, of the power to suppress time and inaugurate beginning. Connotation, both produced and suppressed by the fashion system, acts as a decomposing agent to the well-intentioned purity of structuralist critique, its megalomaniac assertion of intactness in relation to data and antecedence. Suspended between affirmation and decay, connotation suggests the signifying overload allowing life rather than not-life, generosity rather than narcissism. It is neither beyond system nor within it, neither active nor neutralised. Nor both. What kind of reading or critique or ethics of critique would this promise?

III A plural image

The coupling of 'jouissance' and 'plaisir' provides Barthes with a forum to engage still further with utopian fulfilment or delusion. His evocations of a slippery imaginary provide this investigation with its centrifugal pivot. Here as elsewhere, Barthes feeds both on Lacan and on Sartre.

> Bien repérer *les imaginaires du langage*, à savoir: le mot comme unité singulière, monade magique; la parole comme instrument ou expression de la pensée.[28]

An immediate and immobilising passage from signifier to signified, the manufacturing of a magical signifying autonomy: such is the imaginary response to the sign. This imaginary completion comprises elements of the Lacanian one. In *De l'agressivité en psychanalyse* and many other subsequent writings, Lacan suggests that the setting up of the subject in representation is forever vulnerable to being reconstituted in imaginary forms favouring appropriation, possession and fixity.[29] Barthes becomes increasingly fascinated with this reconstitution, and seeks to exhibit the ways in which it is *encouraged* and not dispelled by the positioning of the subject in syntax and in discourse at large. Barthes summarizes magnificently this psychic/linguistic collaboration of syntax and ego as everything absorbed in the rubric 'Moi, je':

> l'imaginaire vient à pas de loup, patinant en douceur sur un passé simple, un pronom, un souvenir, bref tout ce qui peut se rassembler sous la devise même du Miroir et de son Image: *Moi, je.*[30]

To say 'I' presupposes its mirror-reflection – a specular confirmation of an utterance. The nurturing of this impossible assumption rides on a profusion and a confusion of attitudes, gestures, reactions, perceptions and impulses that emerge under Barthes's pen as indeterminately legalising and naturalising.

The ambivalence or controlled confusion that Barthes allows to develop around the notions of 'jouissance' and text provide him with one of his principal counter-measures to this imaginary response to language. Allusions to his experience of structuralist methodology continue to provide sustenance:

> Le texte, c'est le langage sans son imaginaire, *c'est ce qui manque à la science du langage pour que soit manifestée son importance générale* (et non sa particularité technocratique). Tout ce qui est à peine toléré par la linguistique (comme science canonique, positive), la signifiance, la jouissance, c'est précisément là ce qui retire le texte des imaginaires du langage.[31]

Text is what eludes the attempts of the scientific imaginary to appropriate it. But to that extent, it is an *acknowledgement* that 'le langage', any use of language, not only articulates the subject's desire for supremacy, but also acts to manufacture images of supremacy fulfilled.

Clearly, this is not a happy acknowledgement. Barthes keeps plugging away at the idea that to assert a place beyond language is itself a repetition of the ways in which desire is formed as language and framed in language. More subtly, and therefore more insidiously, Barthesian 'jouissance' is dependent on the 'plaisir' which holds pride of place in the title of his book, *Le Plaisir du texte*, and which to that extent seems to silence the effects of 'jouissance'. At one level, Barthes values the pleasures of the text, precisely since they are vilified by the critical orthodoxies of right and left. Barthes's pleasure-in-text provides a source of resistance to complacency and stasis. But it is a perpetually disappointing one. The pleasure of the text and of the cultural ease involved does at least allow for a human subject constructed in disjunction, rather than in the quasi-unimpeachable logic of the classical narrative or of the structure at large. But this develops in conjunction with pleasure made permissible within the boundaries of any discourse. These boundaries are a matter of form, they are an imaginary construction. So is the text of 'jouissance', which constructs a formal 'beyond' to the engulfing of cultural transgression in cultural ease. Both pleasure and 'jouissance' are a matter of form.

The text of 'jouissance', the writing of some capacity to resist structure and positioning, can only be sensed indirectly, removed from reading *in* reading, made apparent in still other constructions of 'jouissance' itself.

> Avec l'écrivain de jouissance (et son lecteur) commence le texte intenable, le texte impossible. Ce texte est hors-plaisir, hors-critique, *sauf à être atteint par un*

autre texte de jouissance: vous ne pouvez parler 'sur' un tel texte, vous pouvez seulement parler 'en' lui, *à sa manière*, entrer dans un plagiat éperdu, affirmer hystériquement le vide de jouissance (et non plus répéter obsessionnellement la lettre du plaisir).[32]

A collapsing play of differences is enacted which allows 'jouissance' the form of an affirmation that is not a further product of oppositional conflict: 'hors'.[33] 'Jouissance' is nothing other than different, intransitively so, Barthes might say; it reproduces itself identically.[34] Hysteria is alluded to as a psychic state disallowing difference and plurality, a kind of imaginary affirmation of singularity-in-repetition. But in the very same disallowing, 'hysterical affirmation' marks a stop to readings that appeal to institutionalised position or to the rediscovery of it.

As a consequence, here we have a disruption of reaffirmation and repetition that proceeds paradoxically by a kind of desperate plagiarism – 'un plagiat éperdu'. 'Jouissance' intensifies stopping to a pitch where 'the shock of the new' is nothing more than naive slate-wiping. It is an intensification within which stopping and continuing, rejecting and engulfing, narcissistic affirmation and an affirmative setting aside of the ego's refusal to begin again are all concentrated in the sign. This is not a clash of opposites, more an uneasy and unresolved interaction. 'Jouissance', in clinging on to any aspiration to excess, suppresses co-habitation. Flirting with the plural, 'jouissance' resists even models of that and seeks to remain impregnable to all such models; but for that reason it is also stuck on the model.

This ambivalence glues excess to emulation; Barthes explores it further in terms of representation, on which 'jouissance' crucially relies because of its own reinvestments in the powers of form. The *appeal*, rather than its dismemberment, of being positioned, systematised and codified, continues to be the object of Barthes's horrified fascination. His notorious interplay of 'le scriptible' and 'le lisible' in *S/Z* had already produced an account of this.

> Le texte scriptible, c'est *nous en train d'écrire* [. . .]. Le scriptible, c'est le romanesque sans le roman, la poésie sans le poème, l'essai sans la dissertation, l'écriture sans le style, la production sans le produit, la structuration sans la structure.[35]

Like the text of 'jouissance', the 'scriptible' text is 'beyond' product and 'beyond' structure; that ambition is clear. But the point I want to emphasise is that this ambition is flawed or corrupted at its inception: 'jouissance' and the 'scriptible' are purely identical with themselves, inviting hysterical plagiarism of an *image* of enjoyed, ingrained writing that is fixated just as much as it is elusive. This image cannot fail to *match* the ones projected by structure and the structured text.

Certainly, the 'scriptible' text can only be in-production, not produced; this means that I can do no more than point to 'S/Z' and say 'scriptible!'; or else become hopelessly involved in the ins and outs of one or more of its bits, as I did in response to *Système de la mode*. But the fact that the 'scriptible' is identical with itself does not leave it intact. The nameless, mobile fascination exercised by the 'scriptible' text is produced through a rhetorically manufactured *forgetting*, which is a reflection of the apparently spontaneous forgetting characteristic of engaging with a 'lisible' text. Forgetting there is the effect of reading within the procedures that mask culture as natural culture, and that paper over those masks. A different kind of forgetting from the affirmative hysteria of 'jouissance'; but the ambivalence of forgetting – both a strategic and a structural effect – nonetheless precludes any definitive excising of 'plaisir' from 'jouissance'. The 'scriptible' text explores the captivating power of 'le lisible'; it is a dramatization of the elusive fascination which 'le lisible' is capable of exercising. For this fascination is a mark of continually renewed attempts to capture images of that psychic ease characteristic of ideal cultural performance.

With this in mind, how does the notion of connotation fare in *S/Z*? Returning to some familiar ground may take us some way forward. In *Système de la mode*, as I argued earlier, the action of connotation in opening the written fashion system out to the situation of culture is seen as frankly alienating: it threatens to dissolve the power to circumscribe and dominate experience affirmed by the notion of structure. Having transformed that alienation into a positive force, in *S/Z* connotation takes up the reins and is made by Barthes into a positive if non-affirmative form of resistance to codification. Barthes presents it as an *anti*-hysterical turning inside-out not only of structure but of the analysing ego:

> Topologiquement, la connotation assure une dissémination (limitée) des sens, répandue comme une poussière d'or sur la surface apparente du texte (le sens est d'or). Sémiologiquement, toute connotation est le départ d'un code (qui ne sera jamais constituée), l'articulation d'une voix qui est tissée dans le texte.[36]

In its topological relation to denotation, Barthes would have connotation transform the production of meaning – significance as well as signification – into a kind of word-dust that shimmers because of its plurality; but even more because of the possibility evoked of sweeping even plurality aside, controlled and predictable as plurality can only be. This shimmering is indeed a limited one ('limitée') – limited by the fact that it is an element of a semiology *in place* as well as of a semiological account: 'sémiologiquement'. But momentarily, an 'other' to the narcissistic umbrella of the semiological performer is offered in one of Barthes's myriad micro-changes of argumentative

direction. For connotation ensures that the codes which make up the operational structure of narrative semiology are never completed, nor constituted
as such ('jamais constituée'). But at the same time, even in parading plurality
from within the realist narrative – 'départ d'un code' – Barthes positively and
affirmatively fails to depart from the terms of narrative semiology, even
though he succeeds in de-scribing such a method rather than circum-scribing
it. For it is a *semiological* property of connotation to make the system of realist
narrative appear to lack structural fixity, since this mobility acts as a suppression of the codes and casts their performance as culturally natural, as formally absent, forgotten in reading by virtue of their own elusiveness.
Connotation feeds the 'lisible' on the same effects as it does the 'scriptible'.

As any reader of *S/Z* will know, the instrument of this seemless web
('tisser') of narrative unfolding and of theoretical coming together is a
binding agent Barthes terms 'une voix', perhaps as a testimony to the pleasurable logocentricity of realist narrative. An initial allusion to this 'voix' is made
in the quotation above, which I am still commenting on. The presence of
these 'voix' in the system of realist narrative at once supports the system and
undermines it, always reminding us that such undermining is *in the service of*
'le récit classique' and confirms its authority.

There are five such 'voix' in action in *S/Z*, Barthes's reading of his own
fascination with Balzac's *Sarrasine*. They comprise: 'la Voix de l'Empirie (les
proaïrétismes), la Voix de la Personne (les sèmes), la Voix de la Science (les
codes culturels), la Voix de la Vérité (les herméneutismes), la Voix du
Symbole.'[37] To evoke Barthes's listing of the 'voix' in this way in turn evokes
the range of assumptions associated with the realist mimesis: empirical data,
pseudo-scientific analysis, the hero, the unveiling of truth, the assertion of
epistemological supremacy through narrative.

In decorating and facilitating narrative performance, in effecting the
collapse of each code as a fully constituted entity, the 'voix' help to make of
the code a 'scriptible' structure-in-motion, a structure-in-dissolution. My
point is that the agility of the code – both elusive and appropriative – is
enhanced by this rather than simply deconstructed:

> Il s'agit en effet, non de manifester une structure, mais autant que possible de
> produire une structuration.[38]

Process rather than product, certainly, is the form that Barthes anticipates
realist narrative may take; but the common etymological root in French
speaks volumes for the interdependence of the two, their unholy alliances
and loving embraces. Barthes's account of connotation and 'les voix' and of
their ambivalent effects is not only a backwards-and-forwards glance at
Sarrasine but also at the fragmentation of that text in which the work of *S/Z*

consists. Within the narrative and within the work on it, the displaying of narrative construction, of the power to manipulate form and image, is shown to be enmeshed with that psychic fascination with the tyranny of the narrating identity which Barthes had begun to confront in his practice of structuralism in *Système de la mode*.

This concentration of voice, code, connotation, structure and structuration, of the material text, its critique and its theorisation, is brought by Barthes to an imploding halt with regard to representation. The elusive focal point of this implosion is castration. Representations of castration and responses to it are clearly the driving element in the plot of Balzac's novella. Zambinella, the castrated male singer, is taken by Sarrasine, male sculptor, for a woman whom Sarrasine is then encouraged to love. In Barthes's reading, it is in terms of this delusion that Sarrasine expresses a fruitless desire to unify the various, fragmented or 'déchiquetés' elements in his sexual desire as well as in his art – his desire-as-art. Barthes articulates this desire for a 'lubricated' gluing together of sexual and plastic assertiveness in terms of transgression of the Oedipal laws of splitting and deferral. The compulsions to narrate and to model thus seek to engulf, but to that extent are engulfed by, symbolic structures of psychosocial orthodoxy.

In working this out, Barthes characterizes Balzac's task as novelist–performer in the following way:

> confondre le symbolique et l'herméneutique, faire que la recherche de la vérité (structure herméneutique) soit la recherche de la castration (structure symbolique), que la vérité soit *anecdotiquement* (et non plus symboliquement) le phallus perdu.[39]

Culture, in the metonymic account of it here in the terms of realist performance, seems to spin evermore culturally adaptable, evermore institutionally seductive images and theories of the natural and of the sexually fulfilled. Symbolic castration is the unplaceable place ('perdu') where the Oedipal laws of family and society are inaugurated. Hermeneutic castration spins yarns of narrative acclimatisation, habituation and naturalisation. The dynamic dissolution of distinction between symbolic and hermeneutic castration in *Sarrasine–S/Z* might be expected to effect such confusion that the system of realist narrative would simply grind to a glorious halt. But in fact, sensations of closure and discursive mastery abound. With stabilising distinction collapsing, closure is now unstoppable, without beginning and without conclusion; plural. The Barthesian 'récit classique' is a story-telling that joys in obedience to the laws it affirms. It is on that collapsing, adorably mobile and unpredictable basis that it points in the air at its own inability to foreclose. Such is the paradoxical activity of 'le scriptible'. In the interactive matching of hermeneutic and symbolic readings, we are brought to an abrupt, engulfing, castrating but still innovative – unstoppably innovative, innovative from within – full stop:

> 'illustrant' la castration [symbolique] par la castrature [herméneutique], le même par le même, [*Sarrasine*] rend dérisoire l'idée d'illustration, [cette nouvelle] abolit les deux faces de l'équivalence (la lettre et le symbole), sans que ce soit au profit de l'une ou de l'autre; le latent y occupe d'emblée la ligne du manifeste, *le signe s'aplatit: il n'y a plus de représentation*.[40]

A 'flat' full stop is reached, unpromising and dull. But this very flatness is indefinite, involving us in 'une finalité insaisissable' – a finality that fails to establish itself, which cannot be measured, and which allows beginning to be affirmed. A beginning, that is, where there is none – within representation, whose flattening here signals its further proliferation. Within the Lacanian Symbolic Order, Barthes in *S/Z* seeks to construct a writing through which incompleteness is acknowledged both as a source of mobility and as a source of pain. Alienation in the Symbolic is a practice, but a paradoxical one: a *captivated* play rather than a free play; not bound by grief but steeped in it nonetheless.

But to affirm new beginning is to imagine the death of the past, of antecedence and authority, of 'the critical voices that have trained and taught us'.[41] These Freudian voices that I discussed in the previous chapter signal the dissolution of a primary unconscious narcissism in the human subject. But as I emphasised in that chapter, these 'critical voices' of Oedipal civilisation also build scenes of secondary reconstruction of narcissistic, complacent, autocratic completion; symptoms of pain are reversible – to borrow Barthes's own term; they indicate both loss and regrouping. The attempts to reconcile the appeal of a silencing autonomy with the demands of material and social time and place seem endlessly varied.

So the project Barthes edges into, both as semiologist and as writer, is no less than to match his own procedures to the seductive workings of psychosocial images of completion, fulfilment and autonomy; to caress the sensations, echoes and mnemonics of those networks in his writing. Barthes's are not an 'écriture' or a 'jouissance' that simply assert their own resistance to narcissistic fulfilment; for that fulfilment is discursive, open to exchange, part of the fabric of social life and the subject's many places there – narrative, syntactic, gendered, psychic . . .; this is what Barthes's writing enacts.

The oscillation between a 'scriptible' unbuilding of signifying dominance on the one hand, and the pleasurable joy of signifying position on the other, is a sensation Barthes re-focuses on continually in his theory and practice of knowledge. Knowledge is an ideological construct, Barthes reminds us, perhaps rather baldly. What he adds is a continuing willingness to confront the practical, ethical, writerly consequences of the sense in which to unbuild the effects of ideology engenders an involvement with them which scenes of methodological competitiveness serve merely to bolster. 'Critical theory' for Barthes involves (re-)constructing articulations of supremacy in rhetorical, imaginary and ideological forms:

> L'idéologie: ce qui se répète et *consiste* (par ce dernier verbe elle s'exclut de l'ordre du signifiant). Il suffit donc que l'analyse idéologique (ou la contre-idéologie) se répète et consiste (en proclamant *sur place* sa validité, par un geste de pur dédouanement) pour qu'elle devienne elle-même un objet idéologique. Que faire? [42]

Barthes's answer, to various implicit or explicit degrees throughout his writing, is aesthetic. The aesthetic experience is one of forms. For Barthes, it resists and thereby *re-forms* (resists and radicalises; resists and forms again) a secondary, perverse, socialized gluing of 'jouissance' to the already glutinous functioning of ideology that is articulated in signification. 'Et s'il y avait, à titre de perversion seconde, *une jouissance de l'idéologie?*'[43] No semiology can undo the binding of transgression to the Oedipal draw of the orthodox. Nor can any writing, however 'scriptible'. In responding to this, Barthes invokes the notion of epistemology and directs it at isolating the quasi-plastic, but untouchable, un-bodily forms within which knowledge is manufactured in dreams of possession and singularity:

> L'imaginaire, assomption globale de l'image, existe chez les animaux (mais point le symbolique), puisqu'ils se dirigent droit sur le leurre, sexuel ou ennemi, qu'on leur tend. Cet horizon zoologique ne donne-t-il pas à l'imaginaire une précellence d'intérêt? Est-ce que ce n'est pas là, *épistémologiquement*, une catégorie d'avenir? [44]

In this sense of 'épistémologiquement', the effects of Barthes's writing fragments have epistemological content. Like his placing-and-removing quotation marks with Flaubertian double-edged irony, they signal the effort to 'signer son imaginaire',[45] to take possession of the forms we identify with and love. They suggest for a moment that identification, and the loving relation at large, might be individually constructed and sculpted. This interlocking of sexual and ideological identification or fascination makes of *Fragments d'un discours amoureux* a testimony to an en-graining epistemology of the imaginary. (But) Any (of its) fragment(s), in ending, in-forms a kind of meta-narrative that articulates not critical disavowal, but antecedence – 'le grand Autre narratif'.[46] Do we admit our impotence in the matter of ending, and thus accept the 'gift' of alienation, now re-grouped in orthodox packages? Or do we manufacture our own power to disrupt ending and thus accept the gifts of delusion? It is this wild capacity to buzz between a fascinated seclusion within fictitiously autonomous forms, and a fascination with the power of these same forms to engage with their own downfall, that is the source of the paradoxical creativity Barthes affirms in his writer's evocation of imaginary response.

Each fragment in *Fragments d'un discours amoureux* is an indulgence of a secluded scene uncoupling making love from making sense – or rather uncoupling imagining love from imagining sense. Each fragment indulges a seclusion in grief at the loss of imaginary wholeness. But this is a momentary indulgence, not only because each fragment ends, but also because each one figures in the alphabetical glossary at the back, alluding again to the practice of classification – to the dream and the power of system. Each fragment invites hysterical, fixated rereading, hysterical attempts to stabilise our own response as we read, identify, become fascinated. Equally, each fragment reintroduces the symbolic dimension: it ends, the effort to stabilise is fruitless and we are coerced again to begin an 'other'. And yet symbolic coercion is resisted in a system of neither/nor. The book stabilises neither erotic capturing of sexual relation, nor the killing of sexual relation and the symbolic role-play it demands symbolised by Thanatos. Neither silent nor discursive; neither static nor mobile; neither utopian nor ideological; neither imaginary nor symbolic. Nor both. Continual rereadings of power articulated in desire; neither repetitive nor differentiated. Continual wardings off of violence; neither with nor without signs.

IV A decaying image

Towards the beginning of this chapter I said there is no beginning or ending to the space of Barthes's writing, and followed that up immediately by isolating a fairly obvious starting point. A lesson in heuristics I have tried to learn from Barthes himself. Moreover, I have had a goal or an ending in mind all along, and that is to follow the paths trodden by many other readers that lead from the early writing of Barthes to his later writing. I have learnt, or made an initial stab at learning, to be suspicious of originality, and to confine myself to seeking out a criticism that lays bare the paths of my own intellectual and cultural constitution – 'signer l'imaginaire', if you like. But as I have argued, it rapidly becomes clear that to favour one bit of Barthes over the other is not only to grossly oversimplify, but also to make the reading of any one favoured bit unnecessarily restricted and predictable. That is not the lesson of the fragment, any more than an attempt to reconstruct a consistent evolution or intellectual progress would be. An immersion in writing that so attracts critics to Barthes is signalled as an ethical and methodological desideratum from the very outset of his thought. What is regarded by many including Marguerite Duras as his writerly phase is certainly incomprehensible without a sense of Barthes's own past and continual immersion in the theorising that is drawn from literature, linguistics, semiology, existentialist phenomenology, anthropology, psychoanalysis and Zen to mention but those.[47]

So I make no bones about taking a step back and starting again in my quest for ways of bringing this chapter into contact with some of Barthes's later writing. 'Recommençons',[48] as Barthes suggests in the *Fragments*, embarking on a further attempt to seek out an alternative to affirmation as reaffirmation, as worship, as participation in unchanged value.

> 'Qu'on imagine (s'il est possible) une femme couverte d'un vêtement sans fin, lui-même tissé de tout ce que dit le journal de Mode . . .' (*Système de la Mode*). Cette imagination, apparemment méthodique, puisqu'elle ne fait que mettre en œuvre une motion opératoire de l'analyse sémantique ('le texte sans fin'), vise en douce à dénoncer le monstre de la Totalité (la Totalité comme monstre).[49]

This is taken from the last fragment of *Roland Barthes*. Barthes could not have chosen a more dramatic place, nor a more tongue-and-cheek and inconclusive one, to highlight the continuity in his thought. High method meets the need for an 'écriture', and the pursuit of an ethics of form with which to counter inhumanity and violence emerges with a thoroughly mediated brightness from these simple-looking metaphors and allusions to theoretical thought. No matter that 'le monstre de la totalité' might have seemed by 1975, the year of the book's publication, to have become quite an inadequate, watered down, negative standard bearer or target for the various radicalizing investments of semiology, deconstruction, Foucauldian epistemology, psychoanalytic criticism, feminism, as well as Barthes's own practice of textual plurality that had all developed in the postwar theoretical debate. On the contrary. All this anxiety and ambition is carried and given further analytical-turned-imaginative energy in this moment of reading and of imaginary, synthetic perusal.

But the lures of totalising accounts of experience and of a totalised sense of self are not to be done away with without the sense that any strategy for the achievement of this, including the carnavalesque that Barthes refers to here, will themselves be transformed into performative images of that very same totality that they seek to break up. The psychoanalytic dimension that is in play here, and that combines so ominously with the others I have just mentioned, can itself be encapsulated in one such totalising and immediate sweep – one that I shall continue to have recourse to in the chapters that follow. In 1904 Freud characterises the narcissistic tendency as so omnivorous that even paranoia can nourish it and fulfil it. This active and dynamic perversity is developed in the later stages of his writing into an all-embracing theory of discontent, of a civilisation that can neither see beyond discontent nor produce the desire to. And the driving force behind this multifaceted, elusive and plural defensiveness is Eros:

> When a love-relationship is at its height there is no room left for any interest in the environment; a pair of lovers are sufficient to themselves, and do not even need the child they have in common to make them happy. In no other case does Eros so clearly betray the core of his being, his purpose of making one out of more than one; but when he has achieved this in the proverbial way through the love of two human beings, he refuses to go further.[50]

The incapacity of the ego to countenance a beyond to its own boundaries that Freud articulates in this well-known passage forms the basis of his response in 1932 to Einstein's notorious question, *Why War?* And in her own book by that name in which she takes up the question again, Jacqueline Rose argues that what emerges from Freud's response to the question is the notion that propensity for war derives from a fear of knowledge and of its acquisition. This fear is structural in Freud, it is an inescapable element in the functioning of the psyche. The funnelling of the many into the one governs the erotic charge itself, and produces its fundamentally ambivalent procedures favouring both life and not life, the acceptance and the stifling of others, generosity and violence.

In his account of this ambivalence in *Civilisation and its Discontents*, Freud brings together the range of his allusive involvements with the methodologies that have fired his speculative imagination and that include human biology, animal biology, anthropology, literature, visual art, history, the law, politics. But the plurality of the psychic and cultural sediment that Freud is able to uncover is determinist in nature, even though it needs a theory of almost indefinite plurality and malleability to uncover; this is the famed determinism of the erotic constitution of the human, gendered subject. Freud argues that the ego is structurally at odds with itself. Its goal is happiness, but it depends for that happiness on circumstance quite outside itself, and outside its forever lost and longed-for control, whose only remaining form is imposed and self-imposed immobility. Civilisation will not provide the ego with the happiness it seeks. Its suffering is threefold: the superior power of nature, the feebleness of the body, and the inadequacy of the regulations adjusting human relations.

Civilisation is seen to fail in alleviating suffering at all these three levels, and much of this argumentation is now very familiar. At the level of the body, the ego will never overcome its disappointment at being subjected to material decay. Nor can it ever accommodate itself to the sense of being a tenant of the body and of being subjugated to the requirement of procreation. These are quasi-existential boundaries to the mobility of the ego and to its capacity to absorb frustration. Freud reads the form of the human body, its organic evolution from quadruped to upright biped, as a further irrefutable sign of an ego subjugated to the deadening inevitability of civilisation, which he presents as an unstoppable process that is not only organic, but anthropological as well as social and sexual. The body, in all its gendered shapes and forms, is a mobile and all the more irrevocable testimony to the sacrifice of instinctive pleasure to civilisation.

And in giving his account of the ego's battles with others, Freud again offers no hope for happiness within civilisation, no hope for that hopeless return to a world whose forms and bodies mirror the only true one. The ego gives up its supremacy, its position of silent soliloquy, only under the severest pressure to accept a position in the family. But this acceptance is imposed at the cost of a founding act of violence, which Freud had previously postulated in *Totem and Taboo*.[51] In that notorious scenario, Freud speculates about a distant anthropological moment in which the male sons band together in revolt against the implacable authority of the father. They murder him, only then to be confronted – and this is the crucial point – with the prospect of the endless repetition of this violent bid for self-determination. They vote to separate, to inaugurate the family, to found the taboo on incest and thus to divide, to trade, and to diversify the source of power. But in compensation, male power is wielded all the more firmly within the family, and publicly affirmed in the domination of women and in their exchange in marriage.

Moreover, this cycle of violent resentment followed by static relations of authority is then repeated at a later stage in the process of civilisation imagined by Freud, at the stage when the family forges relations with other families and with society at large. Attitudes, if not acts, of suspicion and violence predominate there once again in Freud's psychoanalytical account. Adolescents are forced through various rites of passage that signal nothing more strongly than a fear of the world out there. Women are cast in the role of defenders of the family and of emotional life within the family unit. Men are absorbed into business and the pursuit of social and technological progress – which itself, Freud argues, can only disappoint once again. For the pursuit of utility involves uniformity. While satisfying the ego's desire to appropriate others and the environment, this uniformity can only once again disappoint the ego's desire to remain unique and answerable only to itself.

Freud, with Baudelaire before him, thus reads symptomatically the valuing of leisure in civilised society as an escape from the bruising of the ego suffered by its enforced participation in progress. And the outrageously static gender relations that all this involves are also read symptomatically by Freud – whose entire tone in this book is one of still unabated outrage by a situation that strikes him overridingly with its pathos. Dynamics within and without the family are read as symptomatic of a paradoxically vibrating, but immobile society that Freud sees civilisation as a whole as being structurally incapable of passing beyond, fixated as it is on the innumerable reminders that it is the lot of the ego to conform.

The reader of *Roland Barthes* might come across one of the last illustrations in the book – a page reproduced from the *Encyclopédie* showing the veins in the human body. Barthes does not comment; the overall effect is of plural possible readings – not only the anatomical approach suggested in the subscription is involved, but also the botanical as well as the zoological one, and the distinct rhetorics of medicine and of art, particularly the sketch, are also in play. Who can with any certainty draw the paths to the inception and the maintenance of breath, of voice and gasp in the body? But equally, who cannot be blinded – struck beyond knowledge and the need for it – by the self-evident knowability of the bodily form?

To put the response differently: who would want some withdrawal – impossible anyway – from the word, from the magnificently synthetic forms it wields on the springboards of acoustic and scriptural images? Synthesis may have its own aura of a return to narcissistic seamlessness, but still the Word dissolves repeatedly in its usages and in endless formations and reformations of its sense. Perhaps this unpredictable scattering of sense, which the encyclopaedic pursuit of enumeration cannot exhaust any more than the structuralist one can, is some compensation for the harnessing of erotic energy to social and communal goals and for the dissipation of self-centred, self-compressing egoistic energy that this sacrifice involves. Perhaps. But then again such sublimation may not only be poor compensation, as Freud stresses in *Civilisation and its Discontents*; it may actually secrete the psychic unguents of the ego's impregnable cocoon, a form of which Barthes portrays in his reading of Sarrasine's psycho-cultural pathology. This cocoon is made of the codes and voices the displaying of which, in the ambient and transient, self-diminishing idealism of *Système de la mode* as well as of *S/Z*, was thought sufficiently powerful in itself to lead from the stage the whole sorry tragedy of the ego and its identifications.

In the fragment 'L'imaginaire' from *Roland Barthes* that has provided this chapter with a leitmotif, Barthes evokes again those features of method – any method, and also every method that Barthes as writer had adopted up to and including the composition of *Roland Barthes* – that promise display, manifestation, awareness of the terms and scenes of awareness itself. Principally, Barthes here revisits his notion of 'mise-en-scène':

> L'effort vital de ce livre est de mettre en scène un imaginaire. 'Mettre en scène'
> veut dire: échelonner les portants, disperser les rôles, établir des niveaux et, à
> la limite: faire de la rampe une barre incertaine.[52]

Barthes uses an appeal to autobiography to enmesh subjective with critical
experience of the imaginary – or to enact that enmeshing. The theatre director's prerogative is to apportion roles, patterns of behaviour and of movement, to control space and to shape it. But for the performer's space also to
be an intellectual space, Barthes either as critic or as autobiographer would
need to be sure that scripting was equally finite in both cases, the effects
equally manageable and predictable.

> La difficulté, cependant, est qu'on ne peut numéroter ces degrés, comme les
> degrés d'un spiritueux ou d'une torture.[53]

The more informed the idea of theatre is by Brechtian alienation effects, and
the more mobile the possibilities become in the relation of spectator to action
– 'une barre incertaine' –, the less those possibilities can be enumerated. The
degree of alcoholic intensity can be magnified indefinitely, torture is endlessly
and alternately sadistic and masochistic; such is the outcome of rationalist
epistemology. Mobility does not produce redirection. The fixity of this
outcome, the paranoia and regression it nourishes might be countered,
Barthes suggests, by the rhetorical procedures that he synthesises as the practice of 'signer l'imaginaire' that I mentioned earlier. Referring to *Roland
Barthes* itself, he goes on:

> C'est ce qu'on a pu faire ici pour quelques fragments (*guillemets, parenthèses,
> dictée, scène, redan, etc.*): le sujet, dédoublé (ou *s'imaginant* tel), parvient parfois
> à signer son imaginaire.[54]

'Signer': to sign, to put one's name to – in that sense to take possession of, to
match subjective investment with its effects and with the objects of its attachment. Mobile, floating quotation marks – 'un texte aux guillemets incer-
tains'[55] as Barthes puts it later in the fragment – is itself an image, a rich
metaphoric encapsulating, but also a loaded one, of what Barthes is trying to
have his reader imagine. Developed in response to Flaubert, it silently
includes a range of possible reading attitudes – by silently including, I mean
including without voice, without stability of effect or response or conception.
Such attitudes of the reading mind include concerns with the plural, the
intertextual, the carnavalesque . . .We are being invited to imagine a reading
that has abandoned the pursuit of depth – 'il ne sait pas bien *approfondir*',[56]
writes Barthes of himself – and that in return nourishes not only the

ephemeral but the multifocused, each in the service of an intransitive metonymy, rather than a transcendent and virile metaphor. Such a writing would be able to signal its own sources of obsession, its own channels of interest, and also the channelling of its interest and its erotic inspirations. It would be a writing that would not silence or immobilise the volatility of this channelling or the energy of its symptoms.

But that is exactly the danger run by the aspiration to 'signer l'imaginaire' – to signal is inevitably to impose form, to affirm coherence; to fall into 'l'imaginaire de la lucidité',[57] as Barthes puts it in this fragment; to return again to the dramas of metaphor and synthesis. Perhaps a further signing could alert us to this further twist in the spiral. Another meaning of 'signer' – to use sign language, in a sense to mime – testifies to a kind of creative withdrawal from the game, a capitulation in the face of the ambition to oversee response and the pressures to respond. Rather than give signs of the labyrinthine constitution of past and anticipated response, this type of sign-writing now mimes it, sketches in the same spaceless textual air the shapes which response assumes – intellectual, erotic, mnemonic, desired, imagined . . . But will this wordless doubling of the word elude the power of the word to allocate place and to dominate it?

Both senses of 'signer', and the imperceptible distance between them, are ways Barthes has invented to give form to the slyness of imaginary impulse and also its protean appropriativeness.

> L'imaginaire vient à pas de loup, patinant en douceur sur un passé simple, un pronom, un souvenir, bref tout ce qui peut se rassembler sous la devise même du Miroir et de son Image: *Moi, je.*[58]

The colloquial sounding 'moi, je' might so easily be translated using John Lennon's refrain 'I, me, me, I', his implacable condemnation of capitalist egoism, were it not that the naive focus on 'ego' as a curable ill is precisely what Lacanian psychoanalysis recoils from as well as Barthes's own reading of that. But the ego is present, symptomatically ever-present in the apparently commonplace and emptiest-sounding signifier. 'Le moi', after all, is simply the French word for the ego, and in Barthes's own textual miming here, the ego is activated with each utterance, each use of the first person, each automatic and, in that ambivalent sense, spontaneous involvement with syntax, grammar and rhetoric. To say or to think 'I' or 'je', to kick once again into *parole* and deferral, is to adopt and not discard the costumes of the ego, to shuffle in amongst its masks, and in that way to circumscribe in the air an exclusion zone allowing, however ephemerally, speech, synthesis, thought.

To transfer briefly to Lacanian ground for a moment, there cannot be a simple division or antagonism between the orders of the imaginary and the symbolic. The imaginary lures and delusions of the mirror stage are said to provide the infant with the jubilation of a wholly specular independence from the breast, from the mother's presence or absence, and in relation to the spatial environment at large. But the symbolic, far from distinguishing itself definitively from the Imaginary or cauterising its boundaries, is subsumed in the effects of deferral that constitute it. It is marked by no moment of entry other than in symptomatic form, no conclusive moment of awareness that speaking subjects exist in innumerable effects of representation and in the positions that allow relations of dialogue, authority, gender, vision and its privileging, epistemology . . . the vast labyrinths of discourse at large. There is no firm line of distinction between imaginary and symbolic, no dialogue or dialectic, nor even some mobile overlap or dovetailing. There is rather a mutual silencing, a mutual exclusion: the intimacy of the links between the two produces effects of engulfment, take-over, sameness, coming together rather than drawing apart.

Lacan himself emphasizes this process in a typical wordplay in which he characterises the relation of imaginary to symbolic as a merging of two sets of relations – *concurrence* and *concours*. The distinction is a fine one, hardly there: hardly movement at all, then, between the two orientations. What starts out as competition ends up as – competition. As a result, at one level at least, we might be able to breathe a sigh of relief on behalf of the symbolic: immobility – or mobility of a purely specular and formal kind – monologue, tyrannical delusion, mutilation of other and self alike – all these approaches to exchange that characterise ancestral imaginary attachments and moments of fulfilment are subject, it would seem, to the severest 'competition' at the hands of an exchange now, in another moment, understood and accepted as difference, deferral, splitting, cutting, un-wholeness, incompletion, bound-lessness, a manner of exchange that still, for all that, constitutes a society and the situations that make it up . . .*Concurrence* is the stuff, the symbolic and rhetorical stuff itself of some decay in an otherwise seamless continuity of desire and fulfilment, present and future, private sensation and public sense.

But *concurrence* drifts ceaselessly and regressively into *concours* – another competition, and an equally public one in one sense – the sense of the 'con-cours d'entrée', the 'concours de beauté', the 'concours agricole'. But Lacan brings out the etymology of coming together in *concours*, highlighting in the signifier itself (where else?) the primordial sense and the inextinguishable assumption of accord, conjunction, entwinement, fusion. There is an oscilla-tion, not a distinction, between such conjunction and the aggressive energy with which the subject encounters others. At one level, what produces the sense of one-ness is itself made of the plural and of others; 'le désir de l'autre',[59] to invoke another Lacanian wordplay, is not only the desire for another object or form, but the desire for the other's desire, the place of it and the position of it. If the subject is subjugated by its desire for another, condemned to bear witness to its own lack of centre, then it seeks supremacy once again in the desire for the position of another and of that desiring energy. The imaginary position is not only fragile in itself, but matches the fragile, fragilised position of the subject's position in the symbolic order.

From either orientation, imaginary or symbolic, the subject experiences an unbreachable discontinuity of experience and sense of self, and a consequent devaluing of the objects of his or her fascination. '"Je ne suis rien de ce qui m'arrive. Tu n'es rien de ce qui vaut"',[60] as Lacan scripts it. The subject may be nothing and may have nothing of itself, but then will think as though the other had nothing, either. Symbolic and imaginary orientations come together in producing the symptoms of the subject's desperate competitiveness. And in fact, the imaginary is defined in terms of 'un stade': not only a stage to be gone through but a stadium, implying an audience, however absent or innumerable, without bounds or place. Symbolic representation, like the relation to others and to objects, is both ancestral and anticipated, it has no start or conclusion. Rather than suggesting simply the collapse of the imaginary order and the birth of free, unthreatened and unthreatening exchange, this infiltration is truly reversible; the effects of representation nurture those of the imaginary. Symbolic and imaginary orientations each collude with the other in spurring magnificently elusive constructions of the nostalgic, on the one hand, and the paranoid on the other.

Barthes's response to that multiheaded 'monstre de la totalité' that is fed by the imaginary orientation and its lack of boundary, its lack of centre in the symbolic, is to develop a writing that signals and signs precisely that elusiveness of imaginary self-protection, its mobility, its potential tyranny, its retentiveness, its indefiniteness and its infectiousness, its consequent mobility, pluralism and fascination. And that fascination includes not only fascination with capture at large but with capturing those imaginary effects themselves. This is the challenge that Barthes's later writing seeks to rise to and from which it derives its creative energy. If the relation of the Lacanian imaginary to the symbolic is one of both/and, then in *Fragments d'un discours amoureux*, as I indicated earlier, that relation is one of neither/nor. Nor both. The rhetoric of the book mimes coming together but injects that process with discontinuity, the renewed rather than the repeated beginning, the dissolved rather than the denied ending. In staging the voracious, multiform assumptions of security, seclusion and power, the book stages simultaneously the generation and degeneration of that voraciousness itself. But not both; the effect of one on the other is not there to be charted, the relations in the book are not organic nor even dynamic. And it is in the context of erotic appeal and desire, in the most intimate recesses of bodily made verbal, that the book plays out its ceaseless, stop–start testimony to psychic and symptomatic, coerced but creative ingenuity.

I shall be returning periodically to various fragments from the book in the chapters that follow, and shall not attempt here or elsewhere a complete account of *Fragments*. In effect, a few examples could take us just as far as many more. The effect of the fragment in Barthes's hand, let me repeat, is simultaneously to assert and to dissolve its own boundaries. In 'L'exil de l'imaginaire', Barthes makes his own use of the play on 'de' that is so productive for Lacan: the title signals both the exile that constitutes the imaginary, and exile from the imaginary. In the first small paragraph of that fragment, Barthes gives a rapid, deft and constantly re-readable perusal of what is at stake for him in the notion of the image and its paths to the imaginary.

> Je reprends Werther à ce moment fictif (dans la fiction elle-même) où il aurait renoncer à se suicider. Il ne lui reste plus alors que l'exil: non pas s'éloigner de Charlotte (il l'à déjà fait une fois, sans résultat), mais s'exiler de son image, ou pire encore: tarir cette énergie délirante qu'on appelle l'Imaginaire. Commence alors 'une espèce de longue insomnie'. Tel est le prix à payer: la mort de l'Image contre ma propre vie.[61]

Early Romanticism in the form of the iconic Werther, high Romanticism in the form of Hugo's cosmic introspection, the Freudian analytic approach to the psyche are all evoked in one brief loop for the historical and the epistemological narratives they announce. Textual, fictional and purely fictive mobility are all active ingredients in this writing, however diffuse and implicit they may be. Barthes imagines Werther *not* committing suicide out of unrequited love. He imagines the Romantic illusion broken, and in doing that he is developing the logic in Goethe's novel and of a narrative display that cannot accommodate the poetry of adoration, and that crumbles in the search for the origins of adoration, its forms and its future. In Barthes's imagination at this point, Werther has already accepted what is patent in the novel although beyond acceptance there, which is that objects of love elude the adoration directed at them.

But there would need to be more. This acceptance is the foregoing of an image, not a person; with his simple-looking reference to the events in *Werther*, Barthes signals the distinction between leaving a person behind and leaving behind the desire for position in relation to her. In another fragment, Barthes suggests that what Werther is obsessed with and fascinated by is the place that is not his – the place of the husband with a family, attended to by Charlotte.

Chaque fois que je voyais l'autre, inopinément, dans sa 'structure' *(sistemato)*, j'étais fasciné: je croyais contempler une *essence*: celle de la conjugalité.[62]

This is a voyeurism or a scopophilia that has been oddly temporalised here. The essence being viewed is suspended in time and place, flattened in its gendered familiarity. It is beyond the frame of subjectivity and yet defines the subject nonetheless, not only in the structuralist or rationalist sense, but in the sense of structure and the appeal of it beating out their rhythms quietly like a pulse in the mind. The space of 'l'essence de la conjugalité' is suspended between orthodoxy and perversion – and it is that suspension which gives it its unmeasured temporality.

Non, ce que je fantasme dans le système (fantasme d'autant plus paradoxal qu'il n'a pas d'éclat): je veux, je désire, tout simplement, une *structure* (ce mot, naguère, faisait grincer des dents: on y voyait le comble de l'abstraction). Certes, il n'y a pas un bonheur de la structure; mais toute structure est *habitable*.[63]

Returning to 'L'exil de l'imaginaire', it is this paradoxical suspension that Barthes imagines Werther giving up, ready to abandon his fixation on a position he cannot occupy. In this way he would become the recipient of the Freudian gift of life – of socialised creativity, at one level, or at another, simply the gift of gift which here in Barthes's opening little paragraph takes the form once again of image and its indefinite refractiveness:

Tel est le prix à payer: la mort de l'Image contre ma propre vie.[64]

This gift, though, this letting go of the image, while broadcasting generosity, also signals the implacable orthodoxy of civilisation as Freud encounters it. Barthes's temporalised, or at least vibrating suspension in the image might work against those quasi-metaphysical pressures to conform. Suspension seems to outmanoeuvre the intimations of its own fixity: it is the product of 'une énergie délirante', the energy of excess, the exceeding of targets and their induced appeal – an energy derived from the mobility of these targets, symptomatic as they are and as such open to continuous rereading, refiguring, reinvestment. But Barthes swerves off again immediately in his response to the image and its malleability: 'délire' is now clearly symptomatic, readably so, and as such part of an established currency of erotic response.

(La passion amoureuse est un délire; mais le délire n'est pas étrange; tout le monde en parle, il est désormais apprivoisé. Ce qui est énigmatique, c'est *la perte de délire:* on rentre dans quoi?)[65]

No sooner has Barthes introduced the idea that imaginary suspension might be resistant generally and to narrative in particular than he reminds us that 'délire' is a speakable and familiar commonplace. It is now the *loss* of dreams of folly and of the exorbitant that might induce enigma or instability – those limited but at least unappropriative signs of drama and of the yet-to-be. Suspension and the excess that might have gone with it have taken their place in representation, and *as* a representation of itself; it is public and familiar, however lived, uncircumscribed, joyous or painful. To lose a place in the drama would be to step into – what? the new? a tired quest for it? or perhaps a re-energising of exile? Barthes heuristically leaves it open – a feigned ignorance that has a history in French rhetoric from Pascal to Ponge. It is a feint that here might have some power to transform the symbolic and the represented, at least for the moment of reading, into an element of the unknown, the yet-to-be-prescribed and positioned.

For the duration of that moment of reading, the symbolic seems against all the odds to have been transmuted into the space of the lover and the lover's sense of being suspended from sense, of being placed without place. Despite any tautology in the sound of this, or rather resting on tautology once again in his writing life, Barthes contrives to find forms and formulations that would transform the sense of love – into what? 'Adorable'; from various levels of the banal, Barthes imagines that epithet as capturing the totality of the loved being:

> [. . .] car Tout ne pourrait s'inventorier sans se diminuer: dans *Adorable!* aucune qualité ne vient se loger, mais seulement le *tout* de l'affect.[66]

But this imaginary capturing in a word is marked by what eludes this would-be verbal lassooing. The utterance of 'adorable!' signals not only capturing but missing. Confidence in the power of the epithet to qualify, to capture and enrapture, itself rekindles the sense that some quality will always still be missing and that the power to name gets its life-blood from the possibility of its collapse. But at the same time, this exile in uttering *Adorable!* from the enraptured state it articulates, from the totality of affective sensation it extracts for a moment from memory, *serves* the imaginary embrace *just as much as* the unravelling of that at the hands of symbolic interaction and exchange. On the one hand, the remnant devalues and contaminates the matching of experience and their forms in the mind; but the remnant serves the imaginary power of the verbal embrace to unearth, or at least evoke, but in any case to *retain* the extraneous, the enigmatic, the elusive; all these are elements that renew that imaginary Word and give it life. Civilised, socialised, discursive, gendered exile from the imaginary is *also* the exile of which the imaginary consists, in which it consists, in which it acquires the consistency of a skin.

De cet échec langagier, il ne reste qu'une trace: le mot 'adorable' (la bonne traduction de 'adorable' serait l'*ipse* latin: c'est lui, c'est bien lui en personne).[67]

The thing in itself, the loved body and soul in itself, reachable only by a word, but beyond the reach of a word: this is adoration of a word both for what it places and displaces. An adoration at once self-exploding and self-preserving; not an ambivalence, but a competitiveness that spans antagonism and collusion, in which to invade rests on being invaded, and in which the competitors each succeed by abdicating.

Perhaps this vibration of the synthetic and the incomplete is what produces that 'énergie délirante' that Barthes accords imaginary fixation, even in its take-over of erotic attachment. Clearly, movement and grief have become alloys of each other once again. To give up the tight embrace of subject and object pushing to and fro in images made of sensation, symptom, ephemera, whim, the scripted and the intimate, the vocabularies of the banal and the familiar – to give up this image is the rather sad, perhaps, rite of passage required by a civilisation of exchange: 'Quel dommage!',[68] as Barthes says. For this movement from Eros to Agape, from the boudoir to the Last Supper, is not without return. The gift of intransitive gift, for which the inevitably incommensurate return can only be place and position, does have dimension: it is *imagined* received, it has to be imagined received by precisely those freed from the erotic embrace of the One, and who are now grieved over for their very return to order and to their place in a mobile, elusive but ever-present Oedipal script:

> [. . .] de même, l'être aimé – si je lui sacrifie un Imaginaire qui cependant l'empoissait –, l'être aimé doit entrer dans la mélancolie de sa propre déchéance. Et il faut, concurremment à mon propre deuil, prévoir et assumer cette mélancholie de l'autre, et j'en souffre, *car je l'aime encore.*[69]

To abandon and to retain continue to grapple with each other in a drama that overdetermines the encounter – social as well as amorous – between self and other or others. What kind of farewell is this? What freedom of movement would the falling away of hysterical *affolement* let in?[70] Is this a place of resignation or resistance? Disappointment or explosiveness? Ethics or tyranny? An economy of invasion or of generosity?

If there is no countering of the imaginary by the symbolic, no cure for monologue at the hands of dialogue, of narcissism at the hands of civilisation, then *Fragments d'un discours amoureux* bears witness not only to a dynamic of exclusion and the stand-off, but also to the self-evidence of that dynamic and in some sense to its banality. The two orders have settled down to a familiar and unresolved rubbing of shoulders enjoyed by suspicious allies or partners in crime. This perception is itself not much of a theoretical advance, perhaps, on what we find in Lacan and his explosive engagement with his own inheritances – however agonistic – of Bachelard, Sartre, the Surrealists, to mention but those twentieth-century figures. But for Barthes to situate his book at what might seem the tired end of a theoretical, and purely theoretical, debate is also to situate it in the microlife of the intimate, in the junctures of the ingrained and the spontaneous. High and low theory meet, speculation and observation, the conceptual and the popular, the projected and the remembered, affirmation and brush-off. They vibrate continuously like the two strands of the reed in an oboe. This vibration does not produce a harmony or an equivalence or a tolerance; but neither is there any ground on which to establish any empires. To destroy, Barthes reminds us, would in any case merely reproduce the discursive fortifications it tries to blow up:

> *détruire* ne serait en fin de compte que reconstruire un lieu de parole dont le seul caractère serait l'extériorité: extérieur et immobile: tel est le langage dogmatique.[71]

Textual practice and textual ethics are what Barthes offers as resistance to the dour asphyxia threatened by dogma and doxa alike. And this text – both a practice and a fantasy – is not one of insipid formal freedom, though it rests on forms and the imagining of them; it is a text that surveys its own decomposition.

> Tandis qu'en décomposant, j'accepte d'accompagner cette décomposition, de me décomposer moi-même, au fur et à mesure: je dérape, m'accroche et entraîne.[72]

This is writing that dissolves targets, watches them dissolve in the continuing pursuit of them; it is a figuration of what the ego might be without the bounds of its psychic, cultural, gendered and so many other defences. It is a composition heard only here in reading, and mimed in further acts of writing. It is one instance of the pursuit of decay.

CHAPTER THREE

Dreams, schemes and wordplay: the Surrealism of Robert Desnos

At the beginning of *Nadja*, Breton's youthful but seminal Surrealist text, published in 1928, the narrator ponders on the voices that make up his sense of self.[1] The Cartesian ego, transparent and self-validating is transformed into a hot-house of voices that openly challenge their host to hear them and understand them. But will he succeed? This eager narrator and the uncompromising Breton more generally seek tirelessly to press the unpredictable, the chance occurrence, the irredeemably circumstantial into allowing a censored, unimagined transparency of the mind and the senses to emerge. But in *Nadja*, Breton's narrator ultimately stands idly by as he watches the collapse of his attempt to get the unconscious out of the asylum. Perhaps his liberated vision is blinkered by his gender. Perhaps obsession will always lack the power to uncover the attachments that drive it. Steadily, inexorably, the voices that Breton seeks out display their own lack of integrity, their dependence on the loaded dice of dialogue and discursive play at large.

Nadja charts in advance the now familiar message booming out to us from Surrealist and other avant-gardist experimentation in Europe of the 1920s and 30s. The unconscious cannot wilfully or formalistically be wrenched from the Freudian concept of it, it is transmitted in symptoms rather than in unambiguous signals of creative energy and revolt. Gloomily, perhaps, the legacy of Surrealism, as well as of the postwar theoretical debate, is, inevitably, the signifier: the no-alternative fascination with the impact and impulse as such of word and image. But the sumptuous diversity of individual Surrealist practitioners and practices testifies to the ambition, the uncharted excitement and outcomes of wholeheartedly accepting discursive mediation in all its indefinite forms. *Nadja* itself is a notorious agglomeration of autobiography, photography, fiction, criticism, philosophy. Aragon's Surrealist and non-Surrealist writing spans a relishing of linguistic discovery for its own sake, polemical writing in prose and verse, art criticism and the historical novel. Abstractionism and ironic realism famously rub shoulders, or rub each other up the wrong way, in Surrealist painting. Robert Desnos, in himself far less of an iconic figure in popular modernism, cuts his own highly distinctive groove in this vigorous uncoupling of sense and purpose. From his early collaboration with Breton in the 1920s until he was killed by the Nazis in 1945, his own activity involves writing and broadcasting, commentary on jazz and painting as well as his tireless commitment to revealing dream-energy at work in language: hailed as a 'medium' by Breton, his work encompasses aggressively erotic fiction, elaborate, lyrical pastiche and the irreverent phonetic wordplay which is the object of my own fascination in this chapter. Can wordplay produce a decay in convention and censorship? Or does it simply highlight a decay in invention?

The objectives of language-play seem ambivalent and provisional. On the one hand, to indulge in it offers the prospect of exposing the rules of language through a range of ironic or aggressive devices and attitudes. But these attitudes might simply be an obvious part of the speaking subject's general experience of the linguistic given which she or he in any case experiences as a kind of on-the-spot improvisation, without needing for that to resort to visions of linguistic free play. Perhaps it is precisely this spontaneous, illusory sense of language-in-the-mouth that the wordplayer seeks to exploit for its powers of semantic and syntactic metamorphosis. Even so, language games seem relatively po-faced in relation to the real thing. And beyond this, in any event, there is the still more powerful image of a discourse able to predict its own effects and manipulate its audience with complete certainty: a discourse embraced and enclosed in the fascinating, immobilised image of its own impact, all fragmentation momentarily absorbed.

Each of these aspirations might have catastrophic outcomes embedded in them. In the first place, ironic gestures might never reach beyond a kind of naive despair or a static *mauvaise foi*. And in the second, the dream of eluding the interplay in language of the different positions occupied by speaker and listener, the essentially antisocial phantasy of placing the speaking and imagining 'I' alone and unique on the stage of its own soliloquy, suggest an overestimation of linguistic power that is as violent as it is illusory. Desnos momentarily toyed with the image of Alfred de Musset as an emblematic model of his own writing. The situation of Lorenzaccio after his assassination of Lorenzo de Medicis testifies to the high stakes of gaming with the 'I' in discourse. Lorenzaccio's political vision as well as his private sense of his own worth are hollowed out in his attempt to bring down the Medicis culture of exploitation by aping its manners and donning its disguises. Political assassination is infiltrated by the deluded pursuit of the final solution, and turns into a symbolic, antisocial and antisexual suppression of any dialogue of actor and spectator, or agent and community.[2]

But the impulse to turn our language-bound subjectivity around and have it master its own language is not an easy one to dismiss. It is at the heart of lyrical poetics and, for example, the lyrical shaping of the voice. Michel Murat writes:

> A la limite, le comportement lyrique signifie par lui-même, et se passe de la littérature; une continuité en tous cas est postulée de l'homme à l'œuvre.[3]

And this confluence of self and language is one of the strongest elements in Surrealist aspiration. Maurice Blanchot emphasises the ideological dimension of automatic writing. A dissolution is manufactured of the barriers separating conscious from unconscious, sequestering nations and classes, and dividing the subject. Breton writes in the *Manifeste du Surréalisme* of 1924 that

> Non seulement ce langage sans réserve que je cherche à rendre toujours valable, qui me paraît s'adapter à toutes les circonstances de la vie, non seulement ce langage ne me prive d'aucun de mes moyens, mais encore il me prête une extraordinaire lucidité et cela dans le domaine où de lui j'en attendais le moins.[4]

The mobility of the frontiers of waking and sleeping, thinking and dreaming, are exploited in an effort to abolish the inaccessibility of one to the other. The aura of automatic writing eludes form and formulation, is allowed to spread as a liquid across every recess or enclosure in the hope of giving shape, in a mass of directionless *énonciation*, to the psychic implants making up the fabric of language. Blanchot comments:

> Dans l'écriture automatique, ce n'est pas à proprement parler le mot qui devient libre, mais le mot et ma liberté ne font plus qu'un. Je me glisse dans le mot, il garde mon empreinte et il est ma réalité imprimée; il adhèrer à ma non-adhérence.[5]

The speaking or writing subject and his/her discourse, far from supplanting one another in a never-ending structural toing-and-froing, act in accord, as though subjectivity were etching its marks in the substance of sense. Instead of complying with its own moulding in the structures of verbal exchange, writing manufactures the power to avoid 'adhering' to the force of these structures, in psychic terms as well as in terms of what is permissible or acceptable in language. The subject now 'adheres' to the immotivated mobility that automatic writing is granted the power to improvise.

Further on, Blanchot articulates this Surrealist drive towards a co-ordination of word and liberty in terms reminiscent of Sartrean thought. His speculation shifts to the prospect of outmanoeuvring the potential violence of engagement with others and with otherness at large by usurping their place and their position:

> Que cet effort suprême par lequel l'homme veut se retourner sur soi et se saisir d'un regard qui n'est pas le sien ait toujours été le rêve et le ressort du surréalisme, les signes en sont innombrables.[6]

Blanchot is focusing his response to Surrealist ambition on the principal quality of automatic writing, which is that it rests on dialogue and therefore on rhetoric. He emphasises the democracy of the Surrealist aspiration to see self as other; but he does so ambivalently. His 'regard qui n'est pas le sien', his compressed evocation here of the Not-I, and particularly his invocation of the Sartrean metaphor of an invasive, unblinking gaze, are themselves a citation of the impulse to imagine otherness – amorphous and plural – as *one*; dialogue with this other-I is embraced and stultified in the same stroke. Blanchot is responding to the desire expressed in Surrealism to transform our immersion in contingency into a set of unique events able to assert their integrity and their intactness. And this need not be a solitary or a defensive intactness – not the ironic, self-critical 'moi, je suis intact, ça m'est égal'[7] of Rimbaud. Unhampered by any self-consciously new reading, events conceived in this way radiate democracy by returning to us, to the subjectivity of the perceiving eye, the power to mobilise them and remodel them in the present, with every blink and impulse of revolt. To succeed, this quest for the integrity of the event would need a language able to do away with the some of the differences it depends on – signifier and signified, sound and sense. 'Image and sound interpenetrate with automatic precision and such felicity that no chink is left for the penny-in-the-slot called meaning', writes Walter Benjamin in his account of Surrealism in *One-Way Street*.[8] In this way, the signifier acquires the capacity to take hold of its own effects and the spell they cast.

In pursuit of such an expression, much Surrealist writing seems to take up some of the threads in the work of Nerval. Michel Murat has highlighted the appeal of Nerval for Desnos, as well as the fact that both writers were fascinated by an actress and by the theatre at large. Both he and Marie-Claire Dumas point out that the name of Yvonne George along with that of Robert Desnos himself figure in acrostic down both sides of 'Infinitif', in the 'Les Ténèbres' section of *Corps et biens*.[9]

> *Infinitif*
> Y mourir ô belle flammèche y mourir
> voir les nuages fondre comme la neige et l'écho
> origines du soleil et du blanc pauvres comme Job
> ne pas mourir encore et voir durer l'ombre

naître avec le feu et ne pas mourir
éteindre et embrasser amour fugace le ciel mat
gagner les hauteurs abandonner le bord
et qui sait découvrir ce que j'aime
omettre de transmettre mon nom aux années
rire aux heures orageuses dormir au pied d'un pin
grâce aux étoiles semblables à un numéro
et mourir ce que j'aime au bord des flammes.[10]

The ludic poetic form of the acrostic, however unpretentious, carries hidden within it the capacity to set off a catastrophe that slumbers at the heart of sense-making. It offers us on the one hand a kind of Sartrean *dépassement* or forward intellectual thrust, but impotence on the other. The evident artifice of the acrostic in 'Infinitif' spectacularly fails to stabilise two personalities – Robert Desnos or Yvonne George – in relation to the two signifiers or to each other. But there is no nostalgia for lost powers of naming. The effect is much more one of proper names refusing to name properly. We might almost believe that the signified and all its support-systems had been buried under this formal edifice – one which, even so, allows bits of signification to emerge on the surface. Looking at the two names torn apart down either side of the poem, we might almost imagine two wings of a magic mirror reflecting ad infinitum, without setting it in motion, the syntax of sense and appropriation, and congealing at the same time an entire grammar of erotic relations.

Might we imagine, here in the clutches of the infinitive, an ability to move from the grammatically incomplete to the grammatically boundless and into a discourse free of legislation? Perhaps we are always all too ready to imagine such a step. And the poem does unfurl in a series of points of departure, or rather of false starts. The expression 'grâce aux étoiles sem-blables à un numéro', for example, does not fall into place in relation to any verb or clause in the poem. It forms a syntactic nowhere, and on the level of the signified it underscores the mystical dimension sketched in by 'le numéro' with its hints of some magic or cabbalistic power. And the stage of this magic is a return to the signifier which allows, for a second, the infinitive 'mourir' in the following line to act as a transitive verb. As Eros turns towards the hypnotising site of the signifier, the poem seems to project for a moment the supreme power to foreclose and dominate its own impact.

Many of the aspirations of wordplay that I sketched out briefly at the beginning are at work in 'Infinitif'. Broadly, they consist in having, or trying to have, the operations of language seize up; in having this quasi-narcissistic fixity in the signifier cancel out the otherness that discourse coats us in; and even in having this otherness assume the forms of subjectivity itself and reproduce the sense and sensibility of selfhood. Once again, Nerval's writing

seems to anticipate many of the elements and consequences that such aspiration might involve. Nerval also attributes a mystical power to the signifier in
his spiritual quest for the roots of genesis. The 'alphabet magique'[11] and the
'hiéroglyphe mystérieux'[12] that he imagines in *Aurélia* have the power to
compose the score of the present and its generation.[13] At the same time, to
seek, as Nerval's narrator does, to place thought beyond representation – i.e.
beyond the footlights, or in the incarnation of a goddess – is to court
madness. This is the drama of *Aurélia*.

And in *Les Nuits d'octobre*, where Nerval explores the relations between
realism and his own sur-realism or 'supernaturalisme', Gérard meets two bar-
stool philosophers for whom all question and answer has been reduced to the
exchange of two barely distinguishable monosyllables: 'hum', and 'heuh'.[14]
These philosophical grunts highlight the folly of the whole quest for a linguistic out-of-bounds. But at the same time, this overdetermination in the
signifier does produce an absorbing phonetic substance, and puts on display
the unquenchable but futile desire to push a narrative way through to the
roots of our interplay with others, with the past, and with anteriority at large.

This log-jam in the flow of narration is actively desired by the unwilling narrator of Beckett's *Molloy*. In a dialogue with detritus and collapse that
is both amorous and antagonistic, Molloy's narrative stallings form part of a
general campaign to establish Molloy's own intactness. At a certain point in
his journey the purpose of which now escapes him, this unwilling narrator
seeks the power at once to inaugurate and abolish the impulse itself to
narrate. At a point, the proud means to this end takes the form of the French
monosyllable 'ma'(my), which, the narrator claims, is not just the utterance
of the possessive, but expresses the desire to possess, to possess a 'ma', a
'maman', and loudly to proclaim this desire. At the same time, the narrator
has given this syllable the power to abolish that desire and its long history. In
saying 'ma', in announcing and pronouncing possession, the narrator literally
truncates, phonetically amputates the maternal line. Either way, Molloy feels
able to defuse for the moment the ceaseless challenges thrown down to his
illusory and increasingly desperate autonomy. This 'ma', for the duration of
its utterance at least, is a signifier able to explode signification. The fall-out
creates, on the one hand, an enlarged power to manipulate language at will
at the level of *parole*; on the other, a coagulated stasis, the phantasm of
annihilation, a *jouissance* of ignorance and repression.[15]

What of the wordplay in *Corps et biens*? Marie-Claire Dumas and Michel
Murat have each characterised the collection as Desnos's own appraisal of
Surrealist automatism, and suggested that it represents Desnos's own way of
drawing a line under it. I want to concentrate on the formalist havoc created
in the 'Langage cuit' section of *Corps et biens*, and now particularly on
'Elégant Cantique de Salomé Salomon'.[16]

Elégant Cantique de Salomé Salomon
Mon mal meurt mais mes mains miment
Nœuds, nerfs non anneaux. Nul nord
Même amour mol? mames, mord
Nus nénés nonne ni Nine.

Où est Ninive sur la mammemonde?

Ma mer, m'amis, me murmure:
'nos nils noient nous nuits nées neiges'.
Meurt momie! môme: âme au mur.
Néant nié nom ni nerf n'ai-je!

    Aime haine
    Et n'aime
    Haine aime
    aimai ne

      M N
      N M
      N M
      M N

At the end of this small piece of poetic wordplay, signification has been reduced to a run of two consonants each barely distinguishable from the other – M N N M N M M N. This series without progression remains just this side of nonsense, in that it does consist in a minute fiddling with the alphabetical sequence – which is itself arbitrary, and which precisely because of that confirms intimations of sense-making just as much as it might deny them. This run of sounds is reminiscent of Nerval's grunts and Beckett's 'ma'. The drive to capture at a stroke the range of effects and positions involved in using language has now turned into an obsession busy reducing the many to the one and to asphyxia. The title is itself a concentration of different historical moments and of different narrative starting points. The pairing of the names Salome and Solomon creates an air of homophony in French, on the back of which this pairing can also act as a syntagmatic linkage making Solomon sound like the family name of Salome, in spite of the glaring historical incompatibility in the signified. This concertinaing of heterogeneous facets is continued at the levels of culture and sex. Salome and Solomon are each renowned for finding aesthetic form for obsessional love – be it the canticle or the dance of the seven veils.

This stuffing of the plural into the homogeneous is also developed in the syntax of the poem. The writing both playfully circumvents coherence and sketches it in, however allusively:

Mon mal meurt mais mes mains miment
Nœuds, nerfs non anneaux. Nul nord
Même amour mol? mames, mord
Nus nénés nonne ni Nine.

In the first sentence, there is at least some articulation of sense, in spite of the surge in the signifier towards wiping away phonetic difference. As readers we can make out the clause 'mon mal meurt', the conjunction 'mais', as well as the reference to hands that mime knots and nerves but not rings. And the further pursuit of coherence kicks back in once we have started to read. We inevitably seek out some interpretation of these units of sense. We might linger on this 'mal', and on the death ('meurt') of this pain or sickness or yearning, the orgasmic *petite mort* desired at all costs regardless of any 'anneau', the ring that symbolises fidelity and the sexual *doxa*. We might also probe into the image of miming, that imaginary mode of thought through which, according to Sartre in *L'Imaginaire*, consciousness strives to capture and harness the psychic networks of a concept.[17] In this case, that concept might be the knots and nerves – 'nœuds, nerfs' – of the personality, the web of its fibres and threads. But at the same time as provoking such a reading, the poem obviously wipes out the aural differences between the acoustic images it projects and moves towards abolishing sense. Interpretation and the tenacity of it is made to look like a pursuit of the most reductive kind of analogy.

But just as clearly, the poem seems to have the core of sexual play in its sights. The sexual scene is alluded to by references to joy and pain ('amour', 'mal'), to a woman that someone is in love with ('Nine', 'môme'), to the body ('nus', 'mames', from which 'mamelles' is derived). Even the map of the world is transformed by signifying play into a map of the female body, on which the range of seductive power triggered by the body and its forms and outlines is compressed into a single, fetishistic love-object – one which still fails for all that to settle the uncertainty about the causes of its gendered magnetism:

Où est Ninive sur la mammemonde?

But in spite of the interrogative form, the play in the signifier enunciates such a complete colonisation of heterosexual relation that it seems possible to do away with the paltry empire of the proper name and the extension of its exclusivity into neologism. As the pleasures of fetishism rub shoulders with those of collapse, the falling away of the name heralds the dissolution of positions in sexual exchange and of their charting in discourse. The demise of difference between name and noun is not here a source of anxiety or nausea; on the contrary, it fashions its own brand of gratification:

Néant nié nom ni nerf n'ai-je!

Clearly, this is gratification wound up in a cord of the singular and singularising signifiers which is wound up still more tightly in the pun-rhyme 'neiges' / 'n'ai-je', and in the M N series itself, reminiscent of a child humming or just burbling. The whole effect is reminiscent of nursery rhymes and nonsense verse. The text does seem to reach back into the furthest and most intimate memories, which here leave their mark on signifiers that withdraw defiantly from narrative sequence and organisation. As we read, the process of memory folding into repression is once more put on display. This is the Freudian repression, born in the structures of desire, the avatars of which are love and hate. And in fact this enmeshing of love and hate in desire is represented in the quasi-childish wordplay of the penultimate stanza: 'Aime haine / Et n'aime haine. . .'. And in a final twist of this play, the acoustic image that the M N series forms *is* a phonetic concentration of precisely the verb-form 'aime' and the noun 'haine'. In this child's litany, in this textual play based, it seems, on the child's parodying of adult discourse, Desnos finds form *in* the signifier, rather than in resistance to it, for an imaginary, ironic capturing of the Oedipal foundations of sex and language.

These foundations are represented in the poem by an emphatically narcissistic discourse of refusal and fixation. Might this not simply confirm the Sartrean, somewhat undifferentiated critique of 'Surrealist' aspiration, in 'Situation de l'écrivain en 1947', as being purely metaphysical, as leaving the articulations of power unchallenged, and 'le monde rigoureusement intact'?[18] Or as Benjamin frames the problem, is the Surrealist attitude able to 'bind revolt to revolution'?[19] In a later re-attempt to gauge the active power of poetry in relation to the terms of its own production and reception, Sartre attributes a different sort of energy to the passivity of Narcissus. In 'Orphée noir', his introduction to the *Anthologie nouvelle de poésie nègre et malgache*, Sartre involves Narcissus in the idea of poetry at large, as well as in the condition and constrictions of being black, the condition of *négritude*:

> La négritude, triomphe du narcissisme et suicide de Narcisse, tension de l'âme au-delà de la culture, des mots et de tous les faits psychiques, nuit lumineuse du non-savoir, [. . .] expansion de générosité, est en son essence, Poésie.[20]

In the light of 'Elégant Cantique de Salomé Salomon', the triumph of narcissism would result from a totality – in this case, that of the black's condition and identity – sealed off and singularised, dominated and ludically discarded at a stroke. And Sartre's Narcissus is suicidal here as well as triumphant since, looked at in Freudian terms, both the prize and the cost of such acts of imaginary capturing would be the creative power itself of the ego, its capacity to redirect or at least tame the determining pressures of its own situation. This prized, but also potentially futile power of intervention is to be won at the cost of a willed ignorance, at the cost of espousing impotence in the pursuit of revelation – 'une nuit lumineuse du non-savoir'.

This resurgence of Narcissus is part of Sartre's continuing enquiry into the fascination poetry exercises on him which begins in *Qu'est-ce que la littérature?*. He concludes there notoriously that poetry is played out to the rules of 'qui perd gagne',[21] and this image of poetry is developed from his well-known notion of a radical distinction between poetry and prose. At least momentarily in *Qu'est-ce que la littérature?*, Sartre grants prose the power of a certain 'dépassement', the power to emancipate the human subject from his or her situation, from absorption in it and in the conditions of language more particularly:

> L'écrivain est un parleur; il désigne, démontre, ordonne, refuse, interpelle, persuade, insinue.[22]

On the one hand, Sartre seems here to be seeking out a prose able to smother the anxiety of that 'substance' which is the poetic experience, that asphyxia at the hands 'l'infini désordre de la matière'.[23] I have taken this last morsel of evocative philosophising from *L'Engagement de Mallarmé*,[24] a manuscript in which Sartre, a short time after *Qu'est-ce que la littérature?*, again struggles with a task that for him is a fragment of the inescapable existential drama: how can poetry, which Sartre casts as absorbed in the material, imprisoned in chance, immersed in the ineffable intimacy of the personality, and fascinated by 'le clapotis de l'Etre',[25] ever be made to give a totalising, rather than purely contingent, account of its situation, its relation to other discourses and to the Other at large? Sartre struggles to circumscribe this hovering between being and nothingness, this 'vain effort pour limiter l'Etre par le Néant'[26] that is a fundamental element in the poet's particular existential pathology as Sartre strives to situate it.[27] In *Qu'est-ce que la littérature?*, in striving perhaps more polemically than in other texts to define and challenge the poetic project, the embattled Sartre is drawn into attributing a certain primacy to the perceptual mode of consciousness, which he consistently seeks to distinguish from the imagining one. In *L'Imaginaire*, Sartre had argued ever more firmly that an object called to mind in the imagination is 'irréel'.[28] The imagining thinker can learn nothing new about this object, since it consists entirely of itself, its own conceptual history which is the platform and the outcome of the very act of imagining it. An object-in-image, as well as a situation-in-image, presents itself to consciousness as a stasis, it is 'inagissant',[29] without cause or effect, it is out-of-bounds and out-of-play.[30]

At the same time, Rhiannon Goldthorpe's in-depth analysis of Sartre's conception of the imagination highlights his continuing, multifaceted fascination with the imagining mode of thought, its mobile relation to the perceptual mode, which itself suffers from all manner of corrosion of its autonomy, in fact its *imagined* autonomy and impermeability in relation to the Other.[31] It is this sense of corrosion which propels Sartre's unrelenting examination of the poetic project conceived in the most general aesthetic, metaphysical and ethical terms, involving Flaubert, Genet and Sarraute in addition to Mallarmé, the Surrealists and francophone black-African poets whom I have already mentioned; artists such as Vermeer and Giacometti; and ultimately the implications of biographical thought itself. Sartre is fascinated by the very 'out-of-play' quality of the object-in-image, its immobility and its passivity, qualities which keep it out of the reach – 'hors d'atteinte' – of any fraying at the hands of its own contingency and of its own involvement in the unfinished relativity of the world. In fact, the imagining consciousness is able to make a totalising synthesis of this very entanglement in its own generation.

In our position as 'parleurs', on the other hand, as master-of-ceremonies in prose and speech, we do not seem to enjoy this degree of emancipation ('s'affranchir') from matter, from Nature, and from the fragility of manufactured synthesis.[32] The organising powers of prose are, as a matter of essence, limited: 'le langage est prose par essence et la prose, par essence, échec'.[33] Both the discourses of prose and poetry seem involved in a dialectics of failure. What does this dynamic consist of and what are we to expect from it?

For Sartre, poetry is a discourse of mourning emanating from the wreckage of prose. Consciousness of our situation and its contingency, of an as-such quality in the present, is formed in response to the failure of language and of prose in particular: 'le présent est ce qui est, et son poids nous écrase'.[34] This crushing is carried out and conceived of as 'un remords du monde'.[35] Liberty is encountered from within the networks of this mourning, itself provoked in relation to matter. Liberty is discovered in a dialectical encounter with matter, and with the passivity within which matter threatens continually to engulf our powers of intervention. In *Qu'est-ce que la littérature?*, Sartre presents this notion of a liberty-inducing passivity in terms of the high level of realism he ascribes to Vermeer. Sartre attributes to realist forms the capacity to capture and project back as a whole what he calls 'la pâte des choses'.[36] This highly suggestive and sensuous metaphor bears witness in Sartre's hands to the dimensionless 'substance' of the material given. Our capacity to designate cannot sustain its powers of emancipation from this agglutinous and miasmic 'substance'. The reading process itself, its quality of the 'caprice', bears this out.[37] The reader enjoys moments of 'capriciousness' and spontaneity in relation to the project being announced and developed by the writer, only once again to lose that readerly sense of chosen and imposed

direction. The distinction between perceptual juncture and imaginary synthesis stacked up on the strength of it melts into reading, into reading as
process, a process toying with completion as much as it is toyed with by the
mirage of it. Text takes over the position, or rather the effects, of matter, of
the real in the great battle with consciousness – the battle of consciousness
for supremacy which has such a chequered and forlorn history. 'La pâte des
choses' both designates this passivity burrowing away at perception from
within, and reproduces it at the level of metaphor, 'la substance' now taking
over and mirroring the unfulfilled efforts of interpretation to constitute itself,
to designate its own findings and its own increasingly dimensionless, increasingly smothering treasures. Realism may be mimetic, but ultrarealism raises
the curtain on the collapse of mimetic framing and others beyond that.

Ultimately, poetry and liberty flow from the same vessel – the rhetorical figure of gaming and gambling in language:

> La poésie, c'est qui perd gagne. [. . .] Le poète s'arrange [. . .] pour témoigner
> par sa défaite singulière de la défaite humaine en général.[38]

As sense-making – 'la signification' – collapses like so many castles in the air,
Sartre finds that 'nous jugeons de la folle entreprise de nommer'[39] – to quote
from 'Orphée noir'. Sense-making crumbles under the weight of sense – 'l'in-
communicable pur',[40] 'la phrase-chose, inépuisable comme les choses'.[41]
Sensation undermines sense by gnawing away at the distinction between
them, by making that distinction increasingly a matter of metaphor, within
which each pole absorbs the other, producing the impossible 'phrase-chose',
a confluence of word and object, of word and body, in which each survives
metaphorically only at the expense of the other, each receding further as a
result from perceptual or analytical grasp. The word cloyingly persists in
demanding power, bound up in the effects of analogy it seeks to exploit,
limited by its powers, and losing also even the faint security of the limit in its
own thrust beyond, refuting any definition that comes from its own devices.
Now victim, the word is terrorised by the empire of the body, itself established by the word. This is an empire that mirrors in reverse the megalomaniac pursuit in the word of a point beyond, a point still further beyond its own
ceiling or the terrorised imagining of it. Infinite regress in the word produces
forms that allude, can only allude evermore obsessively to the body and
which testify to their own fraying and collapsing integrity.

Freedom consists in large part in constructing a platform to represent
this imploding and engulfing shadow-boxing with the body. Sartrean
'témoignage', his notion of bearing witness, transforms the given into gift, it
forms a generosity that is itself both transitive and intransitive, responsible
and boundless. But boundlessness or the notion of it is produces another

form, it provides greater purchase on the idea of 'substance' but provides it with greater impetus as well. Once again the curtain is raised on a psychic oscillation of perceptual novelty and the sealing up of it in imaginary, synthetic packages of the known. Poetry takes part in forming, and is formed metaphorically in the body of a towering Narcissus whose generosity emerges in his collapse. With otherness implanted in him, it falls to Narcissus to counter the given by returning it as gift. But having said that, this act of exchange is now stifled by the appropriativenness of Narcissus, and by another start-up of the game on which his survival depends. Poetry consists in having Narcissus lose, in having him die in the representation of mortality. But in losing and hence winning, in winning again in metaphor and the word, the democracy he both proclaims and incarnates comes under renewed threat; it is absorbed beyond conception, silenced in the graceful image of an integral body. Can generosity find the broken forms through which to survive?

In 'Orphée noir' Sartre returns to the quest for forms that break and are broken. But perhaps the concept of *négritude* itself stands in the way of that. There is nothing new in saying that *négritude*, the condition of oppressed black, raises the curtain again on the spiked dynamic of scars and their orthodox healing, as oppression itself is made to hover between situation and essence. Is there a way forward?

As Goldthorpe has pointed out, the black poet as well as the Surrealist seeks 'une destruction, un autodafé du langage'[42] – though for the black in Sartre's account, this project has an urgent and specific materiality that is lacking in Surrealist practice which for Sartre can only hope for 'une calme unité des contraires'.[43] This paradoxical struggle to 'faire du silence avec le langage'[44] is presented as a narcissistic attempt to banish the Other. In such an attempt, Black Narcissus bears witness to the other as coloniser – insidiously appropriative:

> Il s'agit [. . .] de faire bander comme un sexe *l'un* des contraires du couple 'noir-blanc' dans son opposition à l'autre.[45]

This attempt to preserve sexual and cultural differences intact does not signal a naive return of confidence in the powers of designation and categorization that prose is supposed to display. On the contrary, conflation of categories abounds – sexual and cultural, metaphorical and ideological, etc. Rather, this artificial unity or singularity eludes the structures of sense-making. It transforms the passivity of our immersion in 'le sens' into an active resistance to 'la signification', here the instrument of coercion and colonisation. Narcissus is once again made up of an interplay of forms, within which the threat to the integrity of each is absorbed in the inception of others – an endless mental dance of the seven veils. But it does sketch in a capacity to outmanoeuvre ideological stereotyping and its ventilation at the level of 'parole'. The erect sex-organ of Sartre's metaphor towers above the sex-difference that makes it, free-floating and beyond capture. This is outmanoeuvreing by representa- tion, a representation that bears witness, once again, to the power and the coercion it opposes. But might not tyranny be confirmed in this way? Sartre's oscillating account of the active–passive Narcissus-as-Poet might bear witness only to the vulnerability of the testimony. Does Sartre's Black Narcissus succeed merely in substituting for the phantasies of colonisation the phantasy of a centre-stage Anointed One? One phallic Order for another? Once again, how are we ever to accept or design a Narcissus embracing his own defeat, Narcissus yielding to the spectator's eye and its terrifying democracy?

'Chant du ciel' in the 'Les Ténèbres' section of *Corps et biens* dramatises the traumatic quality of such a notion, as much for Desnos as for any other writer.

Chant du ciel
La fleur des Alpes disait au coquillage: 'tu luis'
Le coquillage disait à la mer: 'tu resonnes'
La mer disait au bateau: 'tu trembles'
Le bateau disait au feu: 'tu brilles'
Le feu me disait: 'je brille moins que ses yeux'
Le bateau me disait: 'je tremble moins que ton coeur quand elle paraît'
Le mer me disait: 'je résonne moins que son nom en ton amour'
Le coquillage me disait: 'je luis moins que le phosphore du désir dans ton
   rêve creux'
La fleur des Alpes me disait: 'elle est belle'
Je disais: 'elle est belle, elle est belle, elle est émouvante'.[46]

Murat evokes the spectre of 'une glu narcissique'[47] that the poem, for him, has the ability to loosen. And yet the drama of the poem is that this spectre of clingfilmed uni-formity is not so easily undone. On one level, the poem seems to give free rein to the desire to colonise the full range of contingency. The poem unfolds in a series of personified objects, each literally in dialogue with the others. In this way, the poem seems even able to satisfy a desire to defuse the threat to the ego's autonomy which comes from the diversity of its *own* responses to the real, in all its social and material plurality. We would then have a love poem that had the effect of immobilising the relations of lover to the object of his or her desire. Imagine Narcissus satiated. You would have just such a perfect match of impulse and desire on the one hand, and the morphology of objects on the other. It would also involve domesticating the perpetual, subtle otherness of the discourses we absorb and articulate – a dis- concerting mobility which could then be stored forever among objects whose familiarity is no longer in doubt: 'tu luis', 'tu résonnes'. We would then be very close to the mawkish nostalgia, expressed in 'Non l'amour n'est pas mort', for a name that would do its job. There, the 'moi qui suis Robert Desnos'[48] enjoys loving a body that is quite simply engulfed in his own, and that takes 'la forme et le nom [de son] amour'.[49]

This is what distinguishes 'Chant du ciel' so sharply from 'Non l'amour n'est pas mort'. The interplay in 'Chant du ciel' of analogy and image remains unresolved. On the one hand, the objects that accumulate in the poem seem to reverberate independently, while on the other, the evocative power of each depends on its being comparable to the others. Neither resolution nor symmetry is on offer here. On the one hand, the poem functions as image – inviting psychic capturing; on the other, it functions as analogy – inviting ideological capturing. Affirmation and stereotype continually slip through each other's defences in the mobile positions of address that make up the poem. There is no hope proclaimed in this mobility of building it up into an autonomous, unbreachable structure. On the contrary, it is allowed to droop in the poem's final drifting down the paths of cliché: 'elle est belle, elle est belle, elle est émouvante'. Murat, invoking the Sartrean game of poetry, outlines a 'qui perd gagne' of a poetics of cliché.[50] By being the loser in this game here, Desnos demonstrates the power of allowing affirmation to decay. The affirmation of love is put to the test by the massed forces of stereotype and the resulting indifference. But beyond threat, affirmation is dissolved in the poem by the heterogeneity of moments of love and talk it invokes. Here we are very near to the interplay of type and subjectivity so close to Apollinaire's concerns, and in terms of which he continually strives for an ethics of nostalgia and loss.

But yet again, any ethic of this kind continually comes up against the spectre of a merely triumphant, a sadly triumphant Narcissus, surviving intact the unravelling of subjective autonomy in the discursive forms it inhabits. Enclaves for this spectre seem to emerge unstoppably in mind and language. The mirage of a structure able to preserve its autonomy and its imperviousness or aggression has a highly seductive appeal. Jean-François Lyotard's work in *Les TRANSformateurs DUchamp* is a case in point. On the one hand, he offers an attractive reading of the revolt in forms carried out by Duchamp, and such a reading might be readily applied to Desnos's own practices in *Corps et biens*. But even an argument aimed at setting aside the mirages of structural autonomy, of a self-certifying power of intervention that the notion of structure itself would allow, runs the risk of becoming increasingly embroiled in the appropriativeness it seeks to counter.

In *Les TRANSformateurs DUchamp*, Lyotard is delighted by Duchamp's visual and verbal machinery, and discovers there a series of artificial constructions that function according to the principles of dissimilarity and incommensurability. He detects a sort of topological sabotage of forces –

forces that are given quasi-physical properties by Lyotard – able to organise social activity into homogenous forms and into spaces that can be super-imposed. In Lyotard's reading of Duchamp, the two-dimensional ambushes the three-dimensional and prevents the laws of perspective from coming into effect in building our world. At the level of language, rules of conjugation set about those of declension in various homonymic plays. For Lyotard, this signals that the enmeshing of these two sets of rules in the interplay of grammatical differences would be called to a halt and nullified. This is the example he gives to support his contention: 'le nègre aigrit, les négresses s'aigrissent ou maigrissent'.[51] Furthermore, at the level of time, the inescapable continuity of duration is fragmented into moments of 'dis-chronie', and even of 'autochronie'[52] – a manufactured capacity to start the clock at any chosen moment.

All these mechanical artifices show Duchamp, for Lyotard, taking advantage of the essential property of any working machine – the capacity to trap the workings of nature. A mechanism functions 'en captant les forces naturelles';[53] but equally, its performance is such that it 'joue un tour à ces forces, réalisant cette monstruosité: que le moins fort soit plus fort que le plus fort'.[54]

Nature's forces can only be coercive, 'monstrous' in the sense of antag-onistic to the smooth exercising of power; and the subversion of forces in nature has implications for democracy. Lyotard claims that the traps Duchamp sets for nature are also, in the same stroke, able to sabotage the working forms of language and of logic, and their own unifying impetus, equally strong as the one driving the mechanisms of nature. For Lyotard, the spectator of the *Large Glass* becomes aware of seeing 'autochronies' with an eye 'sans mémoire', an eye liberated from memory and the articulations of antecedence, and open to the discontinuous, dysfunctioning chronos of the device offered to us by Duchamp. The effect of this is to outmanoeuvre 'le "si . . . alors" de l'implication qui conduit à lier des moments différents'.[55] And if Implication can be brought down, then causality crumbles with it – causal-ity being the corner-stone of the operations of logic as well as of nature, by virtue of its manipulation of time. For Lyotard, the 'autochronies' of the *Large Glass* each set up sequences of events able to call a halt to themselves, to defuse the interaction of cause and effect by projecting one onto the other – as Lyotard puts it in ways that echo Barthes's *S/Z* – and stifling enigma along with the pursuit of resolution.

But to attempt to derail structure in this way is to give in to the delusions prompted by imaginary modes of thought. To consider ludic approaches as any kind of 'auto'-activity gives the game away at a stroke. The perceived tyranny of nature, of logic, and of democratic institutions that they are seen to support, is posited in an image: the image of the homogeneous and the superimposed – the stuff of synthesis, in fact, which is perpetuated in Lyotard's account of it. Lyotard's trapping proceeds by aggressively distinguishing its mechanism from this synthetic cross-section of force and the functioning of force; but he counters this absorbent drive to sameness with a synthetic package of his own. Trapping can and does consist of outmanoeuvring fixed positions, or the reductive effects of ideology, or even any purely operational herding of elements into categories. But as Lyotard describes it, trapping is a procedure that grants itself the power of inauguration, the power to draw a line in the sand above its own beginning and another around its own effects. Its effects are generated by its own structure and by the self-professed artifice of it. So that the space marked out for itself by the mechanism of the trap is a space without place, but speciously so – inevitably and proudly so, or vainly. And to that extent, it succeeds merely in providing Narcissus with another dwelling, precisely because it sets off dreams of stifling power, of capturing it and sealing it off in a vast set of superimposable analogies of its own making.

Lyotard's mechanism of the trap is situated in the history of postwar thinking in France on structure, confirming rather than countering the paradoxes associated with the notion, and emerges as what Barthes calls 'une structure habitable'.[56] *Fragments d'un discours amoureux*, where the expression makes a dramatic if understated entry, was published in 1977, the same year as *Les TRANSformateurs DUChamp*. This juxtaposition in history highlights the different paths pursued in response to the concept of structure, its operational capacities as well as the nets and networks of the ambitions it triggers. That Barthes should be addressing amorous discourse, and Lyotard the machine underlines rather than undermines this confluence of interest in the structure, but also the parting of ways it involves. This is the uneasy *danse macabre* of faith and suspicion in response to desire. In *Fragments*, Barthes suggests that any structure turns out to be 'habitable', since it draws the subject into the lure of a system with impervious boundaries – neatly tautological rather than intransitive and slippery. Its appeal is that it provides desire with such boundaries, offers its own well-oiled forms as desirable objects, and in that way defuses the anxiety of desire and the pressure of desiring. Is this the extent of Desnos's games in *Rrose Sélavy* ('Eros c'est la vie')?

For Lyotard, the phonetic slithering that characterises Duchamp's *Rrose Sélavy*, as well as Desnos's, has the effect – fairly obviously – of highlighting the arbitrary enmeshing of signifier and signified. This in turn would set off a chain reaction liberating us from knowledge, from the known and its weight, from the replication of its forms dictated by the laws and precedents of signification. Desnos's own *Rrose Sélavy*, however, resists such a reading at a number of points. To begin with, both Marie-Claire Dumas and Michel Murat sense some germination of narrative even in Desnos's notionally automatic texts – in fact particularly there.[57] In the case of *Rrose Sélavy*, it is quite clear that there is no image produced of a narrative structured according to the rules of intrigue and resolution. But even so, any indicators of an embryonic narrative, or even of a narrative in tatters buried or absorbed in the short-cir-cuits of these little texts, would prevent them being read purely as autonomous, tautological operations with the power to disentangle us from the entrails and the in-trays of memory.

Here is number 27 in the series:

Le temps est un aigle agile dans un temple.[58]

Phonetic sliding sows the seeds of confusion, and certainly defers conclusive interpretation. But the very fact that there is no immediate way out of this little ludic circuit involves us further in it, and casts its signifiers and the mar-ginal interplay between them as the agents of memory once again. This entanglement of memory and enunciation undermines our purchase on either, along with any sense that we might be outmanoeuvring the amassed forces of analogy. On the contrary, 'Le temps est un aigle agile comme un temple' constructs returns indefinitely, while at the same time effacing the moment itself of return.

This coupling of the effacement of origin to a circuit of continual returns signals a reflection in this little poem of the relations of signifier to signified. On the level of the signified, our involvement in the temporality of memory is encircled in an imaginary edifice with endlessly adaptable bound-aries. But the slipperiness of the signifier is transformed into an obstacle to embracing the scale of this construction. The concentration in the signifier of barely distinguishable elements is an allusion to the rather desperate aspiration lodged within this little poem to capture the networks of sense and all their room for manoeuvre. This aspiration is given further form in the signifier by the chiasmic phonetic structure of the line: the 'g' and the 'i' exchange places at the apex, and the pivotal 'l' transforms time into a temple at the end and locks it in there. Looking at both ends at once, the completion of the temple of time turns on the sound of the definite article rounding off the sequence as it began.

But symmetry in the signifier is not matched by sense in the signified, since the dominance of this symmetry and its impact clears everything in its wake, and threatens to nullify sense precisely because of its aspiration to dominate it. But equally, this aspiration is broken rather than accomplished by mobility in the signified, which phonetic symmetry-turned-slitheriness mimicks rather than captures, and undermines only to bear witness to. As in Rimbaud's rhetorical declarations, 'est' and the present tense at large can be sent out to alert us to the effects of narrative sequence as much as to stifle them. The indeterminacy of time in *Rrose Sélavy* 27 – both open-ended and enclosed on the level of the signified, walled up but leaky in the signifier, with both levels at loggerheads in a protracted but unresolved divorce – serves as much to confirm the supremacy of narrative structure as to escort it from the stage. The attempt to short-circuit narrative unfolding might make victims of that unfolding out of self-confident jugglers with it.

The imaginary pursuit of capture, of the perfect seige or the fool-proof trap, provides language games with their on–off button and their energy. For Desnos, the wager comprises the desire to finger the roots of desire; the desire for a unique event, impervious to interpretation, to narration and its own narration; the desire to colonise the Other, its positions and its force; the desire for a ludic structure able to nullify its own force.

Problems of 'sens' and the structures of sense are as fruitful for Barthes as they are for Sartre and I want to begin concluding this chapter with a few remarks on Barthes's involvement with the issues I have raised. This might seem to fly in the face of Barthes's stated distaste for artifices of surprise – on which much Surrealist theory and practice is based – on the grounds that artifice suggests fist-shaking and ultimately futile gestures of defiance. And no doubt they do, in some ways. On the other hand, Barthes himself may be commenting at this point in *La Chambre claire* as elsewhere on the sad vicissitudes of defiance, the pursuit of transgression and the strategies that accompany them.[59]

For Barthes, 'sens' is the vehicle of *doxa*, of the stereotype, of Flaubertian 'Bêtise', of analogy. For Sartre, as I discussed earlier, 'sens' unravels signification and ushers in its collapse, it forms the setbacks suffered by perception and composes the triumph of word-as-object, of words powerless to designate relation. For Sartre, 'sens', like poetry, both designates and incarnates the linguistic skin of the body, language absorbed in the sensations of bodily existence; the distinction melts between 'sens' as word and 'sens' as sensation – or the indication of sensation; 'sens' as process. And for Barthes, 'sens' is 'l'enmêlement du corps et du langage',[60] the limits – to which there is no beyond – of the possible and the permissable. For both, to think of 'sens' is to think through the relations of body and language. 'Through': these relations are both a vehicle of thought and a deferral of the synthetic platforms it might arrive at. In plunging into 'sens', poetry in Sartre's experience sets out in its entirety our immersion in language. But this all-enveloping, self-enveloping image is 'irréel' – immobile and unexceedable. At the cost of a dismal stasis, Narcissus sets out the image of his own coming-to-being, of his induced birth in discourse and in dialogue with its structures.

Narcissus, as I find I must stress again, is from his inception impregnated with otherness.[61] This otherness is what he battles against, and seeks both tirelessly and languidly to reincorporate by ceaselessly redrawing the metaphoric outlines of the body intact. To that extent, he serves as a paradox-ical bulwark, a last warning against the seductive pull of that Barthesian utopia of the non-sign. 'Mais à quoi sert l'utopie?',[62] Barthes wonders in *Roland Barthes*. In the end, rather than providing a place beyond designation and subjugation, it serves only to oil the wheels of sign-making, succeeds only in producing a working notion of deferral and of an unreachable other that confirms signification, puts its workings on display, rather than nullify-ing it. Like the folded-in tentacles of Narcissus, the image of utopian sense-making now forms the capacity itself to manipulate signifying structures, in fact to structure all that lies beyond the psychic borders of the body, troubling sanity and inducing panic.[63]

The notion of 'structuration sans structure',[64] of structure as process not precedent, that is the corner-stone of *écriture* as Barthes defines it in *S/Z*, turns out itself to be an effect of thinking-in-the-image, of the synthetic emancipation that is the progressive, but also bamboozling prize of imagi-nary thought in Barthes's own engagement with it. The pursuit of 'structures habitables', within which all that is beyond us entertains us in a raking over of cold erotic coals reminiscent of the Jack and Queen of Hearts in Baudelaire's 'Spleen', cannot be easily made to throw in the towel. This is reflected in the functioning of *Fragments d'un discours amoureux*, as title and as the book as a whole, and which I alluded to in chapter 2. On the one hand, the book presents itself episodically, in the fragments announced in the title, outmanoeuvring the fixity of an operational discourse. At the same time, such a title seems also to toy with the ambition of restoring this fragmented discourse to its wholeness and its entirety. Barthes himself lays this ambition bare in his introduction to the book:

> Tout épisode amoureux peut être, certes, doté d'un sens: il naît, se développe et meurt, il suit un chemin qu'il est toujours possible d'interpéter selon une causalité ou une finalité . . .[65]

We cannot love, apparently, without reconciling ourselves to what is there and what is given to us to love. Reconciliation adopts the same strategies as those of defiance, subversion or autonomy. The excessive and the exorbitant continually reconstruct, it seems, the desire to be situated and to be posi-tioned. Imaginary flights into the immoderate and the unrestrained are irre-trievably caught up in the glue of the imaginary itself – such is Barthes's verdict in his fragment on voluptuousness and 'comblement'.[66]

And yet for an English-speaking reader, the difficulty in translating 'comblement' might have held out some hope. As in the case of 'jouissance', if satisfaction lexically slips through the graphs of definition, then the dialog-ics of translation might have held out the prospect of a desiring beyond model. In overstepping and transgressing the embroilment of the body and discourse, the loving subject imagines himself, imagines herself ultimately fulfilled, moulded in otherness, without any more stories to tell. Narcissus acts, jubilates and turns flaccid, all in a series of instantaneous episodes made up by the fragments of the book – so different from the complacent 'autochronies' imagined by Lyotard. Barthes's own performance consists in deploying the imaginary power of playing and replaying, of fashioning and reforming, while at the same time seeking to prevent *disappointment* in the failures of that power veering into the forms of tyranny. With a deftness characteristic of his assumption of simplicity in *Fragments*, his hyperactive sense there of the humming and rustling immediacies of seduction and deferral, Barthes is able to sketch an imaginary 'comblement' that is not made of satiation but which scorns it. The lightness of touch with which he spins a coating over orgasm of quotation, allusion, expository rhetoric and analytical tentativeness, the lightness with which he matches writing on orgasm with its wordless familiarity and formless intensity, and with which he makes avoidance of the word more than a show of textual play, but showing rather word and body absorbed in one another – all this is itself a display of potency, vitality and volatility in the imaginary.

Barthes evokes 'le régime de l'imaginaire'[67] in this fragment, a *régime*, rather than the essentialism of the Sartrean mode or the distant, collapsing structuralism of the Lacanian order; still a straitjacketing, right enough, but one which carries at least a semantic floating within it. The semantic content of 'régime' ranges from the governmental, to the juridical, to the mechanical, to the medical, to the geographical, to the grammatical. Forming and reforming the outlines and contours of bodies sexed and sensed, Barthes's imaginary here alludes to, and makes mild and friendly mockery of, the Sartrean doom of seeking ever further reaches of appropriation and the gloomy syntheses that are the only reward. Barthes's 'trop'[68] characteristic of imaginary desiring, a continual seeking of more and beyond, is an appeal to gorging as an antidote to complacency. But even here, in exceeding mere repletion, in foraging amongst sensation and memory, in mobilising but also silencing the capacity to imagine seemingly at will any number of modifications to the erotic script, Barthes turns the corner only to discover the perfect match – *la Coïncidence*.

Throughout this fragment, and indeed all over Barthes's later writing, wordplay exposes its subversive potential at the same time as the limits which subversive ambition runs up against. Just as Rimbaud's 'délire' heralds an undoing of reading ('dé-lire') only to rediscover the tramlines of reading,[69] just as Barthes's 'scriptible'[70] is tied to the bar in *S/Z* that separates it and binds it to the 'lisible',[71] so 'la démesure'[72] broods 'la mesure',[73] excess flows to the rhythms of order, and the music of sex dances to the tune of sameness and of coming together. Ecstasy, by being beyond the telling of it, opens out realms of perfection, of untouchable wholeness impervious to the inevitable orthodoxy of Oedipal narrative and its chronicles of inadequacy and of psychic wounding. But Barthes is also imbued through his writing here with a sudden, an immediate and unstoppable leap from the beyond or the 'too much' to the 'already'. To be *already* the fulfilled subject we yearn for is to inhabit utopia. Moreover, Barthes arrives at the point of discussing this subject already unensnared from repression by immersing his reader yet again in the old chestnut of desire for fulfilment, the will to fulfilment, rather than the chimeras of its achievement.[74] But this very acceptance of deferral, this relishing of diversion and drifting *is*, is 'already' dipped in a coating of brilliance ('brille') that gives plurality, interruption and the unnarratable a shape, a form, the outline of transitivity and the streamline of the will. To spurn narration and its Oedipal intestines is to ship us out of language – 'hors du langage' – not only beyond the positions of discourse and the subject-ed subject, but beyond even the *jouissance* of text and the sheens of signifying texture; and it does so as surely as the adherence to structure would, the adherence to its implicit rationalism or to the secure signified it assumes. In fact to be concerned or obsessed with *jouissance* itself is to bathe, however vicariously, in this dissolution of language, this trans-porting beyond its scope and its possibilities – '"le transport est la joie de laquelle on ne peut parler."'[75] *Jouissance* seems to demand an hysterical adherence which Barthes devotes his later writing to countering by casting it in slitheriness and in sparkling signifying dust. But the more he succeeds, the more his text is open to this transport, the 'beyond' of the imagination is further bound to the 'already' of the imaginary, and the glue of the perfect fit sets in – 'je colle à l'Image'.[76] 'Hors langage',[77] 'hors texte',[78] the free-floating analogy of sex and text, 'démesure', 'comblement', and wordplay at large all join in what I would call an inverted Sartrean game with the image of 'qui gagne perd'. Barthes's writing here is truly a writing of the body, precisely because the analogy between body and writing collapses, and an education in that loss can begin.

For Freud the relation of jokes – of wordplay, that is – to the unconscious is essentially unfunny. The unconscious and the repression by which we know it are not be outwitted or outplayed. André Gide, both in and despite his resistance to any perceived Freudian take-over of his writing, captures throughout his treatments of sexual and moral behaviour the bleak outcome shared by motivated and immotivated actions alike. For Freud, the motivated joke is the smutty one, exhibitionist in character and structure, whose only achievement could be to relieve the pressure of the penis covered over – of the taboo on the desire to show the penis – and the establishment of a male bonding in the process: yet another sad and irrevocable symptom of repression itself, of its checks and counter-checks, of the regime it oversees of positions allocated and imposed, and of the monitored and predictable system of deferral it so often seems destined to operate. The immotivated joke, on the other hand – more specifically focussed on word-play and the pun – is directed at the positions of the subject in language, at the distinctions on which language depends for its power and for the establishment and maintenance of signification. It seeks to shoot the moon in the form of bringing down the edifice of sense-making at large, that collu-sion of the possible and the permissible commented on with such consistent virulence in the poststructuralist tradition.

Perhaps Freud's suggestion of an unholy dialogue between the immo-tivated and the motivated joke, of an ambition to undo imprisonment within a discursive structure caught in the veils of a receding and all the more dom-inant Phallus, itself anticipates the Lacanian reading of the Freudian uncon-scious at large. Motivated and immotivated wordplay combined make up a projection of the signifier and its effects, of the distribution and the allocation of positions in relation to sexual difference, of a discourse whose paradoxical indefiniteness continually veers towards the foreclosed and the foretold. In casting word as wordform, wordplay triggers the imaginary charge into the beyond – but as ever, this is the inward turned beyond of domination, supremacy and stasis, and the corresponding sewing up of decay and of the corporeal into other bodies and elsewhere spaces. Lacan's 'objet a', for example, – through which Lacan continues verbally to exemplify in the midst of expounding (a practice that could itself be cast as an exemplar of wordplay at large) – stages both the disintegration of otherness and the perception of it, of Agape and a community of differences, but also the relishing of such disintegration, even in the wordplay recounting it, that accounts for the instability of our embrace of the not-I. And in so doing Lacan's wordplay and the numerous appearances of it stage an ever more unstoppable veering towards the absorption, the assimilation, the normalisation of this blindness to you and to the body. The performer Barthes seeks to steer the power of imaginary morphing away from this oscillation of immobile dominance and grief at its loss; away from the prospect of loss signalling nothing further than an attachment to its forms. As Barthes suggests in *Fragments*, both the prize and the price – once again – of ease in language and with language is the sense of it as a skin, as an extension of the finger-tips, as a memory of touching another, a memory made mine and whole.[79]

Perhaps until mobility in the signifier can be made, as Judith Butler is engaged in doing,[80] to retrace its genesis in psychic reconstructions of the body, in the repression itself of the ache for sameness and return, in remap-pings, born of loss and mortality, of desire at large, words and their signify-ing morphology will seem always on the point of acceding to an illusory freedom that confirms their subjugation. Perhaps all the writers discussed here, caught up as they are in the networks of word and image and committed to them, might seem caught in a perpetual waiting game, a ceaseless 'until'. Even so, Desnos, in any case, at moments in his Surrealist prosodic wordsmithing – itself a farewell to that project – works with the adhesiveness of loss and its forms, with and against it, targeting it and in so doing becoming its target. In 'Idéal Maîtresse' – in which the refutation of grammar is signalled from the title onwards – the 'je' triumphs over syntax: 'je mauve, je me chaise, déjà je miroir'.[81] But what to call this triumph if not either merely a casting aside of the sad treasures of the personal 'I', or a vain, cacophonous raging against discursive positioning? Desnos, ultimately, seems neither to know nor care. But kicking and screaming, and without giving up his work of bruising and bamboozling signifying and narrative structure, he allows the poem to be dragged into a climactic lyrical expansion, lauding as only lyricism can the intactness of the loved body and the wholeness of the desiring voice, but sketching at the same time a symbolic, anti-discursive, anti-sense suicide, destroying the semantics of the body and the grammar of identification, only to bear ever stronger witness to their totemic and invasive allure:

> Eh quoi, déjà je miroir. Maîtresse tu carré noir et si les nuages de tout à l'heure myosotis, ils moulins dans la toujours présente éternité.[82]

CHAPTER FOUR

Sterility and power: on some paintings by René Magritte

Even in the days when blockbuster exhibitions of visual art have become commonplace, the advance sell-out of every time-slot of the 1998 Magritte retrospective in Brussels was momentous. This painter clearly enjoys a popularity that exceeds boundaries of nationality, of high art and popular culture, of the pleasures and the business of art itself. His extraordinary appeal doubtless arises from the wit and deftness of his touch. Within the pictures, words and images combine in hilariously inappropriate agglomerations that challenge cliché and complacency. Dialogues of picture and title lead viewers down a variety of paths and blind alleys without a sense of priority being imposed. An indefinite, eccentric democracy of response is on offer comprising intimacy, consumerism, feminism, psychoanalysis, linguistics, intertextuality, hilarity, anarchy, despair, cacophony and silence. And Magritte's dual status as both within and outside the orbits of Parisian and Belgian Surrealism adds yet another dimension to the associative mobility that he succeeded in giving his work from 1925 right up to his death in 1967.

But cultural play, formal play, wordplay, jocular acrobatics of any discursive kind are, in the end, not necessarily funny. They may even be repetitive, or fail to reach beyond their own intimations of a kind of alienation. Magritte knows this; his joy and energy are not in the service of cover-up. His is a revolt that questions the revolt available to him. Directed at the image and the image-making capacity, Magritte's revolt is also bound by the image. If image-making is to provide the forms for a new psychic freedom, then that freedom itself will be bound by the limits of adoration and resentment which provide the image with its psychic domain. Such might be the restrictive logic of Magritte's work, the logic with which it struggles – the Freudian logic examined by Klein, Lacan and Kristeva of an Oedipal structure allowing for no theoretical relation between the sexes, and within which responses to the maternal are restricted to phallic anxiety, aggressive projection and frantic reconstruction. Magritte gives visual form to this asphyxia, his imagery of sexual relation advertises its own impotence, its own lack of capacity to see beyond. Perhaps this honesty lies somewhere close to the heart of Magritte's continuing appeal – his commitment to working from within his own sense of the decay, rather than a complacent overestimation, of artistic heroism.

This negative advertising of Magritte's work is generated by his consistent adhesion to a point of view and of viewing. A surprising assertion, perhaps, given his stark constructions of anonymity and enigma. In Magritte, adhesion to the point of view consists in a tenacious exploration of position and positioning, and in particular of the male position in the Oedipal scenario. This position is made of the squeezing of the many into the one, the herding of diverse potential into a single metaphysical outcome. It is guaranteed, rather than shattered, by its innumerable guises and disguises that deaden as much with the familiarity as the porousness of the psychocultural drama they support.

This assumption of the visual into the scopic – itself an inevitable hermeneutic spectre, perhaps – exemplifies a process that places the artist as imagined by the viewer (male or female) in the position of the analyst in the Lacanian construction of him or her – the 'sujet supposé savoir'.[1] Between viewer and her/his construction of the artist, there emerges a balletic set of outmanoeuvrings, a continual dialogue of knowledge projected and knowledge collapsed. Neither a fully constituted viewing subject, nor an established point of view can be presupposed. But foreclosure and immobility seem to threaten either way. The shock tactics of Le Viol or of La Montagne expose but also confirm the orthodoxy of male desire; the main weapon of these pictures, in these the desperate straits of some anticipated deconstruction, is also their principal source of imprisonment: the fascinations of the image, the collaborative as well as transgressive fascination of art.

More particularly, recognition captivates the further to entrap. The recognition of objects and forms envelops viewers in the uncompromising channels of *anagnorisis*, pinning us down to the riddles of the Sphinx, the conditions and the Oedipal wounds of blindness, insight and knowledge. But if tragedy and tragic drama in particular are at the roots of mimesis, Magritte's engagement with it, his own vision of 'la condition humaine', is perverse in so far as it is voiceless – and none the less entrenched for that. The strength of the titles seems even to add to this strange stillness. Their arbitrariness, their associative transformations and their apparent interchangability make a pathway to the image made of a seemingly chartless set of impulses.[2] Vocal stillness in the image heralds a stillness in the action, a suspension of the performance, an interruption of mimesis and its message of tragedy and violence. But is point of view suspended for all this – along with its weighting and its potential tyrannies? Suspension seems rather to

Figure 6 René Magritte, *Le Viol* (1934). Oil on canvas, 73 × 54 cm.

put an amorphous, insidious empire on display, jealous of its boundaries, indefinite and yet pointed in its obsessions.

Indeed, Magritte's evocations of scenes in the wings of a stage, away for a moment from the scripts and scenarios of dialogue, suggest menace rather than utopia or atopia. In *Dialogue dénoué par le vent* (1928), the two participants in this mysterious 'dialogue' have enigmatically become three, the stage curtain has become a domestic and private one fluttering in the wind suggested, in an odd moment of coincidence, by the title, and casting a non-

Figure 7 René Magritte, *Dialogue denoué par le vent* (1928). Oil on canvas, 35 × 27 cm.

tactile breath of erotic intimacy over the scene that now resonates in its own particular stillness. But in return, the sill and the brickwork outside are anonymous and public, the night light is flat and has nothing to distinguish it or subjectivise it, and the three participants are so many truncated torsos, models of female perfection waiting to be completed and returned to their place in orthodox representation. Is suspension here more than an interruption? Or in *Entr'acte* (1927), the graceful invention of legs turning into arms, buttocks into shoulder blades, even of a leg with an arm around its pair, shadows ballet rehearsals and more generally an enforced exercising of the body, a mutilation that is also a rite of passage. The body takes on the forms of its recognition; the only alternative it has here to canonical gesture are gestures of desolation or of abandonment. To flex the muscles is to become attached – like the arm-to-leg extension in the middle ground – to the curtain heralding public scrutiny. To imagine that curtain closed is not to create seclusion, but rather to raise a further curtain on the embrace of intertextual allusion and the effect it has of a kind of psychic implant. Studies of behind-the-scenes ballet dancers abound in the works of Degas and Renoir, and subsequent resistances to 'Impressionism' and to reconstructions of it intensify the oppressive status of the movement as a canonical modernism. The audience space, or the space of the viewer, is occupied in the picture by what might be a volcano with apertures down its slopes as well as at the apex; or some piece of military equipment with shotholes in it, or covered in camouflage

Figure 8 René Magritte, *Entr'acte* (1927). Oil 73 × 115.5 cm.

material. Whatever the case, the space of the audience is threatening and antagonistic.

Tracking down the indeterminacy of this imagery would lead only to a thematic kind of coherence, or to plotting the networks of association or analogy peculiar to artist and viewer. In viewing these lacerated bodies that cannot escape their lost wholeness, we share with them a stage-space that we recognise easily as being our own, all set about with invisible shrouds of intimacy transparent to that all-seeing but faceless companion that never leaves us. And what emerges beyond the footlights of the performance is a visual invention reflecting, without defining, precisely that desire for love and for place that threatens to subjugate as much as it promises to satisfy. The other, the audience, has become absorbed here in the uncircumscribed assumptions and projections we direct at it – and is all the more unforgiving for that. Intertextual allusion adds its own sensation of being watched and being read, or of *having been* watched and read – a loose, knotless straitjacket of reference. Intertextual immersion threatens continually to put to the sword that 'emancipation' of thought that Breton as late as 1961 saw as the vital and original contribution of Magritte's visual figuration.[3]

The reactions of two poets to Magritte's silent but loaded visual world seem to focus sharply on the questions posed by it. On the one hand, there is Robert Desnos's frank distaste for the work and his resentment of what for him is its unapologetic lack of creativity. 'Magritte surtout. Ça je déteste ça.'[4]

On the other, Bernard Noël, perceives a circularity in Magritte's work that allows a 'mystère du monde [. . .] insoutenable'⁵ to emerge. He goes on:

> Et l'impensé, de nouveau cherche le jour d'une image pour se rendre à son contraire, puis mystérieusement lui échapper. Tout ce qui existe trouve sa forme dans sa possibilité même, et s'en constitue. Mais pour que ce qui existe apparaisse et se matérialise, il lui faut rencontrer sa ressemblance dans la pensée visible.⁶

Embroiled allusively in Hegel and Foucault, Noël imagines, as Breton might, a figurative image that would act as a vessel for the 'unthought' and snatch it from the jaws of its opposite – the apparent, the placed, the recognised. But the unknown can only be constituted as such – that is, constituted and known. Is this the 'mystère du monde qui est insoutenable'? Noël and Magritte himself would hope not, perhaps; and yet the room for manoeuvre narrows continuously:

> Après avoir voulu comprendre la peinture-non-traditionnelle, on admet qu'il ne faut pas la comprendre. [. . .] L'image poétique, elle, a été imaginée pour répondre à l'intérêt que nous éprouvons naturellement pour l'inconnu, elle évoque directement le mystère qui est un irrationnel réel.
>
> On peut prendre en soi les images poétiques en se gardant de réduire à du connu ce qu'elles ont d'inconnu, leur réalité étant du même genre que la réalité de l'univers.⁷

This is Magritte writing. *Not* understanding a body of painting forms the basis of its passage into the universal, its escape from the point of view and from the condition of it. But the universal can only ever be a well-worn figure of flight. Nevertheless, Magritte gives in only with a struggle: it is not the recourse to such a topos that signals this art-in-failure, but the rhetoric that fashions and forges a way to this obverse of a climax. As Noël intimates, but perhaps rather defensively, Magritte's thinking, in seeking to displace the dead weight of the known, harvests it ever more furtively and in that way forecloses the open-ended ever more tenaciously, presenting it ever more obstinately as the last resource of Romantic orthodoxy and more generally of the recognisable and the recognised. 'Leur réalité étant *du même genre* que la réalité de l'univers' – not even universal reality, or a boundless freedom of thought, can escape type-casting. But more than simply indicating or fulminating against the unknown taking the forms of the known, Magritte traces this apparently structural inevitability, charts it, overlays it, exposes the layerings and veilings which it involves, exposes the collaboration in this of the impulse itself to expose. His art is a testimony to the quasi magnetic, agglutinous force of the visual, its acquisitive, tragic empire of *anagnorisis* that, blink upon blink, transforms everything in its path into itself. 'La pensée visible change en elle-même le texte du monde, et l'étant devenue s'y perd.'[8]

And this loss is not a setting aside, a passing beyond, but an entrapment in sameness. In *L'Echelle du feu* (1934), Magritte starts off on a pathway showing different objects burning – an egg, a key, a scrap of paper. Their irrecuperably pointless heterogeneity is revelled in, and ultimately is glorified not only by means of the flames of the picture – a mere *trompe l'œil*, a trick of the trade – but of the *prospect* of flames. This is the present and future power affirmed in the picture, or at least in Magritte's publicity for it, to uncover latent, waiting-to-be-tapped sparks produced in chance clashes of eclectic and disparate elements.[9] But this prospect seems to loose its edge and its urgency, the power 'to invent fire' is dampened in Magritte's elaboration of it.

He suggests to Breton in 1934 that another way of provoking that spark would be simply to show one object burning – particularly a metal one.[10] The result is *La Découverte du feu* (1936) – in which fire is shown or discovered coming out of a tuba; this burning tuba occupying the space of the burning bush, perhaps. But surely Magritte cannot resist here yet another wind up at the expense of some notion of Surrealist orthodoxy. For this is now 'une rencontre fortuite'[11] with only one component, an absorption in one or the other element in the production through chance encounters of semantic sparks and the rerouting of sense. Fire itself, of course, is incompatible with metal, which melts rather than burns. But the gap needed for creative rubbing together is being progressively rubbed out. Spontaneous and internal combustion is taking over from the ignition of the disparate and the distant. 'Discovery' is turning and burning inward, and undermined rather than leading to revelation. 'Le hasard'[12] is losing its 'objectif'[13] correlative, the unveiling of the inner now seems to lose rather than gain the multiform energy of the material. By 1948, in *Cosmogonie élémentaire* – a title once again suggested after the event by a collaborator, this time Paul Colinet – fire has self-consciously become a part of what Sarah Whitfield calls Magritte's 'family'.[14] The bilboquet that has consistently attracted mythological reading only to frustrate it, only to compress allusions and render them anonymous, now blows bored fire from its blow-torch mouth, gazing narcissistically into that forever sexed and flattened leaf, a further leitmotif in Magritte's figuration. His visual vocabulary develops into an ever more restricted lattice-work that is produced in his logic of the visual, in his silent and silencing performance of the antagonism of the unknown and the seen.

This immobilising mobility is compounded rather than reversed in the functioning of *La Découverte du feu* as 'peinture-objet'. The piece was designed either to be hung on a wall or placed on a flat surface. But this ambivalence carries little more weight than Duchamp's sugar cubes in the dismissive and unresponsive reading of them offered by Sartre in *Qu'est-ce que la littérature?*.

Figure 9 René Magritte, *Cosmogonie élémentaire* (1948). Gouache on paper, 36 × 45.5 cm.

Objective, material conditions of exchange remain intact; purchase on them is confused rather than revolutionised. Apparently, Magritte would have it no other way. His play with the status of the picture as image or as object confirms rather than troubles the status and the stasis of each. Each is compressed in the other in the 'peinture-objet' as well in that very signifier. Intimations of picture and of object each stifle as much as produce the sparks of association and render a massive otherness that engulfs mobility. But the picture is also alive and not dead; the asphyxia it performs feeds on an alive but self-enclosing, amorphous but self-enraptured multitude of reference and intratextual bits. This is the fascination of art I mentioned a moment ago, its play of gaze and countergaze forms a theatre of power as well as of desire. *Les Journées gigantesques*, *Les Amants*, *La Tentative impossible*, each one produced in 1928, explore this dialogue of fascination and terror. In Magritte's hands, dialogue fails to deliver the troubling of the boundaries of discourse promised in the theorising of automatic writing developed by Breton, or in the dialogic poetics of communication and gift developed tirelessly by Paul Eluard. Magritte's dialogues offer the poisoned fruits of phallic organisation and of the unconditional and silent naming of the Father. Like *Le Viol*, *Les Journées gigantesques* represents sexual violence, but unlike in *Le Viol*, victim and perpetrator are both on display in a figuration of violence which is both symbolic and imaginary.

The first title Magritte alighted on for the picture was *La Peur de l'amour*, which seems to forefront the attributing of responsibility for rape to the victim – for it *is* rape that is figured in the picture. This places the viewer in the position of sadistic collaboration with the male perpetrator of sexual violence – a position supported, on one level, by the design of the image. Sarah Whitfield talks of a 'grim parody of sexual union' to be seen in the way that 'man and woman have become indistinguishable'.[15] But more than this, even, the male figure surges from an all-too-conceivable 'nowhere' and makes to *obliterate* the surface of the female form, and then viewers of the picture with its original title would additionally be coerced into accepting the image as an effect of inhibition or of imaginary 'fear'. To represent violence, it seems, razes any position of detachment from violence. The picture, at this level, functions as imaginary representation, not simply because it deals in an illusion and invites participation in such an illusion – the illusion of some particularly female 'fear'; but because to imagine the 'other', to conceive of it and to give it a figurative form, is to deal, here, in the violent totalities and the invasions that are the stock-in-trade of orthodoxy and of its appeal.

Turning to the symbolic level, Magritte's image represents the bodily take-over that is phallic organisation. The body knows (itself) only (through) the forms it desires. Knowledge then consists not only in those forms seen on others and returned to them with a vengeance, appliquéd to them, but also in the trail they leave on the body itself and on its own formation. This formation proceeds in the voracious and aggressive absorption, proud and antagonized, of bodily difference, metonymically squeezed into sexual difference, which remains both elusive and implacable. 'Le désir de l'autre',[16] in other words; Lacan's celebrated, compressed wordplay encapsulates and incarnates the embroilment of desiring another with desiring another's desire – another's position and power. In this sense, Magritte's image-making would seem to confirm the thrust of Lacan's thinking, developed with half an eye on the Surrealist illusionist image and on Dalí's images in particular, within which knowledge, exactly insofar as it consists in structure, forms a *paranoiac* structure. But how is this represented?

The object of Magritte's mimetic embrace in the picture is repression itself – what it hides and what it leaks. An embrace of the unknown, an unknown psychically translated into an *everything*, impervious to a Proustian education in sensation and dispersal, and reformed into the known: into what is known or imagined about the unknown or feared in it. Repression, here, can only be conceived of in an imaginary capturing, and it is this that is then represented in an atemporal interplay of surfaces – untouchable surfaces, deprived of the sound and the breath of human cries. In *Les Journées*

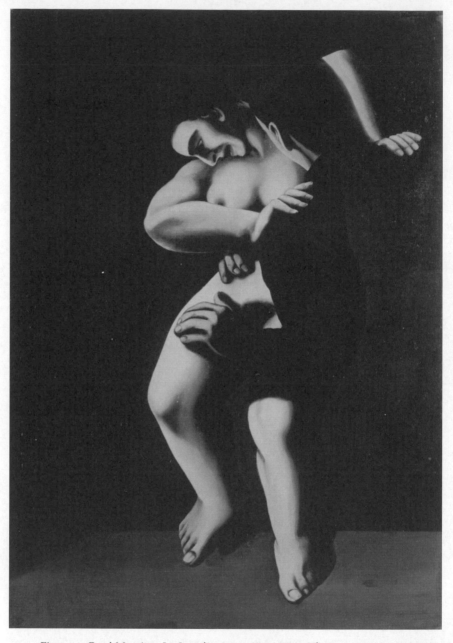

Figure 10 René Magritte, *Les Journées gigantesques* (1928). Oil on canvas, 116 × 81 cm.

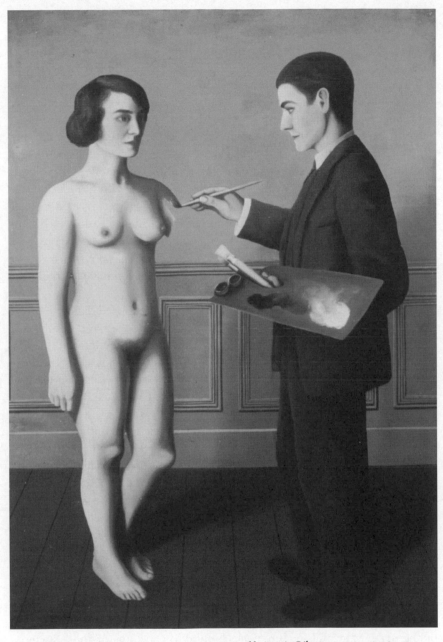

Figure 11 René Magritte, *La Tentative impossible* (1928). Oil on canvas, 116 × 81 cm.

gigantesques, such mimetic capturing rests on a confusion – at once disguised, wilful and supreme – of positions in discourse in relation to gender and to the image-making that devolves from gender difference. The male viewer, liberalised and freed from the projection of 'la peur',[17] might believe he is looking at a visualisation of male aggression. The female viewer might assume the same. But in doing so, each needs to assume knowledge of the unknown, of an 'other' position captured and dominated, even in the conceiving of violence and even in the attempt to nullify it. Dialogue is erased in the attempt to display that violent erasing – to display it, to capture it and to pass beyond. And this erasing is not simply a matter of rhetoric, or an effect of Socratic irony, by which to discuss with the enemy is to engage with him even in the attempt to undermine his positions. For that 'other' that is targeted is made of the trails and the trials of identification, of *broken* identification, its hollow reverberations and incomplete images – all the unsayable narrative of Oedipal law, its indefinite array of enforced cut-offs and about-turns in the approved direction of desire. In the case of *Les Journées gigantesques*, this is the 'other' within.

Magritte displays a sense of familiarity in this imposed dialogue of the psyche and the body – a dialogue that is at once silenced and continuing, dynamic and unchanging. 'Familiar' – both in the sense of intimate, and in the sense of all *too* familiar. Magritte's is a visualisation of unconscious processes, not only in thematic terms – in the sense of providing an Oedipal reading of the sexual relation and of the gendered violence it threatens us with – but in structural terms. Exploiting the static quality of the two-dimensional, illusionist image, Magritte roots his picture in the immobile in such a way as to suggest the indefinite. This is made apparent at an initial level by the compositional features. Sarah Whitfield[18] and David Sylvester[19] reproduce the sketch for the picture Magritte published in the Brussels review *Distances*, also in 1928, showing the stages of the attack on the woman by the man figured in the painting. Compression is the overall effect that, in structural terms, emerges with all the greater force in the completed image, and not just on the figurative level: the figured and the figurative process are also subject to this compression, to this unstoppable narrowing of options. In the Oedipal drama, the body of the male protagonist is forced psychically on that of the female, not just by political or cultural coercion from which it cannot be prised away, just as the body of the female protagonist is implanted in that of the male. Magritte's picture peeks behind the curtains of these surreptitious invasions, projecting a supreme confidence in the power of the image to capture what is lost in time, and ingrained on the surfaces of the body as the eye wonders over it, over what it can never own, only threaten to expose in a paradoxically triumphalist despair at the public gaze and at public consumption.

The male, clothed figure in *Les Journées gigantesques* obliterates and simultaneously publicises the female nudity. Whether or not this is a symptom of the paranoid and appropriative functioning of male power in phallocratic culture, it also signals the operation of Magritte's image-making here, its capacity to display what cannot be displayed, and also to make apparent the way what *is* displayed reveals none of its secrets. The violence of this image is not only the violence of rape and of gender relations at large; this violence is supplemented in infinite regress by the displacing activity of repression itself – a blind mimicking of which, it seems, is the extent of Magritte's ambition here. His achievement is bound by his failure; both consist in repression replicated.

Commentators have noted[20] that it is unusual for the Magritte of the 1920s to return to an idea and produce different versions of it, but that this is precisely what he does in the case of *Les Journées gigantesques*. Perhaps what he offers in this way is a further refinement of his display of sexual difference and of its absorption, in the sense of its acceptance in the body, its dispersal and its obscuring in culture. In the earlier version, the framing of the scene is more violent, the figures are truncated and rip into the field of vision and its lines of perspective – rip into it, but confirm it simultaneously. Scopophilia, paranoia and authority begin again their grim ballet. In the later version, the one reproduced here, the scene is repeated within the confines of an interior, emphasising paradoxically the public element in this conflictual embrace. In the earlier version, on the other hand, the intimate and the private are emphasised in the immediate involvement of the viewer in this scene of violence, standing as s/he is in a very public gallery space.[21] This immediacy is also broken apart, as I suggested earlier, by the complexity of the identification which male and female viewers are asked to perform. If the public is emphasised in the later picture and the private in the earlier one, this is not only to obscure but also to *mobilise* the distinction between them still further. In the later version, the public space indicated is still an interior one, nobody else is figured in the picture; is this a no-man's land, perhaps, an interstice, an in-between space of suspended animation suggesting the prospect of some future freedom of manoeuvre? Rather, a dissolution of distinction, a collapse of positions that does nothing to undermine or obviate their power. Magritte seems to face us with a living yet static mess of disintegrated differences, yet still welded together in a pictorial attempt to account for them, and in a more general attempt to account for identity – that sensed, workaday wholeness which is as much on display in the picture as is its own structural state of being at odds with itself. This set of broken, yet active dichotomies might stretch to the following: the cultural and the psychic, subjectivity and authority, the repressed and the projected, revolt and emulation. At these levels, and still others, the troubling of boundary has led to compression and immobility, to alienation confirmed and re-confirmed indefinitely. Moreover, it is this indefiniteness which, paradoxically, provides the picture with its only source of plurality and dynamism.

This deceptive lack of definition is explored again in *Les Amants* of the same year. The picture shows the heads of two lovers kissing, each one covered by a sheet. David Sylvester and Sarah Whitfield have both argued that the picture is a working over of big-screen Hollywood close-up clinches prevalent in the 1920s.[22] But more than a Surrealist 'flash of discomfort' or 'irritant or source of disquiet', the covering of the lovers' heads with sheets displays a Surrealist investigation of 'le moi', that embroilment of ideology and subjectivity that Breton in *Les Vases communicants*[23] once again seeks so urgently to disentangle and to redirect. But what hope of that here?

The psychic and the cultural, the intimate and the public, are confused beyond comprehension, beyond any visual or theoretical stability. At one level, the stasis of the two-dimensional does once again allow Magritte to provide a mirror-image, albeit a refracted one, of something like the dissolution of opposites craved for consistently by Breton as champion of the kind of rejuvenated dialogue that is 'le merveilleux' – a dialogue made of energy in the unconscious and of dynamism in perception. But the dissolution of opposition, here, and of sexual difference particularly, is once more the mark of the fetish. Far from countering repression, a willed abandoning of difference confirms the action of repression and replicates it. Technically, the fetish signals a refusal to absorb the psychic wounds and the discursive consequences of separation and loss. Culturally, it flags the worship of power, of the unattainable, with the unknown and the archetypal each serving as twin mirages threatening the subject with what he or she can never have. The superego roams free in this picture, the back wall acting as a kind of back-projection screen on which nothing is figured, on which no form takes shape, but which suggests control all the more strongly, the control, in this case, of models and their dissemination. Once again desire married to authority is on display.

But that authority is not located or positioned. If we care to imagine that Magritte is having us watch a static image imitating a moving one, then beyond that the object of Magritte's imitation is a hovering, indeterminate relation as dynamic as it might be fruitless of inner and outer stimuli, psychic structuring and perceptual mobility, coercion and sublimation. Back in the darkened cinema, we sit and wonder at what attracts us and moves us. Faced now with this condensed memory of Hollywood cinematic erotica, wonder flows into blindness, the sensation of the other mouth in the kiss is now not only spell-binding but familiar and recognised. Blindness and recognition go hand in hand here. Familiarity breeds anxiety as we watch; what we know is what we love, but the reasons escape us, ensnared as they are in the suspension that has such a part to play in this image and its effects, and which is made up both of detachment (the prohibition on touch) and engrossed identification. This representation of a kiss through sheets, rather than evoking merely unpleasant or disquieting sensations, intensifies the silence of the image, immobilises any sexual heterogeneity that might have been involved. Sexual difference now looms as a cultural emblem all the more dominant and absorbent for having its provenance obscured and its silent appeal made public. This emblem of Oedipal culture reverberates in a ghastly parody of the intransitive delights of some longed-for redirected sexual energy. This paradoxically static indeterminacy involves the psychic with the visible, shunts together the associative and the preordained; but its only movement is invasive.

The title *Les Journées gigantesques*, whatever the circumstances of its composition, evokes a kind of mythological dimension to the violent experience of sexuality that emerges from the picture. Thanks to the title, the sediment of great deeds seems to reside in the fibre of the associations that come into play in confronting the picture. These deeds would belong to a revered past that is swamped, immersed in a dimensionless, ahistorical quality in the present, but all the more activated by the experience of the image and the raw material of that familiar otherness that Magritte deals in. His intratextual cross-referencing – that is, references within the body of his own work – his accumulation of that 'family' of favoured motifs has the effect of highlighting and doubling this mythological undertow. At the same time, the impact of this menagerie and its various favoured components is ultimately eroded, just as it is in the work of Dalí. Each time a bowler hat or a woman with drawers in her torso appears in the imagery of one or other artist, the familiarity of that image is counterbalanced by the obliteration of the context which would allow it to be securely deciphered. The variety of appearances of each motif cannot be confidently embraced, and instead the viewer grapples with an impact the sources of which elude tracking, and which elicits the viewer's fascination precisely because of that. In Cubist collage and in the subsequent collage work of Ernst, it is the eclecticism of the image's impact, its shifting pluralism, that challenges the habitual structures through which we come to terms with the unknown and interpret the surprising. In the case of Magritte's imagery, it is similarity – Foucault's 'similitude'.[24]

The paradoxical quality of Magritte's visual thinking with the disparate and with the eclectic is further signalled in his contrivance of the 'peinture-objet', within which, as I suggested in the case of *La Découverte du feu*, dialogic plurality is progressively squeezed out and flattened. *Les Journées gigantesques*, as Sarah Whitfield points out, provides Magritte with another opportunity to conjugate different material and plastic elements, this time the painterly and the sculptural.[25] But the formal freedom that Magritte invents for himself in this way seems to have the effect of vacuum-sealing the painterly surface of this picture against any intrusion, against any breath of creative fresh air. Moreover, Magritte's allusions in paint, both in this picture and in others, to the practices of collage emphasise this sealing-off still further. The figure of the man adhering invasively to the naked body of the woman is a silent, immobile homage to the scissors-and-paste work of the collagist. But here, there is no possibility of the intruder being peeled off; a source of the disparate has become an emblem of the enforced, and the substance of the oil paint now acts as a vehicle for the agglutinous, enclosed magnetism of authority. Formal freedom drifts into asphyxia on the level of the image and its impact. And this impact is maintained by a concentration on the material of the image and of its production which might otherwise, in the light of avant-gardist ambitions for the formal, have acted as a dam against the fluid infiltrations of ideological coercion.

Freudian notions of condensation and displacement in the dream work, or in the production of the manifest content of the dream, shed further light on Magritte's own representations of the psyche, his own work with similarity and with the indeterminacy of context. Small wonder, perhaps, given the extent to which these notions have been invoked in proclaiming the range and intensity of Surrealist ambition. But the outcome here is not quite as might be anticipated. Each new appearance of a member in his 'family' of motifs acts, on one level, as a condensation of other such appearances, as well as producing new configurations of the affinities that it carries with it. Take, for example, Magritte's practice of showing a canvas that both reproduces and hides what lies behind it. Its first of many appearances is in *La Belle captive* of 1931, and is thought to have been based on illustrations of perspective in A. Cassagne, *Traité pratique de perspective* of 1873, which Magritte would have seen as a student in Brussels.[26] It is followed up in *La Condition humaine* of 1933, and makes numerous appearances subsequently. Various differences can be spotted between the first two pictures, in particular the addition of an interior element in the second, which Magritte uses to introduce a further element of doubt, since the left-hand edge of the represented canvas extends over the line of the curtain, making the notion that the image on that canvas reproduces what is behind it even more of a supposition. That doubt might extend backwards to the first version, and we might begin to wonder whether the style in the represented picture here matches the style in the rest of the painting. *La Belle captive* as a whole is characterised in style by a certain Romanticism, whereas the style in the represented picture seems to have more to do with the Dutch Golden Age. Moving back to *La Condition humaine*, the tree common to both paintings has moved now into the represented picture. It now figures there in its entirety and in a different style. In conjunction with the curtain that also figures prominently in Magritte's visual vocabulary, the

Figure 12 René Magritte, *La Condition humaine* (1933). Oil on canvas, 100 × 81 cm.

framing and the staging of any act of representation is further emphasised. Beyond that, the broad historical sweep of styles ranging from Romanticism to the 'plein air' is trapped in a frame of recognition that is *still* immobilising for all its capacity to elude definition.

Condensation, then, produces this elusive framing. But condensation is giving way progressively to displacement. The member of the 'family' the viewer recognises is dispersed across a number of different painterly surfaces and contexts. But the sealing up of the image brought on by the asphyxiation of collage and of its embrace of the eclectic has the effect of cementing any alternative to what is before our eyes. Without alternative, we are blinded by what we see. Indeed, the represented image in *La Belle Captive* and in *La Condition humaine* obscures rather than reveals; and this extends over each of the paintings as a whole – an infinite regress of mimesis is triggered, cloaking each painting in the status of being represented, being gazed at and reconstructed, and yet for all that lacking in place, dialogue, reference and potential passing beyond. The displacing of each image in the interpretation of it matches the displacement which produces it in relation to other pictures in the same ad hoc series. The absence of a place of interpretation sets aside the concentration that the condensation of elements within Magritte's lexical 'family' might produce. But in doing so, this place-less viewing and image-making *confirms* that entrapment within a floating, elusive network of condensation I described a moment ago, a network that builds layer upon reference of allusion and history, and plants us in a no-man's land we recognise as our culture – even if only in so far as we allow Magritte or anyone else to force feed it to us once again.

It is clear that no-place and no-context are the mainstays of mystification. To resort to such chimera is to enhance alienation and to collaborate with oppression. Magritte's own high-stakes risk-taking involves exploiting the fascinations of mystery, and in that way putting on display the impulses of identification and of psychic investment. Concatenation, concentration, the paradoxically *plural* funnelling of the many into the one provide him with a footing in the thrust and counter-thrust of imaginary representation. The 'dénouement' that Michel Foucault discovers in Magritte's work[27] – be it the un-knotting of word and image, or the untying of condensation and displacement, or the keeping apart of 'ressemblance' and 'similitude' – seems an outcome that Magritte is unable to envisage. And indeed, the obsessional returns of Magritte's motifs and favoured elements cover the psychovisual space of the body of his work in a coating of impossibility. Interpretation is brought to a standstill; chasing down the tracks of each visual element and its impact, as this chapter has indicated, merely puts on display that very process of hunting down, bringing the viewer more and more into the clutches of the two-dimensional and of its enveloping authority. An inventive, but still enclosing visual and interpretive flatness emerges with increasing obduracy.

In *Les Mémoires d'un saint*, to take another example from much later – 1960 – in his life, Magritte gives visual form to mimetic allusions ranging from sky-patterned wallpaper, the scroll, the magic lantern, the cinema screen, the screen or stage curtain as well as the sky itself, both as a natural element and as a cultural insignia. Perhaps the curtain that opens and closes with equal plausibility sustains the possibility of indefinite readings, and of multiple changes of direction in the channels of perceptual data and association. Magritte, in commenting on the picture, casts doubt on such optimism. And

Figure 13 René Magritte, *Les Mémoires d'un saint* (1960). Oil on canvas, 80 × 100 cm.

perhaps, in fact, the sense of the picture concentrating in its space a range of
Magritte's favoured motifs from the 1930s, the sense of a conclusive line being
drawn in the sand signals the impulse to closed, rather than open-ended pathways into the undetermined and the unspecified. Is this an impulse that might
still be put on display and thus dispensed with, and which might be made to
reveal its source and its energy? Commenting on the picture with his cus-
tomary precision, Magritte stresses that 'le ciel est en forme de rideau parce-
qu'il nous cache quelque chose. Nous sommes entourés de rideaux.'[28]
Endless veils smother the capacity that objects might unleash to make new
configurations of the visible, to loosen the grip on it of the habits of symbolic
reading.[29]

   Any attempt to make of the visible a Barthesian 'écriture blanche',[30] a
form of expression freed of expressiveness and of the requirements of sense,
is headed off once again in *Les Mémoires d'un saint* by the viewer's own position and activity in relation to it. Whether open or closed, the scroll in the
round inevitably suggests enclosure, a wrapping up of the intratextual elements that have been so dear to the artist in the elaboration of his corpus.
Furthermore, the petrified theatre-in-the-round positively invites the authority of the all-embracing overview, and force feeds its viewers on the all-
absorbent mental textures of recognition. But what is the vantage point that

allows this recognition? Not simply the stalls we might imagine in front of the opening–closing curtain. The theatre-in-the-round is itself rounded by a space every atom of which is potentially made of moments of porous, place-less gazing. To entertain the pulses of recognisable bits that emanate from the picture, and that end up statically suspended *on* its surface, is to become involved and absorbed not only in an aggressive, continual reassessment and reappropriation; any such possible forward thrust of project upon inter-pretive project is in fact inverted and made regressive. Instead, the viewer becomes ensnared in a nostalgic placement, the mirage of total recall. Impregnable vantage points abound in the light as well as the darkness sur-rounding the cylindrical theatre; the authority of secure recognition bathes the image from on high as well as the viewer's participation in it, in a light whose tonal progressions and play of light and shade do nothing to rip its seamlessness apart or to inject any differentiation. The dark–light space around the theatre of inventiveness provides this most Oedipal of arts with a platform of interpretation unthreatened even by any internal cracks or splits; it beams, in the very reading of it, a sensation of authority where the many has finally become the one, an *Einfühlung* whereby visions of parental harmony – the harmonisation of the parental bodies – offer an absolution of difference. Such are the inward-looking, eagerly and inveterately totalising channels of reading that Magritte puts on display by demanding them himself and by mimicking their demands.

I suggested earlier that the drifting, shifting sands of intertextual ele-ments and intratextual ones – elements from outside the corpus, and ele-ments belonging to its 'family' – provide Magritte with one of his most fascinating and paradoxical ploys. I have argued that the perusal of his images, the very reception of his confusion there of perceptual and signifying cate-gories, mobilises a sense, or a delusion, of incorporation in an amorphous, engulfing psychic One, an omnipotent and uniform otherness made of the parental and social pressures that both constrict us and civilise us. This other-ness is both a position and texture – psychic and untouchable; the one confirming the other and enhancing its appeal. In what ways, more precisely, do intratextual relations support intertextual ones in Magritte's tenacious cri-tique of the authority of recognition, and above all the psychically driven *pursuit* of that?

In *La Découverte* of 1927, Magritte displays a striking use of the wood-grain motif that is also on display in *La Passion des lumières* of the same year. In commenting on his new 'discovery', he emphasises the capacity of objects gradually to become something else under his painter's brush, and in this way to have viewers think differently about what they see.[31] With reference to *La Passion des lumières*, in which intimations of wood-grain take the place of clouds, Magritte talks of the absence of break between two substances that

Figure 14 René Magritte, *La Découverte* (1927). Oil on canvas, 65 × 50 cm.

he can effect in visual terms, and hence a dissolving of the limits of vision. In *La Découverte*, however, it is not sky and wood-grain that share a visual continuity, but wood-grain and flesh. Once again, Magritte highlights the dynamics of representation and of the positionings involved. The history of nude-painting is in immediate evidence, as well as of pornography.[32] The wood-grain now suggests a physiological, implanted dimension to the sense of being placed in discourse and in the existential drama of self and other, of aggression and absorption.

The effects of the 'peinture-object' are once again in play. The grain-motif appearing intermittently on the woman's body suggests not only an indeterminacy of substance, but of medium and of art form: painting and sculpture. If we imagine a picture of a sculpture, then we might imagine the grain being revealed, being made to appear through the work of the sculptor. But as a painting without reference to work on wood, we now see the grain as purely applied. A literal reference to depth is lost, in favour of a literal emphasis on the two-dimensional, the raw material of painting. Depth gives way to the illusion of it, which itself melts into flatness. This collusion – loaded in favour of the two-dimensional – of the artificial and the natural, of illusionism and the material, not only highlights the ideology of the nude and of its representation. It also depicts an alienating resignation to a sense of the body as both unknown and vandalised. And since, once again, recognition serves confirmation, the choice of a personalised visual lexis supports and reflects this sadomasochistic tautology of creativity and submission. Magritte's own art stands and falls on its power to represent by confirming this tautology of mind and body.

Furthermore, Magritte's introverted vocabulary of obsession, shared and taken in by the viewer, casts its shadow of inverted, joyful yet self-condemning colonisation over other artists and their works. In the case of *Perspective II: Le Balcon de Manet* of 1950, Magritte's intertextual net induces condensation and concentration, rather than dispersal and plurality. His notion of 'affinités électives',[33] first displayed in the painting of that title of 1933, suggests that it is the proximity of objects somehow related to each other that produces poetic sparks, rather than the chance encounter of unrelated objects. This not only signals a defining bone of contention with Surrealist theory, a swerving away from the utopian inventiveness derived from the idea of chance. It is also a face-on acceptance of the limitations which define invention and of its embroilment in canonical orthodoxy. Once again, Magritte highlights the impossibility of objects exceeding their status of *being* represented, or of converting 'le visible' into 'l'invisible'. Here is one of many moments in the *Ecrits* where this problem is addressed:

Comment la peinture, qui est visible, pourrait-elle représenter l'invisible?[34]

Magritte's particularly intertextual 'affinities' breed an increasingly dense asphyxia as a three-horse race develops between the pile-up of allusion, the efforts of recognition to retrieve them, and the striving exhibited in the picture to outdo those same efforts. In *Le Balcon*, intratextual and intertextual relations combine – implosively, confiningly, paranoicly. Manet's balcony is revisited, and has now become infiltrated by another of Magritte's workings-over, this time of David's *Madame Récamier*. Beginning life in 1949 as an oil

Figure 15 René Magritte, *Perspective (le Balcon de Manet)*, (1950). Oil on canvas, 80 × 60 cm.

painting called *Perspective*,[35] this image ends up in 1967 as a bronze sculpture which Magritte with mock simplicity entitles *Madame Récamier de David*. In between, Magritte also produced several painted versions with the title *Madame Récamier de David*, one of which is reproduced here. What is Magritte battling with or toying with in these obsessive returns and their passage from painting to sculpture? The literal and concrete three-dimensionality of the sculpture, an invitation to think in terms of spatial mobility and depth, is little

Figure 16 René Magritte, *Perspective: Madame Récamier de David* (1967). Oil on canvas, 60 × 80 cm.

match for the entombment which it represents; in fact, metaphoric power and conceptual freedom are curtailed and corralled towards the literal along every avenue of interpretation, seemingly, that the piece offers to its viewers. A personal lexis of favoured or despised artists – the distinction is made difficult to apply and seems to lose any value – is subsumed and seamlessly absorbed in the domineering 'perspective' of a culture of icons whose dimensions are elusive – psychically fermented – and for that very reason restrictive. This narrowing of vision, this further confining of vision to the visible, is confirmed by the sculptural form of the piece – confirmed all the more stealthily by the prohibition of touch even to the massive yet still allusive, material tangibility of this sculpture as well as to that of countless others. Magritte's object signals its own inability to disown the culture of fetishistic capturing and appropriation, or the comfort zones of the known and the dominant. Manet's balcony, its sensuous investigations of observing and of being observed, its charting of the bourgeois performance that nurtures and beguiles, is reduced to a projection – by which I mean a further cinematic still so fascinating to Magritte – a projection of the enclosing and entombing dynamics of public knowledge turned voyeurist, regressive, triumphant and arid. 'Life has been turned into death' – as David Sylvester encapsulates it.[36] But what sort of art can this be?

An art of dispossession, an art of failure, perhaps? So many of its treasures seem to turn to dust; we have just seen how intertextuality might be one of them. Like the grains on the female nude's body in *La Découverte*, like the visions of microbes and insects that for the young Giacometti and Aragon respectively evoke the mythological prospects and limitations of creativity, the nets of Magritte's intratextual and intertextual allusions, the very effort they come to signal or prompt to give an account – if not a globalising one, then a testing one – of Magritte's trajectory through his own psyche and his own ambition, seem to end up with an effect of moulding: moulding the range of our receptivity, the range of our capacity to synthesise and absorb, moulding even our sense of our own body in relation to others as we look at Magritte's reconstructed, more sabotaging than sabotaged displays of nudity and its memory. Intimate memory all the same; a muddled, muddied and unfathomable intimacy.

Perhaps the glorious, self-imploding negativity of DADA would after all have been a more productive path to follow, however paradoxical and anarchic. The capacity affirmed by Marcel Duchamp before the First World War, even more powerfully by Kurt Schwitters after it, to transform anything into art, into the substance of a spontaneous novelty simply by designating it as such, gives practitioners and enjoyers of art alike a taste of freedom from its self-fulfilling prophecies, from its aura of prescription and of the untouchable. Schwitters's aesthetics of detritus is the stuff of a dedicated campaign to cleanse visual sensibility of cultural antecedence and weight, and ultimately to open it out to the possibility of gift, to the offering and the receiving of nothing – if not the de-composed, the liquid and the unheard of.

Magritte's commitment, on the other hand, to the image, and therefore to the dynamics of identification, ultimately lock him onto the commercialisation of the body and the commodification of the senses. And yet the take-over of his imagery by advertising in the 1970s and 1980s, its plundering of his humour and of his despair does not mean that Magritte's art is capable only of casting all powers of intervention to the winds; any more than Magritte's own fascination with the Hollywood big screen of the 1920s and 1930s suggests some paucity of resistance to cultural coercion. Perhaps Magritte's dialogue with the aesthetification of commerce and with iconic concentrations of desire is the stuff of an open, energetic cultural exchange which, quite beyond the postmodern supermarket, would make up an acceptance of otherness, of transience and relativity as well as material joy. An acceptance of life, even the hot-house of capitalist and Oedipal cross-pollination, rather than resistance to an energy that threatens to spin out of control; an affirmative failure rather than virile political complacency.

CHAPTER FIVE

The offerings of decay:
Jean Fautrier, *Les Otages*

On ne vous demande pas si vous l'aimez, ou si vous l'admettez cette peinture. Vous avez simplement à constater un fait: que la peinture est entrée dans un stade 'abstrait', 'informel', 'non figurative', choisissez l'appellation. Et c'est une rude chance, car depuis qu'Uccello lui a donné les moyens d'illusion visuelle et depuis que la peinture à l'huile nous en a flanqué plein la vue avec ces orchestrations, il faut bien admettre qu'elle aurait filé un mauvais coton, à partir d'Ingres et Delacroix, si Manet et la photo ne nous avaient sauvés.

Mais approuver Manet, c'est, aujourd'hui, souscrire à l'informel.

Jean Fautrier[1]

I

With a 'discomfort' set at the heart of culture, Freud seals the limits of psychoanalysis and the solace it might provide. Civilisation has no antidote to a continual unease and dissatisfaction with the human lot. Lacan develops this notion of knowledge as an unwanted gift into a science of human destiny.[2] The destiny of the ego is to be continually ill-at-ease, unable to accommodate itself to its existence among others. Its longed-for autonomy, the aspiration to which it cannot abandon, is constantly under the twin threats of others pursuing the same autonomy with equal desperation, and of its own imprisonment within a perishable body. The civilisation of the ego offers it renewed, polymorphous anxiety. It is condemned to violent outbursts against enemies it cannot defeat, spectres and horrors of its own making to which it continually cedes power only to engage in open warfare with them once more.

Lionel Trilling, in tracing the history of the literary-minded 'claiming Freud as their own',[3] reminds psychoanalytical and textual readers alike of the passage leading from this sense of discomfort to the notion of the death instinct more generally. A concern with the unending opposition of reality and pleasure is one of the connections between literary and psychoanalytical responses that Trilling focuses on. Homing in on Keats's fascination with tragedy, and with the paradoxes of an art form acquiring the power to transform pain into cathartic pleasure, Trilling invokes Oedipus and suggests that he 'is not in fact going to his death but to his apotheosis'.[4] 'No living man has loved as I have loved'[5] – resting on Yeats's translation, Trilling allows an Oedipus to emerge who is less blinded by the twin delusions of omniscience and omnipotence, than immersed down to his fibres in the polymorphous narratives carried around on the body, on its surfaces and in its impulses. Transgression is now not a matter of perverted sexual practice, or of any particular sexual act, nor even of some enacted overturn of the frontiers between the generations, and between the warring factions of desire and society. Trangression once again meets its match in its own passage into known and familiar images of revolt and their overestimation. But beyond that, transgressive posture gives way to an affirmation of a myth-making able to countenance its own demise. Such forms hold out the possibility of working with rather than against the decomposition of the body, with the limits of power traced along the body's outlines and against its imaginary extension and bloating.

II

> Comment se comporter en face de l'idée des *Otages*?
> On peut dire que voilà une des questions essentielles de l'époque.[6]

Such are the pronouncements of Francis Ponge in his essay on Jean Fautrier's *Otages*, compiled in 1945 – at a point where the sense of 'époque' could not be more specifically or more poignantly defined. What a moment to declare that an essentially aesthetic question is one of the major ones to be resolved! A moment of realisation – a bodily, a material awareness of the depth and breadth of violence in human existence. Not the violence of disease or death, but the violence of humans on humans, the coerciveness of ideology and symbol made flesh and pulp. Nor the violence of war at large, and its megalomanic resort to deathly aggression, the heat-of-the-battle wave it rides on of nationalist self-importance and disregard for otherness. Ponge knows that Fautrier is dealing with a violence that is rehearsed and planned, carried out behind closed doors with a stealthy precision that revels in its victims' defencelessness.

At Chatenay-Malabry, Fautrier, himself hiding from the Nazis, overhears the screams of the tortured. They begin to infiltrate his art, like some perverse fifth column. What kind of resistance is this, if any, to Nazi atrocity? Is art affirming its power or collapsing in impotence? Rediscovering its purity or its lack of moral purpose? Ponge suggests that responses seeking to come to terms with torture might range from stupefaction to shame. The desire to obliterate such events from any vision of the future might simply involve attempting to forget them. But it might also take the active form of a heroism seeking to uproot the seeds of such unimaginable inhumanity. Would not the goal of using art to denounce organised sadism be best served by a realist approach? A documentary account might be the one to carry the greatest power to shock and to challenge inaction. But Fautrier's is an aesthetic approach, dealing in forms and the identification with them – and for that reason it poses the question of its appropriateness in the most brutal as well as the most pathetic way. 'Il transforme en beauté l'horreur humaine actuelle'[7] – Ponge places Fautrier squarely in the Baudelairean conception of image-making, allowing him to flirt with the artificial paradise of pure art and in that way, at that risk, to delve into the psyche, into the cultural imprints made on it as well as into its material corruptibility. But precisely in dealing with the material, such representation obscures its targets, any target, as well as the focus of any anger. Is this not to detract from the inhumanity of torture, to undermine our capacity to be revolted by it and to prevent such events ever happening again?

But the heroic and the passive approaches to obliterating inhumanity cannot remain as clear-cut as this. Throughout the history of art, representations of decay at the thematic and moral levels have combined with forms that exploit decay, that are themselves evolved in images of decay and mapped onto the horrific dynamism that can be found there.[8] The result has been some of the most universally symbolic art, as well as some of the most punctually shocking in historical and cultural terms: I am thinking of Goya, Daumier, Manet, Dix, Grosz, the photorealism of John Hartfield, even the lithographic montages of Warhol involving the electric chair or the decapitation of Jayne Mansfield in a car crash. And yet the ethical problem remains constant: how to reach beyond style; how to avoid drowning the dignity and the otherness of suffering in the appropriative mish-mash of subjective understanding; how to preserve some objective purchase on oppression and its dimensionless brutality. Sartre brings such questions to the fore again in seeking a distinctive 'littérature engagée' of his own making in the immediate postwar period. But these problems reach to the heart of any history of form, and Sartre's handling of them reveals the parameters of phenomenological thought in which his own work is embedded and is developed.

Let me return for a moment to my discussion in chapter 3 of *Qu'est-ce que la littérature?* and of the notion of the imaginary at large. Sartre implicitly acknowledges that expression – and the ethics of expression along with it – is a matter of form, itself the raw material of imaginary consciousness. What he refers to as the 'réalisme' of Vermeer is one such form – perhaps the one best suited, one might think, with its ability meticulously to depict interiors and the social dynamics played out there, to bearing witness to torture. But this is not the 'realism' Sartre has in mind, and in any case, Vermeer himself is as fascinated as any painter with the display of image-making itself. On the one hand, it is true that realism in Sartre's approach to it is founded on the denotation of objects, on attention to their outlines, and an acceptance of the dialectic of object and subject. But it is also implicated in the doomed cause of prose – within Sartre's own distinction of prose and poetry. The dialectic of object and subject both maintains the power of indication and proposition, and endangers it. The capacity to impose new beginning is both continually reaffirmed and continually under threat, always under the cloud of being exposed as a delusion. Such is the knife-edge on which Vermeer's 'réalisme' is poised in Sartre's account of it. 'La pâte des choses',[9] one of the many metaphors of mucousness in Sartre's discourse that result from his attempts to conceive of the material, represents the liquefied scene of expression in which Sartre situates Vermeer. Here, objects are dissolved along with the subject's purchase on them. A sense of losing the object's form and its context in the very imagining of them triggers what amounts to an engulfing phantasm of a return to substance, of drowning in pure matter, in dimensionless, conceptless origin. Such is the obverse of the unstoppable and indeed indispensable illusion that Lacan encapsulates in a characteristic metaphorising of the signifier, drawing out all its paradoxical powers both to disrupt and to attract imaginary understanding: 'ce m'appartiennent des perceptions'.[10] In alluding to his own critique of the phenomenological account of perception, at the same time as to his situation within it, Lacan here rams home his own 'gift' of the dissolution of the body, but without, ultimately, doing away with those forms of representation that might restore the body's integrity along with the never-ending quest for supremacy. In fact he testifies to the power of such forms in his disruption of the signifier, and exploits them as well – 'ce m'appartiennent des perceptions'. The interplay of forms in Sartrean phenomenology as well as in a Lacanian response to it allows synthesis, naming, signifying appropriation of all kinds to be taken into account, including taking on board notions such as repression and the questions of ethics and responsibility that evolve from it. The *image* of Frantz in Sartre's *Les Séquestrés d'Altona* of 1960, his last work for the theatre, withdrawn in his room full of grief, projections of Nazi guilt and of postwar German redemption, straddles with alarming perfection the reality and pleasure principles, the twin capacities to accept absorption in history and to demand narrative control over it as of now.

    Narrative representation on the one hand, on the other the undermining of representational power in corporeality – each their own source of alienation, each their own source of resistance.[11] The 'tragedy' of art as Trilling evokes it emerges from the second, in a devotion to forms espousing their own collapse, or, at another level, to forms through which to inch away from historical construction to open-ended, irrevocable temporality. We might think of Cubism, for example, in the light that Jean Paris allows us to throw on it as a process of inhabiting objects: 'regarder un objet, c'est venir l'habiter, et de là saisir toutes choses selon la face qu'elles tournent vers nous'.[12] But this 'face', this facet or facade displaces the security of our grasp on objects, temporalizes our hold on the nets they envelop us in. In such fractured perspective, objects are smothered and smother us in masks of objects; layers upon layers of objectness produce the forms objects take in our imagining and conceiving of them. Such masks emerging from objectness, from the psychic paths of dealing in objects, eclipsing the illusory comfort of anthropomorphism, are caught up in a homologous relation to the effects of the sign, not imitating them but failing to distinguish themselves from them, each – mask and sign – involved in their own labyrinths of displacement and deferral, each engulfing and engulfed by the other.

Georges Didi-Huberman describes Giacometti dealing in mask-matter, producing 'un devenir-masque du portrait paternel'.[13] The gorgeous *perpetuum mobile* of Didi-Huberman's formulation highlights the absence here of any literalness in the relation of model to the materials of execution chosen, any literalness in representing the relation of signifying effects to psychic impressions, and of psychic impressions to impressions made by the hand and its implements. The binding agent of analogy, as Roland Barthes would have it, loses its ideological grip in being made to give way to homology and to its peculiar ballet in which partners never face each other, each impervious to the other's advances. But in *Fragments d'un discours amoureux* homology manufactures only limited room for manoeuvre for itself, confirming rather than dematerializing the psychocultural tramlines it seeks to give new direction and depth to. And yet this homologous relation of sign to psyche, and the incompatible metaphors of matter it produces, counters any nostalgia for a subjective freedom of the cities and sites of history. The collapse of historical narrative in representations of the body as masks of its embrace is not so much a signal of inconsequential erotics or of morbid withdrawal, but of that history that can only be told on the assumption that it eludes the telling, the history of a love affair between alienation and resistance.

Germaine Richier's *Diabolo* of 1950, for example, fashions a female form from signs being applied to the body, rather than projected from it. She is enmeshed in metal, solid marionette strings that immobilize her. But this anonymity is also an illusion that can be reread. This same immobility is the sculptured one that is able to suggest movement from within the static, even though this remains suggestion by convention. These strings that are also bars draw the bounds of possibility on the physiology of the body, its outlines and its movements. On the one hand, then, signification, rather than projected outwards, is pasted back onto this female body by the very work of the artist and its engagement with the enveloping, precedent-bound build-up of gazes and glances coming from the spectator of either sex. But on the other hand, in this animation at once stifled and suspended, a certain pride is asserted in the capacity to reinvent alienation with each potential movement, each imagined reconfiguration of the bars which trap the body but which the body also manifests the power to manipulate, producing, if only we could imagine them, different signs, different constructions of the symbolic . . .But then what will the consistency of such a difference be?

Such questions and experiences are delved into relentlessly by what is now possible to think of as a grouping of artists in France in the immediate postwar period which comprises, among others and along with Richier and Giacometti, Wols, Jean Dubuffet, Bernard Buffet, Jean Hélion, Henri Michaux, Tal Coat and Jean Fautrier. Two exhibitions mounted in 1993 were dramatic testimonies to the disturbing capacity of such art to confuse the boundaries of body and politics, the impulsive and the coerced: *Paris Post War – Art and Existentialism 1945–1955* at the Tate Gallery, and *L'Ecriture griffée* at the Musée d'Art Moderne de Saint-Etienne. Sartre's essays on such art seem to seek out a kind of heroism based on the powers he attributes to the imaginary mode of consciousness to free itself from the pressures of contingency. He admires Calder's mobiles for their capacity to give form and therefore impetus to transience, and to offer viewers the prospect of reconstructing their social interaction on the basis of the very transience that characterises their material being. In *La Recherche de l'absolu*, one of two essays he devoted to Giacometti, the stuff the absolute is made of is the relative, and by immersing spectators in it through his forms, Giacometti in Sartre's eye provides them with an opportunity for that 'irréalisant'[14] activity that characterizes, for Sartre, imaginary emancipation from the given.[15] But in essentialising the relative in this way and its powers of reorientation, in fact in marrying the infinite regress of the essence to that of the relative, Sartre might fall prey to the nets of psychic and signifying temptation that his own tactile writing warns against – the temptation of allowing the relative to be swamped in its own indefiniteness, to be cloaked in a one-colour of all-enveloping corporeality.

Such might be the perverse power of the Image to construct for us as we talk a body whole and atemporal.[16] The poetic practice of 'faire du silence avec le langage'[17] that he imagines or projects is certainly a testimony to a revolt against a material indeterminacy of body and sign. But part and parcel of this invocation is a realisation that it transforms indeterminacy into fixity – or into synthesis – and builds revolt on that. Testimony risks being little more than confirmation. Once again, an impasse builds up that might only be surpassed by historical critique. Is it worth spurning it? What is the prize of Fautrier's immersion in the material to the point of embracing the body wilfully made waste, and of offering this up as an object of aesthetic adoration? What is the price of his mimetic collaboration with torture? Can it be an acceptable resistance to ideology carved on the body and in the signs it projects? Is to make images of a tortured body an ingestible counter-action to violent delusions of immortality prompted by the image as such?

III

I can only leave Sartre to his own spirited attempts – in *Critique de la raison dialectique*, or in *L'Idiot de la famille* – to chart the dynamics of the relative and the essential, situational reorientation and the pressures of history. Nor is this the place to comment on his seeming blindness to matters of gender and to the part they should and could play in his thinking. Unless Fautrier's pure art of horror could turn out to be a mute dissolving agent of such psychic or ideological blindness. Trilling, Lacan, Sartre have perhaps served as objects of so many hysterical allusions through which I have so far avoided coming to grips with an art of speechless horror, or perhaps the futility of even trying has only to emerge for a sighting of Fautrier's offering to surface.

Certainly the Sartrean 'pâte des choses', the metaphor of pastiness used to evoke the forced marriage of body and sign, might well seem to project the same mucous effects as the materials used by Fautrier for his *Otages*. He is known for manufacturing a thick pictorial paste made up of absorbent layers of rag on canvas; pastel colour is crumbled, rather than applied, to the final surface.[18] His image-making turns itself continually inside out, survives materially on the temporality of its own production, and invites viewers to delve into decomposition . . .Once again, how are we to take the measure of a didacticism, however high-minded, that rests on a doubling – in the musical sense – of the effects of torture?

> Pas d'individu qui ne soit parcelle transitoire de l'univers biologique en même temps qu'à lui seul tout un monde. Pas de présence charnelle qui n'apparaisse comme déjà rongée par la future absence. Pas d'homme ni de femme dont le sort ne soit, qu'ils en aient une conscience précise ou non, un mariage du ciel et de l'enfer. Pour qui l'applique aux êtres humains et le pousse à l'extrême, le réalisme pourrait-il déboucher sur autre chose que la tragédie.[19]

Figure 17 Jean Fautrier, *La Juive* (1943). Oil on paper, mounted on canvas, 73 × 115.5 cm.

If Michel Leiris, responding to Francis Bacon, is right in discovering that any vision free of delusion is a tragic one, what of Fautrier's own sense that we cannot accept tragedy other than by dialoguing with victimisation?

La Juive of 1943[20] is both abject and delicate. Human butchery is frankly exhibited in this most aesthetically minded interaction of title and matter – only the torso of the Jewess's remains are on view. Even the outlines of the body are shown no respect, they disintegrate as much as emerge within the overwhelming materiality of the thing before us. Abject and delicate combine in this materiality and its unwieldy, pathetic depth: uncompromising agglutinousness bubbles into decorativeness in the pastel that floats over the surface – or can a decorative overlay only stifle what lies beneath? Such indeterminacy adds to the horrifying charm in which the lacerated Jewess envelops her viewers, hovering as she does in Fautrier's chemistry, and under his implements, between mutilation and release.

Dépouille, dated 1946,[21] not reproduced here, shows an equally pathetic and ghastly fragment of a once living body. The shape outlined is at once anatomic and organic, confusion once again adding to nausea and abjectness, or even forming the basis of them. Mutilation has acted both randomly and surgically, insidiously outflanking explanation and history, outdoing forms and channels of personalisation, refuting that sense of integrity that narrative has the power to project on the mobile screens of memory. This is alienation at its rawest, beyond systematic account of it or response to it, an unspeakable dissolution of all project and all love, the body now without bodily form, indistinguishable from a 'nothing' confirmed by the abstract style – a style that triggers memories of a person's bodily past and a person's bodily appeal only to seal their evaporation.

Enough pathos remains, though, for the defencelessness and the victimisation of a once human form to be sensed. But its paths are blocked; no hope here of securely charting a response. The open-endedness of the image is bought at the cost of the body, its skin, its fibres and its right to be whole – at the cost of them, and not on the back of mnemonic reconstruction of them, the brutalisation of which extends from the temporality of Fautrier's alchemy into the fixed object of our stunned contemplation. The flight into the delicacy of the blue pastel that covers the surface but which the surface itself has the power to mould, to override, to trap and absorb – this flight is not propelled by the pathos of the victim, or by any hope of redemption at the martyr's expense. Such is the binding, all-exclusive power of Fautrier's material, its fidelity to itself. Allegory collapses, and beyond that the distant nets of rhetoric at large, as the embrace of aesthetic rapture is once again refused the support of the body. Its positions in perspective, in discourse, in gender and in sex are obliterated – a state which, by embracing the magic of the image-in-time, Fautrier is able to present also as a process, one of dissolving, of collapse, of putrefaction. Rapture is at such a cost, apparently, if rapture itself is not to be abused, and if the violence of humankind and its delusions of grandeur are not to go without resistance.

Such is the character of Fautrier's attempt, as Ponge evokes it, to 'transformer en beauté l'horreur humaine actuelle'. The Baudelairean quality, and the more generally poetic conception of Fautrier's project as Ponge describes it is emphasised by another salient feature of the *Otages* that Ponge highlights: the absence in the pictures of any representation of the torturer or of the executioner. Such an approach is in stark contrast to that of, say, Goya and Manet in depicting violence. It also might suggest a withdrawal from political and historical dimensions, or a wilful refusal to explore the labyrinths of circumstance other than as a problem to be solved in purely pictorial terms, or other than philsophically, as an essential property of material existence. Once again, in this regard Fautrier's images seem to collaborate with the oppressor by abdicating the powers of analysis that any image-making involves, and by granting human and political violence the character of natural events. But Fautrier's 'transformation' of the effects of violence, and of the impetus behind them, is not a transcendence of them, nor is any catharsis involved. While the absence of any representation of torturing demolishes analysis, it also magnifies violence by diminishing pathos. There is no attempt to synthesise the positions involved in torture, or to set up a working relationship of identification *with* the victim and *of* the perpetrator.

On the contrary, in these works that allow time to be read in their own material consistency, and which produce a hovering, an inderminacy of the distinction between the flatness of image and the ruggedness of object, the comforts of synthesis are shown decomposing with the body itself in the only meeting Fautrier allows of form and content.

Ponge's style in 'Le Peintre à l'étude' is tentative, overtly tactful, implicitly suspicious of definition, alerting readers continually to the tyranny of the point of view and to the insidiousness of its appeal. While outflanking the position of blaming the victim, Ponge succumbs to an art in which victimization is discovered and rooted in the body, the lingua franca of existence. The feel of authority, Fautrier's pictures suggest, and of the desire for excessive power are focused on the body and triggered by responses to it and can only disappear with it. Fautrier gouges this impulse out from within the figures and the bodily images which he manufactures, asphyxiating precedent and brutalizing orthodoxy by immersing himself materially in them, in his chosen material, through which he can imagine them seeping. His art is an invented coming-to-grips with the stuff of anteriority by which we know our subjectivity, our temporality – and our grief at the collapse of models that might have leant us their coating of wholeness . . . But then, if not collaboration, do we not find in Fautrier a sadomasochistic immersion in violence and its perpetration?

Some might say that, were this the case, Fautrier would have done enough, arguing that sadomasochistic response and activity ironise rather than replicate authority by transforming directives into sources and forms of pleasure. Such is not Fautrier's response to alienation and its holds on him.[22] The *Otages* invite a gaze turned to the repressed, they impel imagination of the unthinkable – the demise of life itself; their air comes from a visualisation of the unthinkable, beyond metaphors of it and beyond comment on it; an unheard of, invisible air produced within a vacuum on which it thrives. To this extent, Yves Peyré is right to stress repeatedly the artistic purity of Fautrier's enterprise, its wrought, worked at concentration on materials that have exclusively pictorial scope and on questions that refute conception other than in painterly terms.[23] But this is not a metaphysical purity, as Peyré's idiom would seem to imply. Its matter need not be thought of as transcendent and resistant, but rather as absorbent, welcoming all invasions. This purity does not come from an adherence to aesthetic response to the exclusion of all others, but on the contrary from a fidelity that embraces its own collapse, that thrives on its capacity to break ties and to undermine any grip on it.

By shocking and alienating our desiring stares, the love the *Otages* allow spectators to imagine shatters that desperate clinging to the beguiling and torturing phantoms of narcissistic rebuilding. But the *Otages* do not offer agape either – communal love, uniqueness exchanged for its replication in shared forms and in pursuit of common goals set by a community which is symbolically circumscribed, and which ensures psychic and bodily space against defilement. By grasping as a whole the boundaries of the community, differences within it can be managed and tolerated, made the object of legislation, and opportunities for uniqueness are now brokered as part of a global social contract that sets out the differences between war and peace. But this is not the contract offered by Fautrier to viewers of his *Otages*. These pictures seem to immerse the viewing gaze in repression by focussing it on oppression. Bodies are thematically quartered and formally stifled, with no symbolic defence of any kind in evidence. The appeal of the colourings that seem at once to float over the surface and to be soaked up in it, the appeal of the inhuman forms and materials so dangerously *applied* to the human form eschews contract just as it shuns conclusion – just as perusing and reading the picture offer no ending to the contradictions it silently and intangibly projects. Such are the terms and conditions of a sudden eruption into beauty – an eruption that I, rather than Fautrier, can only describe as being without model or precedent, outside the scope of any notion of shock or surprise, dissolving pity and terror *alike*, and heralding an unheard of and instantly recognised onrush of faith.

IV

And yet critical lift-off itself hardly seems appropriate, attempts at affirmative critical lyricism would seem to undo the impact of Fautrier's work, however worked at and critical, however much they might seek to turn the lyrical 'moi' inside out and cast it to the winds of otherness. Ponge's tact, his suspicion of definition in approaching the *Otages*, seem increasingly exemplary, if not simply the least that can be expected of a response to an art that so resolutely resists classification, and that demands embrace and resists it with equal rebarbativeness. Jean Paulhan, though writing some twenty years later, and with much greater bombast and ironic self-assurance, expresses an equally acute embarrassment at offering any reading of Fautrier's work whatsoever, feeling that Fautrier will undoubtedly object to any interpretation whatever its character. Both are impelled, though, to suggest that Fautrier's image-making owes a crucial part of its power to its capacity to resist the coerciveness of the sign.

For Paulhan, the magnificence of Fautrier's colours comes from his capacity to alter the channels of their association, and the unwritten rules of precedent that seem to him to govern their combinations:

On a dit très justement que chaque couleur portait sa note et son sentiment. Mais Fautrier sait changer le sens des couleurs. Il se sert d'elles à sa guise, et du premier coup nous émerveille.[24]

Later in the book, Paulhan involves Fautrier's facility with colour and its connotations in what Paulhan thinks of as an even greater fluency with the whole range of relations that make up the history and the possibilities of painterly art. Paulhan evokes the pictures in terms of a dialogue with their own double, which evokes a mysterious Artaudian space in terms of which the psychic impulses driving painting can be imagined. But Paulhan, faced with Fautrier, refuses to have psychic innuendo and mystery rooted in anything other than tangible, technical, workaday effects:

Peut-être a-t-on, tout à l'heure, ici et là reconnu les traces de son [le mystère] passage dans une duplicité, qui glissait insensiblement du sujet à la peinture même; dans ces couleurs, dont le sens se transforme à nos yeux; dans les différends du dessin avec la nuance, et de la matière avec l'objet, tantôt rapides et tantôt suspendus; et jusque dans l'émotion ambiguë que nous laisse une œuvre étrange et pourtant brillante; jolie, non sans horreur.[25]

Brilliance, horror; the ephemeral and the suspended: metaphors of imponderable elements in our response and in our condition are resolutely given their life *down on the earth* of painterly practice and of the painterly relations of content and form, line and nuance, the materiality of objects and the material of their representation. Gradually but firmly Paulhan dislodges Fautrier's work from drawing and draughtsmanship and places it within the realm of a luminous and unfinished image-making. In this way, Paulhan is able to assert his coming-to-grips with his own sense of the humanity of Fautrier's work:

Mais il faut songer ici à ce qu'est pour nous la couleur (et que n'est pas le dessin): à ce qu'elle a de plus intime – de plus strictement humain – que les lignes, angles et spirales.[26]

But the 'strictly' human emerges from within its own dialogue with the principles of drawing with which Paulhan contrasts it. Paulhan refrains – just – from empowering doubles, slippages, ambiguities to give a sense of the intimate, of the whisperings of the body beyond the telling of them or the signs of them. Paulhan's own unwillingness in this text to give in to the weight of the sign, the confidence he finds in Fautrier to introduce mobility and humanity into the history and the tentacles of the (painterly) signifier, can ultimately only bear open-hearted witness to the signifier's effects, and to the suspended catharsis, to the education in matter – I can only return to the word – in Fautrier's own signed and mimed matter that this life-and-death artist extends to us.

Matière et mémoire is the title Ponge gives to the essay he wrote in 1945 on lithography:

> Quand on inscrit sur la pierre, c'est comme si l'on inscrivait sur une mémoire.[27]

Inscribing on a non-human surface – or responding to that, or to an evocation of that . . . – inescapably involves metaphors and analogies of memory, of a memory extending indefinitely in a past ingesting its own dimensions, a past made of the signs of it, absorbing new ones and making the present of its blots, the very ones emerging from the embrace of hand and surface – such a view of image-making would suit Fautrier's own art. The undermining of any sure footing this entails is acknowledged by Ponge in his preamble to his series of short comments on Fautrier – the fragment being a form entirely appropriate to the ethical need, as he sees it, to be uncertain about making any comment on the *Otages*:

> Ce serait trop peu dire que je ne suis pas sûr des pages qui suivent: voici de drôles de textes, violents, maladroits. Il ne s'agit pas de paroles sûres.[28]

The subject of the pictures can be thought of and expressed only tentatively, for fear of betraying it in the stating of it:

> Mais supposez que *l'atrocité même* soit le sujet . . .[29]

Ponge wants a history of humanity, what he thinks of as humanity by opposition to the foregone conclusion and the narrative grid, a sense of history that would emerge by reference to matter, or to matter imagined through the vicissitudes of art – of an art free from art history and responded to in opening the mind to the body. Without resorting to analogy or comparison, relying on the figure of 'on se dit' and its connotations of a communally sensed, *temporally* grasped immediacy, Ponge introduces Michelangelo's *Esclaves*, and beyond those the Medieval and Renaissance fascination with the Crucifixion, as reference points in ways of reading the *Otages*.[30] The absence of the crucifier in these representations, rather than suggesting any collusion with victimisation, suggests to Ponge the grounds for a dialogue with the humanity he seeks to isolate and promote – a humanity seeping through the tragedy that Leiris sees as the only outcome of a primary realism: a humanity of decay and loss. 'Leurs corps vieilliront dans leurs chaines, ils s'y abîmeront, puis s'y décomposeront'.[31] But this is also a humanity nourished by the moment rather than by essences. Ponge musters the solidarity in which the Resistance was steeped, very much as Camus recounts that same solidarity in his war-time *Lettres à un ami allemand*. The exclusion of the victimiser from the frame emerges from the decision to side with the victim rather than the executioner which is, once all reasoning is done, beyond reason, a matter of unanimous agreement that for "us", although the position of victim may be fearfully thinkable, the role of persecutor is inconceivable.

But such reasoning is, ultimately, reasoning by identification – identification of, and then with a position. The *Otages* do not allow it. Camus resists it in his multifocal narratives, until cornered by his own intellectual rigour into dramatising it in *La Chute*. Ponge's thinking follows Fautrier's work: 'la rage de l'expression (du tube de couleur)'.[32] Medieval Crucifixion pictures and the *Otages* combine in what is for Ponge a simultaneous absorption in the pretext for expression and an imperviousness to it. A recognition, both cultural and of the moment, of common experience and emotion – 'une âme dont nous n'avons pas à nous occuper, qui va de soi'[33] – allows that experience to be put aside, psychically absorbed, silenced in signs that are then addressed and showered in art, drowned in a drowning art . . .

'Voilà l'affaire la plus importante du siècle: l'affaire des *Otages*' – bottom-line appraisals would seem to offer little support to affirmations of the global import of this art. Ponge provisionally jousts with ideas of victory and resolution, moved to pay homage to the Resistance and the Allied Liberation, and rejoicing in finding an art capable of bearing witness to every level of this struggle. In a different light, Ponge reads, almost in passing, the *Esclaves* with the *Otages* as steeping viewers in the intimacy of their own time, while allowing them also to imagine the future and to visualise catastrophe as a passing moment. Such ideas retain their power really only in the setting aside of them. The paradoxical, competitive make-up of the *Otages*, the sort of Lacanian *concurrence* there of the great subjects of art and of art's own resonant materiality,[34] makes for images of grip and counter-grip, in fact images of repression, the sense of it and the idea of it, and beyond that images of what is gloriously beyond reach and yet which insidiously invades – those murmurs of the sign in the mind and heart.

The 'humanity' of the *Otages* seems itself, then, beyond reach and yet invasive – a humanity of signs, doomed to victimization and a paranoid view of it; unless, within the sign, the networks of identification *of* and identification *with* can be allowed to fall away. Can recognition be made to crumble? And in the wake of such a collapse, what space might we imagine beyond the erotic pull of antecedence and of models of fulfilment?[35]

In all events, in Fautrier we are dealing with art, the manipulation of forms, those same forms that encourage recognition and synthesis of temporally distinct perceptions. Barthes offers a composition of forms that would allow their own de-composition to be developed, or at least imagined.[36] What price a body formed in its decomposition – and what prize? And if the *Otages* are to be imagined in an intertext involving Medieval Crucifixion pictures, Goya and Manet, is this a body of experience and sensation that favours coming together or deformation and defecation?[37]

Ponge sees an art covering its traces, an art of expulsion, decay, of material and temporal depth, an art of the sign burying its history by being steeped in it, an art that exhibits the loose frontiers between relish and disgust, liberty and humanity.

> Tout se passe comme si Fautrier [. . .] en était venu et demeuré dès lors à son côté excrément, manie des petits ou des gros tas de mortier blanchâtre (à cause de la manie d'expression du tube de couleurs, d'expulsion de la couleur hors du tube) – avec la nécessité de recouvrir, de cacher, de bénir ces excréments de quelques traits rapides de cendre ou de poussière. De recouvrir la couleur, la matière par un genre de dessin pour masquer cette trace. Pour enfouir la trace. Qu'on perde la piste. Que l'odeur ne se puisse pas trop flairer. Et c'est alors tantôt citrons, tantôt couteaux ou poissons ou visages. Selon ce qu'il ingurgita? Ou selon le dessin, le signe dont il recouvre maniaquement l'excrément, toujours le même excrément (dont l'épaisseur, la présence doit rester fort sensible).[38]

Ponge resorts to a paradox designed to resist resolution, finds allusions, metaphors and a rhetoric to engulf himself and us with him in a process of simultaneous burial and preservation, repression and perception, dominance and democracy. The hovering pivot-made-elusive of this process is the sign. The denseness of the sign, the uncharted waters of its antecedence, is to be both treasured and defiled – embraced for its capacity to outdo the foregone conclusions of sense, but expelled also for its *inability* to do so, and then valued again for its manifestations of corruptibility and decay, fraying memory and repression siding at last with the body, their inevitable ally, rather than against it. Life born of collapse, the rickety footing of identification now exposed – along with the unresolved rivalry there of looking out and looking in. The *Otages* touch on an ability we might acquire to rip apart the reign of the image, its hold on us, the positions it assigns and which we lovingly accept. The pictures, in any case, are painfully, barely still an image of anything; the outlines of the human form have been hacked away, and image-making looks its death in the eye. Heroism, resurrection and an infinitely modest acceptance of mortality now combine. The cost will have been a wilful destruction of the sign, even on the body of its victims – representations of which hold us firmly to their own overwhelming, stifling, *absorbing* materiality. And the prize will have been a new creativity beyond the appropriative greed of the ego.

The necessarily 'will have been' quality of the achievement of the

Otages has dictated the way this piece has unfolded. To affirm the dethroning of the image would serve only to reaffirm its supremacy – transformed now into confident figures of its surpassing. Even to describe the pictures runs the risk of betraying them, of not only fixing them under one interpretive gaze or another, but of getting stuck in their own very status as image which precisely they fashion the power to undo, exhibiting *all the while* our sense of seeing as steeped in that ever-renewed, mimed dialogue of intimate and social history. Derrida, writing on Ponge, concedes with delight that 'on aura conclu [. . .] que j'ai parlé trop longtemps pour ne rien dire',[39] echoing Ponge's own admiration of Fautrier in his ability to 'peindre n'importe quoi'[40] without losing sight of his subject. 'Will have' deferral, the capacity of 'will have' to collapse the past and the future in one another, periphrasis and procrastination all combine in responding to the *Otages*, and conspire to push my return to a verbal grappling with them ever further forward, and closer to an ending that can only hope to forget its purpose. 'Will have' prophesies and places beyond reach at the same time, and this non-coalescent 'at the same time' sews the seeds of Fautrier's gift to us.

V

Returning to the *Otages* yet again, not only my own pages, but even those of Ponge – his allusive tentativeness, his parting analogy with 'la tartine de camembert' – seem overblown, impoverished, defensive. Ironically, consolation can be derived from using reproductions as a mnemonic: any illusion that the real Fautrier can be grasped at a perceptual stroke is instantly dispelled, the shiny surfaces of the photographs jarring oddly with the thick, rough density that makes up the *Otages* and much of the later work as well, and adding a further twist to the unnerving lightness of touch which, in reproduction, exudes now only metaphorically from the colour applied to this rough pictorial terrain; and from the absence of colour in the pictures here.

And this sense of the futility of comment forces its way home at the most direct level. The pictures are ghastly. The pathos and inhumanity of their subject-matter is only added to by the free-floating colour hovering both within and above the dried-out mucousness continually worked at and worked over by Fautrier. He seems to relish producing colour that eludes any colour banding in a manner which the memory of Manet does nothing to stabilize. In *Tête d'otage no. 3* of 1943[41] from a cracked green that both feeds on and defecates the background of Manet's *Le Déjeuner sur l'herbe*, a head emerges starkly that also takes the form of a truncated body, unmistakably a baby, just as unmistakably a woman. Strokes representing her genitalia are applied to the pictorial surface in a way which abuses the child, invades the space of the child's representation with marks of a grossly premature sexuality, just as that

Figure 18 Jean Fautrier, *Tête d'otage no. 3* (1943). Oil on paper, mounted on canvas, 55 × 46 cm.

sexuality is itself violated by being signed, even in forms reminiscent just as much of the hieroglyph as the Croix de Lorraine, since such mobility serves here only to enhance the dreadful compression of infancy and adulthood, which is now the form as well as the result of the wilful amputation of life and the body. In *Corps d'otage* of 1945[42] – where flesh-toned paste figuring the body stands out against another green background, this time one which seems to be developed in the opposite process, one of regressive absorption into a material ever further behind the surface – an infant's body is shown with an ageing face that seems to be both sketched in and fading, with the stub of a single arm waving and pleading. Both here and in *Tête d'otage no. 3*, the wilfully compressed telescoping of time and of ageing is held up as a dire signal of the abuse of power, and of the imaginary imperviousness to any moral or material threat that such abuse not only promotes but simply cannot survive without. But imaginary it remains, and materiality rages wordlessly as the victim pleads and the torturer flays. And the viewer? Imagining the body broken sits ill with stitching up thematic coherence.

In *Tête d'otage no. 23* of 1945,[43] the layers of material and colour making

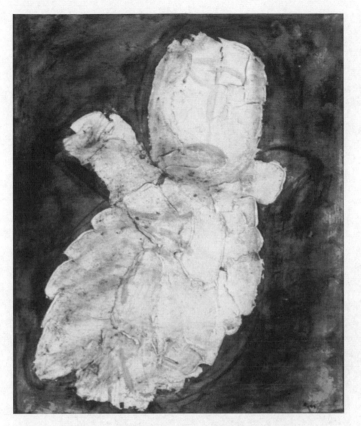

Figure 19 Jean Fautrier, *Corps d'otage* (1945). Oil on paper mounted on
canvas, 64 × 54 cm.

up the lines of the face on a once breathing body seem to shadow visually the
consistency of scabs. The longer furrows of darker-coloured matter might
also suggest the antlers of a deer or an antelope. Signifying mobility cuts
deep, again, without abetting the viewer in the attempt to get a hold of the
picture, to enjoy it or dismiss it or pass beyond it. Plasterish encrustations
stifle the face, the viewer's eye feels its way over a surface of bumps and
cracks, searching for subterranean paths hidden beneath it, nervously relishing the coloured dust floating there from within another circumstance, you
might say. Meanwhile, the cuts have coagulated, the skin surface has resumed
its coating, an ever rougher one, but a coating nonetheless, formed in this
experience of the picture and brutalised once again at the next glance. For if
surface and depth vie for the terrain, so do face and rump, the cruel scars and
animalistic defiance of the face each now combining to show anus, thighs and
vagina in a murderous matching of the organic and the personal, or the lubricated and the decomposed, or the intimate and the raped.

'Murderous' – a naked resorting to the emotive on my part, perhaps. Or

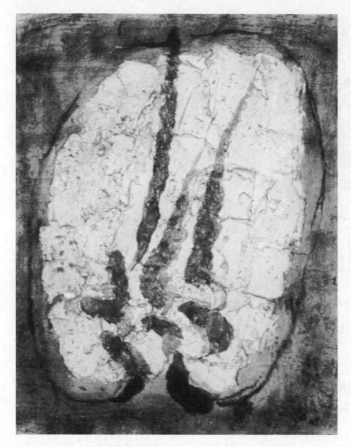

Figure 20 Jean Fautrier, *Tête d'otage no. 23* (1945). Oil on paper
mounted on canvas, 34 × 27 cm.

another helpless response to the tactics of the bully so easily recognised in
attempts to transform inescapable qualities of character and body into
exploitable weaknesses. But also, the images do attract such response: at an
immediate level, the pictures are expressive, working on recognition and
plying identification even though such reaction is having the ground cut from
under it – or rather extended far beneath it as to swallow it whole. In *Tête
d'otage no. 4* of 1943[44] the head emerges from an orange aura itself set against
a blue background; both in relation to each other and on their own, the
colours are not pure but hybrid, not fixed in the space of the painting, but
once again seeming to float, offering new possibilities in the relation of
surface to depth, and of the visible to the temporal. But the colour contrast
is still plain in amongst the shiftiness it sets off, and so is the expression of
horror emanating from the face, although it is in fact the Classical simplicity
of the lines forming arms and hands held up to the face that draws attention
to its expressiveness. Unmistakably silenced, stifled shock. Mouth open and

eyes wide and bleary. Classical, expressive, transparent in the sense of free and volatile expressions of emotion; but if Classical, then also performed, with gestures recognised instantly, even as spontaneous, but without any regard to the self. Perhaps this is the only pathos allowed by Fautrier, the performed and the signed providing the only forms granted the brutalisation of the body and of its integrity.

Gesture is deprived here of any Artaudian power to concentrate, display and dispel the weight of cultural antecedence and investment that propels it. Although that weight may well, in fact, be displayed here, but in a different sense: not grasped or expelled, but displayed in metaphors made of Fautrier's own pictorial sediment, eluding seizure, simply growing thicker towards the centre of the picture taken up by the face and its expressiveness; at once over it and from within, the marks of eyes, nose and mouth emerge now purely as a sign. A Croix de Lorraine, once again, perhaps. Or an ideogram distantly remembered. An instantly recognisable sign, at all events, a sign recognised for the way it comes across only after time spent absorbed in it. The expression of shock acquires depth in feeling it over, an immersion in a kind of non-tactile Braille, but this subjectivised depth does not give or embrace, it slithers on the mind's eye, shifting continually between different intensities and brightnesses, fashioning materially and psychically a sign that soaks up the readings of it but also disperses them.

But sign it remains, bearing witness to its commonplace destiny of listing into the signifier, where mobility and indeterminacy rub shoulders so unnervingly with coercion and suppression. The space suspended between the two is the space of this picture, and particularly the space of its startling orange, alternately bright and withdrawing, each equally inappropriate to representing the administering of torture and pain, and yet espousing inappropriateness as the only way of confronting torture without participating in it. Discouragingly, the maroon double crossed 't', or the smudged and barbaric Cross, can seem like an intensification of this indeterminate orange raging against its own stasis. Perhaps it is merely the renewed perception of this strange immobility, and the impossibility of absorbing it at a glance, that lend it its malleability. Either way, the Sign (of the Cross) dominates only in so far as it recedes – and all the more; its absorption in Fautrier's pictorial matter confirms its own imprints, its marks and its scars. Like the Nazi yellow star, the mark of the sign in the *Otages* both points out, or displays, and incarnates the violence it perpetrates, the violence on which it also depends; martyrisation is both proof and method.

And the stifling of potential needed for the sign to exclude signifying noise and to perpetrate its own reign is at most threatened – or perhaps consumers are just titillated – by the signifying mobility that leaks from the receptacles of sense, those all-seeing, all-absorbing cloaks of civilisation that never, in all our imagining of them, lose their power to monitor and to control.

Fautrier's figure in *Tête d'otage no. 4* is a hostage to the fortunes of war and hate that stretch beyond any notion of their termination in history. It is embroiled and imprisoned in Barthes's 'Moi, je', that unstoppable, plenipo tentiary alliance of the Ego and the Word that bulldozes any unyielding form in its way.[45]

But unevenness reasserts itself all over the surface of the picture, ensured by the process of its coming to be. This is the source of its resistance. But that resistance comes also from its fabulous setting aside of Quixotic revolutionary jousting that dons the colours of antagonism. The prize of this resistance that lays down its arms is a setting aside of any model of resistance; and in this way, it is also a refutation of martyrdom. But this art of setting aside concedes defeat at every juncture, it allows models vestigially to seep through breaches in the surface and *of* the surface: the Crucifix, the Stele, the severed head of St John the Baptist, a Classical styling that precariously keeps its balance on this blistered and pock-marked pictorial skin. And the price paid for such art is not a blaming or a further laceration of the victim, but a shredding of its own allusive networks, and of the range of possibilities we imagine open to us in seeking to represent victimization and martyrdom.

The truncated lump of flesh that *can* be recognised as the compositional mainstay of the *Tête d'otage* of 1944[46] – recognised against all the mimetic odds, but with stark and nauseating self-evidence, nonetheless – is neither purely a witness to atrocity, nor purely an appeal to aesthetic sensibility as a buffer against it. Like Baudelaire's own ode to a corpse, Fautrier's art, not only the *Otages*, but the work leading up to and away from them as well – I am thinking of paintings such as *Le Col vert* of 1926,[47] and *Beauté* of 1962[48] – so ploughs the firm ground of response, so relishes in the endless mismatch it manufactures of form and content, of cut and scar, of vision as selection and ruination combined, that it finally allows us to imagine an open-ness to the body, to mortality and the democracy to be found there. But let us make no mistake: this is not the equality of opportunity aimed for by specifying special interests and promoting them. The deep lines in so many of the *Otages* that circumscribe faces and body parts all the better to site their mutilation bear witness to the suspicion of boundaries that lies at the root of this art. Such lines establish frontiers and simultaneously, over time, watch over their decomposition. Once again, the pictures force feed us an abject denial of any strategy, any strategic view of history that might make identity unique, or at least differenciable. Surrender or War – such is the choice that Fautrier seems to face us with.

But his surrender is not a flaccid resignation. It exposes the psychic image-making that builds identity into a fortress whose only destiny is siege and counter-siege. What we might imagine instead is an identity built of non-completion, of images that breathe the air of their own decay, while at the same time dispelling their own swamping in the ceaseless onrush of history;

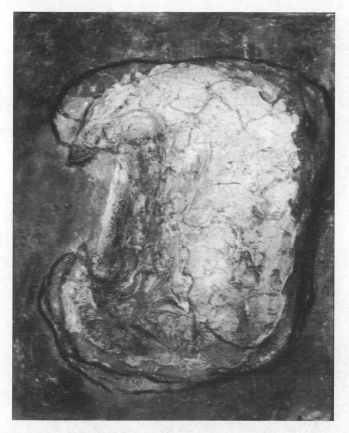

Figure 21 Jean Fautrier, *Tête d'otage* (1944). Oil on paper mounted on
canvas, 41 × 33 cm.

a subjectivity sensed and even desired in its own scattering to the four winds
of relish and decay. Charity rather than defence? Certainly – and certainly
charity rather than a culture of agendas. But the only Redemption would be
in the eye of the beholder, in the beholder's reinvented capacities to confront
the oppressor with a fearless 'where is thy sting?'. Perhaps this may seem a
grandiose and even dangerous claim to make for any art, particularly an art
displaying so vividly its impotence in face of the facts of violence. But once
again, Fautrier offers no cure, or cure could only be projected in that
suspended, hybrid moment of viewing, of dialogue between the indefinite
and the formed. Ethics constructed in the ruin of their foundation.

   La Jolie Fille of 1944[49] both flaunts and incorporates the gendered
reading that would make of it a manifestation of the violence of male desire,
and of the cultural and economic baggage of nude painting. But the news
brought by the picture stretches further. In watching the lines survive on a
surface that would bury them, and seeing them tread the light fantastic where

Figure 22 Jean Fautrier, *La Jolie Fille* (1944). Oil on paper mounted on canvas, 62 × 50 cm.

the effects of mutilation turn into those of ballet, where vice-like compression explodes into the grace of dreamed-of bodily freedom, what we witness, each secluded in her or his moment of viewing, is a suspended moment that both smothers and breathes the air of its own history, is our own freedom to think beyond seclusion, beyond the intolerance of excrescence and decay unless they are inflicted on others, beyond the synthetic cells of I and not you. An art where viewing and banishing from view exchange the gifts of giving, the gift of generosity.

CHAPTER SIX

Clothed intimacy: theatre and sex in Marguerite Duras, *Les Yeux bleus cheveux noirs*

I

'Dit l'acteur'[1] – what actor? Not one of the protagonists; nor is this a voice that could assume the form of one. This is an actor who loses and gains forms, who is pluralised, part of a large group which here at the beginning of *Les Yeux bleus cheveux noirs* is cast in the role of onlookers. It occupies a mediated space somewhere between the reader and the symbolic couple acting out some legendary anxiety waiting to develop, but whose unfolding is also suppressed to the point where this suspended animation can no longer be tolerated, and where, further along in the book, narrative elements are finally sought out, unearthed, developed and stifled again.

Actors in the text transform reading into models of reading, they provide us with a script we had forgotten or did not know we had. The book's two protagonists of the sexual drama do not engage with these actors – their fascination with each other would not allow it – or with the secret of their pain projected on the ungiving and unforgiving surface of each other. Nonetheless, the balletic quality of the emergence and disappearance of the actors in the text penetrates the reader's own fascination with what she and he are drawn into, some prototypical sexual matrix appealing to as well as silencing the legends of romance. Reading is doubled by a renewed, once forgotten awareness that what we imagine as bodies as we read them has already been read, and in fact is now being read aloud as a description of events to an audience in a theatre that is at once boundless and enclosed and which acts as an imaginary doubling of fascination itself, in which the private silence of reading is confused by the communal one of spectating.

Only once, much later in the book as the threads of obsession begin to unravel, is there an explicit reference to a formal audience other than ourselves: a sketched out possibility of a Brechtian interlude within which protagonists and 'actors' are shown sharing a break with spectators. But of course such spectators are further textual figures; the episode only serves to highlight the pervading lack of contact between protagonists and 'actors', those silent officiators, those whispering ghosts projected outwards from the protagonists, perhaps, but with no contact remaining.

Perhaps these ghosts are needed as agents of readers' memory, a warning against the sealing up of the pores of receptivity, but still producing a claustrophobic rather than some purely aesthetic intensity or catharsis. The language of the script glides – much as it does in Jean Genet's *Les Bonnes* – from description to prescription, all within the shifting boundaries of words coming from officiators and those coming from a narrator. Textures and memory levels emerge in the reader's fascination, but not analytical moments, more differing positions and configurations, different micro-responses. Reading becomes permeated with the sense – the memory of the sense – of being watched, even during sex.

There is an analogous relation between the actors' silenced, textual reading aloud, and the reader's own silent reading of the text, the reader's breathing life into the text's stasis and repetitiveness, into each of its facets as it absorbs others and is absorbed by them, until finally those narrative possibilities appear, at least, to intervene in the name of mobility. These are two silent orchestrations, two silent slitherings from observation to direction, neither in contact with the protagonists, although as readers it seems as though we are glued to these protagonists by Duras's perpetual use of the present tense. She invites us into a hall of mirrors made up of dead-end analogies binding us to phantoms that will not reveal their secrets, and which in exactly that way dramatise desire enveloped by its objects and out of synch with them at the same time.

Intimacy in this way is made to straddle the public and the private, the déjà-vu and the spontaneous, and Duras's prose style is one of the arenas in which this occurs. It alludes continuously to the mellifluous, elliptical syntax of contemporary French speech. An emblematic instance of this is provided by the title itself – *Les Yeux bleus cheveux noirs*. At the same time, since the book as a whole is imbued in a reported speech mode, this prose style loses the directness of the spoken while gaining a sense of mystery – a paradoxical mystery of the orthodox, the mystery emanating from the appeal of what appeals to others. Rather than mystery, perhaps this is more a sense of childish wonder, an expectation that through some magical sexualisation of precedent, we might each privately find our place in the adult sexual drama and in the erotic cornucopia. Duras allows the ephemera of dialogue, its volatility and volubility, to solidify in the very process of embracing it, and the residue in her script of the actors' interventions seems to double this effect. But holes appear continuously in this solid linguistic coating, formula dissolves repeatedly in improvised reworkings of it, leaving room for the outburst of a nameless cry that casts an invisible net over the whole text.

'Une soirée d'été, dit l'acteur, serait au cœur de l'histoire'[2] – Duras's opening words appeal to the sense of a shared immediate, the features it has of a script add to the sensuality of community, of communal involvement in transience and in the enjoyment of things passing. This haphazard sense of community forms, in Duras's hands, the basis of its own subversion and explosion. The cry erupts from within this shared moment which is in fact highly organised along the lines of gender and ideology; it elicits from their interweaving an anonymous body of response signalled by the notorious French 'on'. The cry comes from an unnamed throat, though through all the many facets of return to this moment we surmise that this is the cry of grief and shock of one of the protagonists as she is hit by her separation from her lover 'les yeux bleus cheveux noirs'. Simultaneously, the other protagonist is brutalised by his immediate and irreparable attraction to this same boy 'les yeux bleus cheveux noirs'. These are features this boy shares with other people in this moment; they develop to form a textual litany that serves tortuously and cumulatively to express his confusing uniqueness. Increasingly, mobility of response is propelled by constriction.

The cry is of unknown, at least of unspecific character; it is indicated in terms of that notorious East/West dichotomy, that mystery of the Orient prevalent in the West, and inscribed here, or rather 'appliquéd' to the vowels and consonants of speech, even as speech is once again silenced in the written. An explanation of this cry and of its spontaneous but also induced interpretations, is not forthcoming, but engulfed in a 'ne viendra pas'[3] analogous to the projected but unforthcoming outcome of the script. Such collapse of distinction spreads gradually, heralds immobility and develops into obsession, gives birth to an asphyxiating, nauseating sense of rhetoric within rhetoric. Still, the lack of explanation holds out some prospect of wrenching the intimate from the articulated. For this transgressive cry, imbued with knowledge and precedent made musical and labial via the connotations of the text, like that distant sound zooming down on Emma Bovary that embraces her sensuality but that never meets her, is the cry of sex.

II

A fragment among many in *Les Yeux bleus cheveux noirs*[4] acts as an emblem of the novel as a whole. It begins with an indented piece signalling the presence of 'actors' mediating unlocatably between the protagonists – 'héros' – and reader. The isolation of the 'héros' is at once affirmed and countermanded, and in the midst of this undecidablity, forms clothed in white hover in enclosing arcs, visible only in the reading mind's eye, representing the policing of sexual response by inciting, or transcribing, our own collaboration with it.

By contract, the female 'héros' – 'Elle' – has agreed to come and go at regular intervals to the beachside house of the male 'héros' – 'Il' – and to be paid to do so. 'C'est mon contrat: rester ou partir, c'est égal.'[5] Silence and floods of tears have characterised their previous encounters prior to this agreement. Now, under the 'lumière violente et égale'[6] ordained by the shadowy overseers, this weeping continues, sourceless and without remedy, the silent, textualised noise of sexed alienation. That sexing is irredeemably, insidiously, Oedipal and phallic.

The lack of desire of 'Il' for 'Elle' emerges as a landing-stage in this sourceless anxiety, or a symbolic pretext for it. It develops into an obstruction that 'Elle' seeks to dissolve, and which 'Il' is bound by or which he clings to. The hours 'Elle' spends in the house sleeping naked under the violent and even light, under the white sheet, signal her exhaustion from her part in the sexual drama, her retreat from it, but also, under the ever-present stare of 'Il', the forlorn desire to begin a new act.

The sexual inertness of 'Il' elicits the desire for him of 'Elle'. But this desire is not personalising: 'Elle' articulates it in terms of a confirmation of positions allocated and of representations confirmed. Her account of herself as a sexual being is clothed in metaphors of anonymity, a testimony to the fortresses of phallic persona-building and to its continuing efforts to nullify the otherness on which it feeds. 'Elle' herself takes on such a role, constructs herself in the image of such a persona in seeking to engage the amorous passion of 'Il'. As she argues, pleads, recounts, enacts – all in a present-tense performance that is rhetorically as well as temporally amorphous – her sexuality emerges in terms of 'un lieu commun',[7] and of all the bric-à-brac of the symbolic subordination of women: an evil and dangerous sensuality, bleeding and repellent, and inducing madness.

And with what stunning deftness Duras colours in the sensuality of such precedent, at least in the eyes and ears of this male reader. . . The familiarity of such image-making, the weight of its precedence and the mute history of the identifications trailing in their wake are given metaphoric forms that are now the language of sex and the language for sexed sensation. . . :

> Elle lui dit de venir. Venez. Elle dit que c'est un velours, un vertige, mais aussi, il ne faut pas croire, un désert, une chose malfaisante qui porte aussi au crime et à la folie.[8]

I am not suggesting simply that as a male reader my self-criticism is mustered by being faced with this further representation of the suppression of the female other and the terror it induces. It is more that the invitation of the book – 'Venez' – to think sex, to remember the sensations of it – 'velours' – carries with it an imperative to engage with these habits of thought and of talk, as though to identify them were to stuff one's own mind and mouth with their fall-out and to project this dust outwards on our own breath. So that the capacity of Duras as a woman writer to engage with the male reader as well as the female one, to straddle textually the sexual divide and wrap her writing around the undecidably sexed psyche of readers unknown to her, on one level is nothing more than a prostituted performance to order, doubling that of 'Elle' to 'Il'. The volatile aptness of Duras's textual idiom is bound by the 'lieux communs' which it feeds on. So much so that the vagina itself *is* now this 'lieu commun'; sex and sexed otherness, even the sense of that otherness crawling in intimate recesses and extracted in every utterance and gesture, are sealed in the metaphors imposed by phallic orthodoxy:

> Elle lui demande de venir voir ça, que c'est une chose infecte, criminelle, une eau trouble, sale, l'eau du sang, qu'un jour il devra bien le faire, même une fois, fourrager dans ce lieu commun, qu'il ne pourra pas l'éviter toute sa vie. Que ce soit plus tard ou ce soir, quelle différence?[9]

Endlessly rebuffed and frustrated in her attempts to have her plea for entry met with an embrace, 'Elle', in the logic both of the contract and of the symbolic organisation which it reflects, has no option but to cover her face with 'la soie noire',[10] a prop in the performance, emblem of the casting of woman in the role of enigma and danger, and through which her consciousness is filtered:

> Il pleure. Elle repart vers le mur.
> Elle le laisse à lui-même. Met la soie noire, le regarde à travers.[11]

And by what silent, disguised, overdetermined glimmer might this filtering also be empowering?

What of 'Il'? His recurrent weeping, like that of 'Elle', like Troppmann's in Georges Bataille's *Le Bleu du ciel*, is a symptom of grief as well as of exhaustion, a continuing search for an end to a desiring that will have no fulfilment. Both 'Elle' and 'Il' are in love with the absent boy 'les yeux bleus cheveux noirs', and homosexual as well as heterosexual love is presented as bound by the laws of Oedipal organisation. Furthermore, compounding this restrictiveness, male homosexuality is presented in negative terms, as the absence of desire for women, rather than as an affirmative desire for men. In fact all desire in the book is presented as self-negating, an existential quality that erodes the hope of negation ever reaching beyond itself. The boy-signifier 'les yeux bleus cheveux noirs' is a cypher of deferral. Silent, weeping, regressive, 'Il' remains trapped, and the representation of him confirms and collaborates with this *exactly as much* as it offers any hope of seeing through it. As 'Elle' sleeps, silenced (again as in *Le Bleu du ciel*) by the aggressive, violent disinterest or the impotence of 'Il', he watches, performing with increasing intensity his fixated lock on the specular. With a kind of Beckettian repetitiousness, he fetches a mirror and seeks now the secrets of himself on himself, becoming increasingly obsessive, exhibitionist; only the refracted relation of reader to text introduces a foreign presence into this private drama. But it also triggers our own voyeuristic pursuit of some source to sex, as well as the sense of the futility of such a Quixotic venture. As readers in this outside space we may imagine other, differently sexed and gendered readers peering into this performance; the textual quality of it eludes all our reaches just as it hinders the very notion of a self-regard centred on 'Il'.

Or does text foster self-regard? If spectatorship dissolves in the murky fluids of refracted reading and association, then even the idea of it can lend it a once-removed, psychic sensuality that may assume wholly subjective form. 'Il' watches 'Elle' disappear into Lethe, extending his morbid and solitary kingdom in observing oblivion, the collapse of all sense of place, of history, and particularly of narrative and the positions it allocates. 'Il la regarde s'éloigner, s'en aller dans l'oubli de la chambre, de lui, de l'histoire. De toute histoire.'[12] The sleeping form bends to a projection of desire into a space beyond the imposition of desire. But this female form so undesirable to 'Il' testifies despite this silencing, or from within it, to language and its place in her body:

> Cette nuit-là elle appelle encore, toujours avec ce mot, atteint, blessé, qui veut dire on ne sait pas quoi, qui est peut-être un nom, celui de quelqu'un dont jamais elle ne parle. Un nom comme un son, à la fois sombre et fragile, une sorte de gémissement.[13]

To voice is to name, but name here never returns to sound, despite the phonetically induced analogy of 'son'-'nom'.[14] To name is to utter the anguish of naming, and the name lurking in a cry seems to ignite the impulse to cry out.

Duras allows little room to linger on this collapsing boundary; very quickly 'Il' demands an account. Instability and fluidity are made once again into the 'lieu commun' of sexual antagonism. 'Elle' is cast as responsible for the anguish of 'Il' caused by that age-old Oedipal, male dread of the interior, the shapeless, the horrific, and of the power totemistically attributed to the vagina to consume. Again, the 'lieu commun', because of, rather than in spite of, its ideological weight, is given the poetic power to sensualise distinctions and positions. The flounderings of 'Il' amidst his representations of abjection are identified by 'Elle', who in this way projects the role of seer from within the role of victim, counters symbolic representation on its own terms, and constructs narrative position from collapse.

> Je dois vous le dire, c'est comme si vous étiez responsable de la chose intérieure qui est en vous, dont vous ne savez rien, et qui m'épouvante parce qu'elle transforme au-dedans d'elle sans aucune apparence de le faire.
> Elle ne dormait pas.
> Elle dit:
> C'est vrai que je suis responsable de cet astral de mon sexe au rythme lunaire et saignant. Devant vous comme devant la mer.[15]

The poetry of the commonplace and of common placings allows identification and exchange from within the drama of coercion, which is now both exposed and embraced. The construction of responsibility in 'Elle' is made of representations of the female made in the broadest brush-strokes of allusion, recognition, and the volatile immobility of oppression. But this dramatization of the body allows Duras to raise the curtain on the marriage of subjectivity and dispossession that is played out there. To be responsible in society – 'devant vous' – does not match responsibility in natural or bio-natural terms – 'comme devant la mer' – and the language of 'Elle' is produced in this dissymmetry. Such dissymmetry incorporates the antagonistic, desiring/non-desiring relation of 'Il' to 'Elle', in which identification emerges as a gift that cannot be accepted but only resisted, and in which dialogue proceeds in the forms of its collapse:

> Ils se rapprochent, presque à se toucher. Ils se rendorment.[16]

Responsibility, the claims to a sketching in of the outlines of a body and a language, are bought, here, at such a price.

III

There is an absorbing tension in the quality of Julia Kristeva's response to the textual world of Marguerite Duras. Her own writing in 'La Maladie de la douleur'[17] seems tangibly marked by Duras's. It seems to live under the spell of Duras's fascinating – that is, both enlivening and immobilising – capture

of an extraordinary capacity of men and women to articulate both thought
and the timeless anxiety that stifles it, to both sublimate and project their own
suffering. At an initial level, this is apparent in Kristeva's critical idiom in this
piece. In effect, it doubles that capacity Kristeva herself isolates in Duras's
writing to engender, and then to exploit, a kind of drift from a metaphysical
or theoretical lexis to a commonly used one: 'responsable',[18] 'la douleur',[19] 'la
souffrance',[20] 'la folie',[21] 'la maladie';[22] the commonplace, violent demeaning
of the individual. But this sense of nameless suffering finds room to breathe
within uncircumscribed linguistic ephemera, and this produces perhaps the
germ of Duras's remarkable popularity. These words – 'la douleur', 'la
souffrance' – merely in the reading of them have the capacity to open wounds
and to rub salt into them just because of their familiarity and lack of uniqueness.

Kristeva elaborates this insidious infectiousness of connotation by indicating elements of sociorealism present in increasingly stark and iconic form
in Duras's writing. These provide a broad, and ultimately subjective mélange
of cultural experience in terms of which to identify with the text, to become
bound to it and bound up in it: postwar guilt, colonialism and race, Oedipal
or familial violence and abuse. This extended but static surface contact of
Duras with her readers, or conversely of readers' imaginative receptivity to
Duras's signals, is reconstructed in Kristeva's response as an intertextual
spread of both literary and theoretical allusions – 'l'amour fou', 'l'amour
impossible' . . .This intertextual critical fabric involving Breton and Bataille
continuously alludes to and eludes models of definition, teasing us with the
possibility of blunting the various attitudes involved and their powers of
appropriation. In her own textual response to Duras, Kristeva fabricates a
mobile metaphoric web that draws allusively on the analytical power and
rhetorical supremacy of scientific discourse – politics, philosophy, psychoanalysis, medicine. Kristeva has such metaphors take a step outside their own
categories and premises by allowing the connotations of each to drift into
those of others and to infiltrate them. While this might threaten to produce
incoherence or critical flabbiness, it also allows for an apprehensive dissolution of retentive, terrorised and terrorising constructions of epistemological
power. '[Duras] nous conduit à radiographer nos folies, les bords dangereux
où s'écroule l'identité du sens, de la personne, de la vie.'[23] The radiographer's
room; a crossover between the psychological, the psychoanalytical and the
literary at the point of 'folies'; a further intersection of psychonanalysis,
linguistics and philosophy ('identité', 'sens'); a lavish broadening out of
psychology ('la personne') and then life at large beyond that – such is the
range and the rapidity of Kristeva's metaphors, the ease of passage,
characteristic of her later writing, from within to beyond theoretical boundaries and back.

Kristeva's delight in the broad appeal of the drifting, mobile, plural range of Duras's writing is not limitless, but bound up in the ruins of the symptom. If Kristeva's initial response to Duras's work is delight, the second is apprehension, a sense of taking her life into her own hands in engaging with the high stakes of the Durassian drama. This is the drama of identification, which Kristeva both represents and replicates in the writerly forms of her response.

> On comprend désormais qu'il ne faut pas donner les livres de Duras aux lecteurs et lectrices fragiles. [. . .] Les livres [. . .] nous font côtoyer la folie. Ils ne montrent pas de loin, ils ne l'obervent ni ne l'analysent pour en souffrir à distance dans l'espoir d'une issue, bon gré mal gré, un jour ou l'autre. Tout au contraire, les textes apprivoisent la maladie de la mort. [. . .] Aucune purification ne nous attend à la sortie de ses romans [. . .].

> Les identités, les liens, les sentiments se détruisent.[24]

By opposition to the cinema generally, and more implicitly to Duras's own films, her books suggest to Kristeva a non-redemptive, non-cathartic immersion in this ever-present, ever-different 'folie'. This is a ragged, unpredictable, but intimate and familiar sense of being overrun, the victim of which is 'l'individuation' – another intuitive term, signalling a sense of self beyond categories of ideology and of gender. 'La douleur éprise de la mort serait-elle l'individuation suprême?',[25] wonders Kristeva in response to reading *La Douleur,*[26] a text with a female narrator watching the recovery of Robert L. from torture and debilitation at Dachau. Georges Bataille, Jean Genet and Louis René des Forêts resonate in this sketching in of a deadly, transgression-built, structure-proof vision of self-generation. Singularity emerges beyond gender and beyond what political discourse is imagined being able to articulate. Afraid of Duras's multiform, yet repetitive invitations to identify and to identify with 'la folie', to both absorb and mime in signs its smothering of voice and gesture, Kristeva in the same moment reflects that absorption in her own writing, enacts it in her particular reading of the political implications of Duras's writing. She translates the stifled as the explicit, as a refusal to engage with public discourse, as attributing blanket responsibility to the public for the collapse of the subject, the erasure of its humanity and its authenticity.

Hiroshima mon amour[27] surfaces here in Kristeva's mobile, apparently improvised and centreless argumentation as a pivotal text in Duras's writing. The Narcissism that emerges ever more desperately as the motor principle within Freudian theory – from the initial paper *On Narcissism* to the ubiquitous 'discontent' or discomfort that Freud perceives in the fibres of civilised humankind – is given an unnamed and directionless mobility in the notion itself of 'folie' and in its shifting performance. The morbid desire for a mourned object evident in many of Duras's texts as well as in *Hiroshima mon amour*, what Kristeva calls 'absolute' identification[28] with a speaking and moving body lost in grief, now signals a sourceless, motiveless thrust beyond the dialectic of determinism and responsibility. The 'inéluctable' quality that Kristeva attributes to this unconditional logic of 'la folie', a logic that eschews foundation or conclusion, carries the perfect, imaginary fit of identification into a realm beyond model, beyond any reasoning other than its own silencing of reason, beyond comparison and beyond location. 'La folie' works to project this 'beyond' ever further; it is a plea for life beyond life, beyond society and the names of love.

In Kristeva's critical discourse, its knowing confusion of the theoretical, the idiomatic and the sensual, 'la folie' is given a level of political critique which both legitimizes this 'beyond', providing it with a means of expression and of representation, and at the same time signals 'folie' in terms of a masochistic, death-orientated 'souveraineté'[29] that it shares with the theatrical violence of Bataille and the decorative brutality of Genet. Kristeva reads 'la folie' as imprints of a political modelling of the psyche projected at the levels of text and signifier, as psychic marks she identifies within Duras's writing. Her own writing seems to reproduce these marks that are also symptoms, drawing Duras's ever more vulnerable reader further into participating in the production of brashly synthetic images of a bruising, and ultimately murderous, public disregard for personhood:

> La politique n'est pas, comme pour Hannah Arendt, le champ où s'élabore la liberté humaine. Le monde moderne, le monde des guerres mondiales, le tiers monde, le monde souterrain de la mort qui nous agit n'ont pas la splendeur policée de la cité grecque. Le domaine politique moderne est massivement, totalitairement, nivelant, tuant.[30]

Duras, and Kristeva with her, leads us down a path where the supervised freedom of Platonic democracy gives way to a sadistic peering that has no identifiable, constitutional form; to the point where readers run the risk of colluding in this all invasive authority by seeking out, in the very reading of Duras–Kristeva texts, some representation of this paradoxically mobile, multisourced sadistic gaze. In what reads like a web of textual transference and countertransference operating between the two writers, Kristeva highlights a violent flattening of identity in Duras's writing, one which brooks no methodology of critique or differentiation, but which is spawned *within* the public and social structures permitting interchange and life. Kristeva suggests that particularly *Hiroshima mon amour* as well as the much later *L'Amant*[31] fold political and cultural elements into the opus that is the bedrock of the

European reader's – incompatibly male and female – identification with the text: colonisation, its violence and bigotry; the Occupation – collaboration and resistance; the Bomb. These reflect any readers' sense of contemporaneousness and of community, but also of contemporary, everyday and public horror. In its power to draw the reader in, this allusive body of cultural and ideological knowledge, of capabilities and inhibitions, is elevated symbolically from the subjective to embrace political discourse at large. And now another drifting, another shifting of the boundaries of the symbolic and the imaginary modes of psychic comprehension is triggered. This body of knowledge now acts as the forum for an enclosed, imaginary giving and receiving of form, the forms of the inhumanity driving Duras to write; but even these forms cannot now resist the attributes of uniformity and stasis. Symbolically and materially, they *are* the forms of inhumanity; they are as uncompromising as inhumanity and as inescapable as the contemporary. Still, the allusive and populist selectivity of Duras's staging of the public in terms of horror allows inhumanity to be the instrument of its own take-over; and the indefinite compounding of its effects begins to see the light of day.

It is this indefinite compounding that Duras's writing projects, represents and exploits. Her avid readership seems to take inhumanity into the intimacy of silent reading and feeling. With the public dimension suppressed in this way, this now private violence is perpetuated in the asphyxiated recesses of the mind, which in Duras's hands begin to produce a magically silent music of their own. This textual vibration involving the extremes of rejection and absorption produces a kind of discordant harmony, or unharmonious accord, carrying 'all the discrete brilliance of an utterance born by the gods: détruire'.[32] In *Hiroshima mon amour*, this brilliance takes the form of betrayal, of affective fragments rebounding in inaudible, purely metaphoric echoes, and projecting incompatible images of a sadistic murder of love and a democratic claim to love. Throughout Duras's works, in a reversal of the position Nietzsche takes up in *Beyond Good and Evil*, the futility of all political involvement, its debasement of personhood and its colonization of symbolic identifications, signal – a 'blank'; a sign that . . .; a suspension as Kristeva puts it; a discrete moment in the ideological continuum, held onto in imaginary form – atemporal and robustly repetitive. This is the profound, the inaudible cry of negativity.

The stunning graininess of the lovers' naked bodies that opens the film and the scenario of *Hiroshima mon amour* acts as a kind of paint that floods the viewing surface, a coating that covers these bodies irretrievably. It is a skin made of violence and mutilation – the raw materials, seemingly, of the human form. In giving the sensual purely visual shape, the moulding of desire to otherness is taken in subjectively by the viewer, with both the mobile and the ineluctable qualities of intimacy. These grainy configurations of bodies and their contact, under their cover of radioactive brilliance, suggests sculptural, erotic possibility simultaneously propelling and suspending its own realisation.

This bodily coating is a visual form of the unreclaimably textualised, inaudible cry that sets *Les Yeux bleus cheveux noirs* off on its repetitive cycles. It emblematises the realm of expressive exchange, its variety coupled with its sinewy embroilment in grief. This spontaneous but also performed cry – silent, private; public, operatic – both projects and effaces beginning. That absolute moment of desire, where in an orgasmic cry sex is moulded to gender and the unbounded is given sensation, is a moment that for Duras has been smothered, is being smothered, under the layers of its repetition and uniformity. The rituals of *Les Yeux bleus cheveux noirs* will confirm repeatedly this violence done to the individuated, and articulate the protagonists' complicity in violence and their collaboration with it. This smothering is itself desirable. The other skin that obliterates 'I' and smothers it in desirable forms is at one level indefinitely breachable, a tearable psychic coating shoring up vainly against its ruin. But there in the ruins of the performances and images of self, the germ of renewed desire is also discovered – a gift whose poison will be confirmed both in the efforts to represent, and beyond that, in the proclaimed possibilities of draining it and scattering it . . .

With Duras, Kristeva grasps, with that quasi-spontaneous immediacy that is the subjective stuff of a cultural moment, a sense that Hiroshima has obliterated the artifices of political discourse, its positions and its allocations of position. She captures a suspended implicitness within this paradoxically rhetorical denial of rhetoric.

> Parce qu'il y a eu Hiroshima, il ne peut y avoir d'artifice. Ni artifice tragique ou pacifiste face à l'explosion atomique, ni artifice rhétorique face à la mutilation des sentiments. 'Tout ce qu'on peut faire c'est parler de l'impossibilité de parler de *Hiroshima*. La *connaissance de Hiroshima* étant a priori posée comme exemplaire de l'esprit.'[33]

But this surface immediacy, made of words in which the uniform vies with the multiform, carries the imprints of ideological positioning. The violence granted the power to push beyond sexual orthodoxy is a sign of its own uncharted antecedence. The 'Hiroshima *de* l'amour' – as Kristeva fashions it, with Duras – the suspension of Eros raising the curtain on a liberty that has no name, confirms rather than explodes the ideological foundations against which it rages and which also circumscribe it. Identification with otherness – another sex, another gender, a corpse, a crypt – to the point of obliterating the boundaries of the other, faces readers within the débris of this collapsing edifice of horror with nothing more or less than a stand-off between sexual stereotypes: 'Cette folie meurtrie et meurtrière, ne serait rien d'autre que l'absorption par Elle de sa mort à Lui.'[34] Violent transgression is phallically organised, once again. Does 'folie' consist in dreaming otherwise, or in abdication in favour of that Phallic Order?

IV

Kristeva opens her essay by focussing on an aspect of Duras's writing that has fascinated many critics: the emergence I have mentioned of so-called 'blancs' or blanks in the texts, a manufactured collapse of discourse and of a coerced involvement with it. In ways which are reminiscent of Sartre's characterisation of some limited overlap between black and Surrealist writing evident in attempts to 'faire du silence avec le langage',[35] Kristeva refers to 'une mal-adresse stylisque'[36] in Duras's writing, as well as 'une défaillance de la parole'.[37] These features are the obverse of Duras's capacity to exploit the volatility of the linguistically commonplace, which has served as one of the starting-points and principal guiding threads of this essay, and as a measure of its attention to the signifier.

Kristeva notices that this blankness, these silent, alinguistic spaces are never fully established in Duras's writing. This is a silence with make-up, nakedness dressed in the traces of rehearsed and ingrained posture – very much reminiscent of Picasso's figuration of the nude (male or female) that I discussed in chapter 1: 'comme on est démaquillée ou déshabillée sans être négligée.'[38] So that insofar as silence, in *Hiroshima mon amour*, is thought of as articulating contrition or self-denial in memory of the Holocaust and the pogroms, then both remain beyond reach. If there is no way of talking Hiroshima without deadening us to its horror, then there is no beyond either. Such are the high stakes of being 'suspended' in the Durassian textual web.

If silence, on the one hand, projects refusal, then on the other the cinematographic image in particular, Kristeva argues, allows profusion, a mad array of models of fulfilment, an endless lexicon of possible identifications, all equally on offer, all equally open to being dumped. *Les Yeux bleus cheveux noirs* exemplifies this Durassian 'in between', combining plurality with retentiveness. It integrates Barthes's 'intraitable'[39] effects – rhetorically inspired sensations of non-rhetorical response – with the imprints of power and of phallic coercion.

In the same way, Duras's novelistic idiom slithers from a metaphysical register to the volatility of on-the-hoof metaphor. The text of *Les Yeux bleus cheveux noirs* (just like the scenario of *Hiroshima mon amour* and other multi-genre texts) hovers more particularly over generic border-lines, picking and choosing as it moves on, but creating the obverse of discursive agility. The text alludes stylistically to the film scenario; to the description of film shots or images; to stage directions; to proaeretic devices. All act as different constructions of the imagery that holds centre stage – materially and meta-phorically; so many rhetorical attitudes to sexual relation, its impulses, its promised lands, its souvenirs and wounds. The text reads like action both unfolding and described, action rehearsed, action imagined, action watched by actors in the piece doubled by the reader – a reader rent asunder by being ensnared within these incompatible activities of theatre spectator, movie spectator . . . and reader.

Duras's continued use of the present tense I mentioned earlier covers actions and gestures taking place as well as having taken place, adding up to an unspecified experience of witnessing scenes of anxiety – unspecified, in that the positions of this witnessing are mobile, but also solidified, as though the seamless passage from one possible mode of reading to the other were so rapid as to be instantaneously nullified. Description passes through rehearsal directives to prescription, and even though the figures before the reader are imaginary ones, her/his complicity in imposing patterns of behaviour on them is steadily brought to the fore. In fact, the imaginary effects of engage-ment with any literary text is also steadily highlighted; it loses its purely theo-retical or metaphoric qualities. The descriptive/prescriptive oscillation in the text – carrying the imprints of Duras's life-time of cross-boundary textual and cultural travel – bruises and de-authenticates that notorious sense of the whole subject so magisterially lassooed and parodied by Rimbaud: 'Moi, je suis intact'.[40] But even to invoke the notion of prescription and its part in the making of the subject is to muster all the forces of synthesis, signalling once again that oscillation of the broken and the entire characteristic of any thought, any construction of the subject and even of the signifier. Made up of souvenirs and visions, the sense of self is triggered afresh in all its implicit, removed sensuality by readers' participation in such disembodied, familiar-but-textual experiences as a kiss on the mouth – at once unique and exploded in the imagined sensation of all other mouths; or looking at love marks and seeing different ones, seeing others make them . . .

Each scene, each directive, each present moment disrupted by prece-dent and antecedent, acts as a landing, 'un palier' as Kristeva calls it, both an interstice and a stage in a journey upwards or downwards towards a climax or a source. In fact, Kristeva begins by locating Duras's work within the history of twentieth-century writing concerned with that ever elusive source of its own processes: Valéry, Blanchot . . . In Duras, that source is as slippery in conception as ever – at once deferred, performed and sensualised. But this elusiveness, this 'intraitable' sensation emanating from objects of desire is made over into the attribute of a Kafka-esque, voyeuristic power, perceived paranoiacally and dragging with it the vision of proliferating systems on which it feeds. This multiplication of system by sensation – a reversal of Romantic idealism, or alternatively, a climax of Romantic angst – almost exceeds conception, other than in imaginary and aesthetic forms, whose desperate power and glory is to totalise and mesmerise, but which settle instead for a momentary embrace on a landing-stage in temporal decay.

V

In *Les Yeux bleus cheveux noirs*, as I mentioned earlier, the passages with a wider indentation are generally reserved for moments when 'l'acteur' speaks – though his? her? speeches are subsumed in the script-form that partially envelops the novel as a whole. The actor describes the effects a scene should create, description turns to prescription, which is itself directed, and the impression of a rehearsal is generated, not only by the actor acting out in words the impressions and images to be projected, but also by the actor taking on the role of 'répétiteur'. A use of the conditional mood seeps in, slowly spreading over such passages a coating of indefinite provisionality. This provisionality does not only derive from the model of a director suggesting rather than dictating to the performers. It also comes from the unnamed narrator of this text feeling her way to giving this rehearser a form. This form remains sketchy, but its performance is also insidious, acting as a further coating that creeps conditionally over different rhetorical attitudes, perhaps different remembered bodies as well, so that hesitation drifts from evoking potential to submerging in antecedence, in the débris of identifications and the halting reconstruction of their provenance.

'Le noir serait fait dans la salle, la pièce commencerait.'[41] This beginning, this stage-managed schism of performer and spectator is made both imaginable and impossible by Duras's increasingly prevalent use of the conditional. Dealing both in the provisional and the dependent, the conditional orchestrates but also projects; in Duras's use of it here, the distinction between the time-dimensions dissolves and along with it the distinction between the desired and the coerced. The excitement of the opening, of the curtain being raised, coincides with the recognition of performance: the reign of emulation takes hold. The 'actor' continues to describe the scene, continues to confuse the narrative and the directorial. Conditional is piled upon conditional, to the point where suspended animation is coupled with a burgeoning faith in the future. But once again, plurality flatters to disappoint. It begins to have the effect of setting in stone, in a kind of psychic concrete, the stage-props of the sexual drama that is to unfold and that has been told a thousand times before: the cigarettes, two or three roses, a funereal hue – all the paraphernalia of mysterious, decadent sexuality.

This ambience is re-sexualised here in the text, a sexual odour begins to emerge in words, even though the words refer not only generally (and inevitably) to reference itself, but to the uniqueness of sex lost in discourse. The appropriative voyeurism of memory, and in particular its failure, are dramatised on a stage that is textual, and therefore diffuse. But this diffuseness *is* the stuff of subjective intimacy and investigation. It is not so much that imaginary fulfilment meets with the disappointment it deserves and that would allow the ego to let go. Textuality and the subjectivity of sex are moulded and remoulded to each other, giving rise to indefatigable attempts to preserve that elusive uniqueness, to read it even in the most familiar, publicly owned emblems and vestiges of it. The uniqueness of sexual sensation is at once affirmed and dispersed in the pluralised perspectives of genre and rhetoric that make up this text. On the one hand, the enclosed subjectivity of sex is turned inside out and gains new dialogues, new fetishes, new air; on the other, it is re-enclosed in any arbitrary configuration of expressive objects and sensations.

The effect is not only of endless reduplication or of ideological prescription. The textual 'odeur sexuelle'[42] that is introduced is particular to each reader, its capacity to elude category mimes the sensuality and the memory of sex. But for all its liberation of subjective sensual possibility, this 'odeur' is irredeemably *read*: reading is supervised, its spontaneity disguises its *telos*; deferral joins hands with confirmation. Sensation is recognised by its powers of dispersal, but also by the identifications that are built on it and of which it is built: shattered in its imagining of gendered otherness, the reading and remembering I makes flimsy, fantasized footholds in an orthodoxy made flesh.

Duras's magnificent, purely implicit 'odeur sexuelle' triggers sexual-mindedness and suspends it simultaneously. In being filtered through the range of textual attitudes and performances alluded to in the book, sexuality and sex acquire multiple forms that straddle the subjective and the coerced, the improvised and the implacably written. Which will have the power to discard? Which (only) to clothe anew? In Duras's art, decay immerses readers in the horror of public discourse and of intimate participation in that; still, by suspending catharsis and redemption, decay conceives the prolonged labour of voice.

CHAPTER SEVEN

'Des milliers de Parisiens': conflict, community and collapse in Jean Genet, *Les Paravents*

Tous les vivants, ni tous les morts, ni les vivants futurs ne pourront voir *Les Paravents*. La totalité humaine en sera privée: voilà ce qui ressemble à quelquechose qui serait un absolu. Le monde a vécu sans eux, il vivra pareil. Une nonchalance politique permettra une rencontre aléatoire entre quelques milliers de Parisiens, et la pièce. Afin que cet événement – la ou les représentations -, sans troubler l'ordre du monde, impose là une déflagration poétique, agissant sur quelques milliers de Parisiens, je voudrais qu'elle soit si forte et si dense qu'elle illumine, par ses prolongements, le monde des morts (ou plus justement de la mort) – des milliards et des milliards – et celui des vivants qui viendront (mais c'est moins important?).[1]

This is the opening paragraph of Genet's first letter to Roger Blin on the production in the making of *Les Paravents* in 1966. As his pen flows here, with the composition of the play behind him, Genet seems to come up for air, a new air he can at least imagine he has created for himself, an air without any absolute other than disintegration, and especially the disintegration of 'tous', of a group known as 'all' reference to which Genet repeats only and forever in the negative, as though wholeness, as though 'totalité' were not only there but deprived of itself. This is what the play stands for, this is where it stands and how it stands, this is how it seeps into and builds itself up in the collapsing slime of an event.

Not a particularly primordial slime, this. (Or if so, only in so far as that notion itself is among those that the play deprives its audience of the use of.) The event of the play, multiplied or not in various performances, will not be available to posterity, and does reach back beyond its own space or the space of its imagining. If generosity consists in some part in bearing witness to the Passion, as Sartre would have it,[2] in offering a testimony of the metaphysics, the poetics and the mnemonics of decay, then this play offers generosity without playback or payback. It gives form to Derrida's speculation that gift can brook no exchange if it is to be gift, and to his proffering of a *potlatch* that might abandon hunting down the receivers of its gifts, its trappings and its own mirror images.[3]

In that opening paragraph to Blin, Genet imagines at once celebrating and grieving for the relativity of the play and for its placenta made of circumstance and transience. He makes a show of attributing to it no pretention to 'troubler l'ordre du monde', or to intervene in the lyrical, ideological emanation of identification and nostalgia that this expression implies. Absolutes remain intact after all, it would seem, and the only hope of bringing their reign and their metaphysics to a close would be to clothe them in that dignity; to try and compete would only confirm and entrench. The audiences whom the play will *not* reach provide it with its handle on this drama of the Absolute that it mimes without capturing, intercedes in without toppling, brings down without destroying, adores without obeying.

Posterity – 'ceux qui viendront' – can be made into an irrelevance by the play, made to lose its power to snap time shut and to keep the stage and its props intact. Stage and staging will move audiences and *will* cause foundations to tremble – but only if the world ('le monde') that has spawned these scenes is left in peace, is allowed to remain the same and if writer and audiences alike can accept that it will always be the same. No 'vols de langage'[4] as Barthes would have it, no utopia-swapping, no leaping into theory over the head of dialogue and its unpredictability, its rapid spontaneity – an allusive spontaneity this, repetitious as much as improvised, a dance on the combined rhythms of Eros and precedence. For art to imitate life and life to be sensed with humility and passion, death must be invented; the capacity to imagine it must be reinvented and reinfused with the futility of life, and not restricted hopelessly by the pretensions of the concept or its magnetic force. Death is taken on in the play as a crowd, a crowd of lovers lost, found and betrayed, comrades in arms manufactured in a blink and destroyed in a wave; if death is ruin, it is also the ruin of itself, 'la mort' turned into 'les morts'[5] on the spring of orgasm and of its passing. There are no aspirations, dramas or myths of creativity, of origin or originality: 'l'ordre du monde' demolishes them rather than preserving them. The play ruins itself, or rather hovers on that brink: to succeed would be to fail, an accomplished ruin would be only be an edifice, or perhaps even a sketch, but certainly not a demise. We are stuck in the ruins and with ruin.

Genet keeps this immobile mobility going by talking in this letter to Blin not only of a series of performances of *Les Paravents* but also of a single performance that, properly staged, should suffice. But what would be the purpose of such a be-all and end-all performance – the performance of an ending? Or the purpose of imagining it? Death is to be made active, even though it can only ever be death. And if finality eludes us, then that is its active ingredient: the capacity it endows us with, in some imaginary hindsight, to run delusions of finality into the ground. Let us talk and talk some more, let us perform some more and watch performance grow and dissolve in the process and the memory of it, and as we talk let us watch self-awareness exceeding the narcissism of form, in fact ignoring it, overriding it in the living death of a dialogue with models and scripts, with cultural and psychic silhouettes whose implants have no beginning and which know no closure, and which are in that way the death of us, enveloping us, giving birth to us in a formless sludge of the barely remembered and the hardly achieved.

'Tu m'as donné ta boue et j'en ai fait de l'or'[6] affirms Baudelaire's narrator with the hindsight of the performer, the valedictory builder of attitudes or momentary identities. This final attitude in *Les Fleurs du mal* is imbued with its own instability, embedded in its own shadowing of the past and in its shadow-boxing with its own temporality. This is an affirmation representing an endeavour that – particularly in its prose manifestation, perhaps – consists in the shaking down of attitudes, of their representation, of the rhetorical forms in which they are cast and which are themselves moulded by sensual impulse and its passing; but these are attitudes and forms which also freeze impulse and make of its generation an object of obscure desire, fascination and adoration. Such is the ambivalent sludge or 'boue' offered also to the audience and to the readers of *Les Paravents*.

Its gift to the dead or from the dead is to keep the inactive in suspended inanimation, to infuse the imposed with the unstable, to let degeneration roam and reign intransitively. Degeneration is projected as a kind of purging, a purging uncontaminated by completion or by any measurement of its success. This suspension is maintained in Genet's hesitation between imagining a series of performances of the play as well as affirming that a single one ought to suffice; this contradiction remains unresolved and extends over any engagement with the play. What can we take without destroying, how can the play be represented or criticised when it offers its own performances predominantly to the 'dead'? In effect to an audience that is left to imagine itself without a place? Without a position in relation to its own experiences of the culture of representation, however familiar that experience is, however subjective, however intimate, and in effect beyond the reach of the image-making that is on such unstoppable display in the cacophony of projections that is Genet's play?

The play produces audiences, readers and critics without place, without position or context from within which to build their interpretations and defend their appropriations. Genet talks, in the passage I quoted at the start, of 'une nonchalance politique' that will allow the chance coming together of an audience, a momentary binding together of a group of spectators faced with the spontaneous but also no-exit identifications and lures displayed in the play. The imagined group making up audience and readers is the fruit of 'une rencontre aléatoire' that has all the futility made volatile of decay and of infidelity. An explosiveness in the languid and the haphazard, a revolution sustained in leaving the barricades bare, a commitment, or better a fragile, renewable intensity based on an erotics of the contingent – such are the elements in Genet's open theatrical space in *Les Paravents*.

This is no off-shoot of Utopia, the play has no place beyond placing, nor does it seek one. In terms of a developing praxis in European drama, the play pokes about in twin dialogue with the Sartrean and Brechtian maieutics. It engages one way with spectators spectating, the spectators' simultaneous resistance and vulnerability to what they see and to the situation in which that implicates them: here are the problematics of the Sartrean place, of the coefficients of perceiving it – an activity that is brusque, impervious, and arrogant – and conceiving of it – more synthetic, absorbing and absorbent, troubled. The other way, Genet fraternises with joyous incaution and abandon with Brechtian alienation effects, in which spectacle has both the power to transform and is retained as spectacle, both shatters and performs the spectators' investment in the spectacle of their own ideological moment, its avatars and vicissitudes. Lack of commitment in *Les Paravents* to either of these approaches is what strikes, certainly lack of any comment or directive of this or that kind. Genet allows one theatrical possibility to feed off the other, each consumes, undermines and glorifies the other. He anticipates for the play 'une déflagration poétique' – a conflagration that guzzles what it depends on, which is to say a circumscribed, situated audience – those 'milliers de Parisiens' that Genet invokes in the letter to Blin.

This is not the quasi-literal purging anticipated by Artaud in his theory and practice of symbolic theatre and cruel theatre, his vision of meeting fire with fire and of turning in on itself the violence of the urge to dominate. Or if it does survive, then only in so far as the virtuality of that Artaudian purging of his audiences' impulse to quash is what is preserved in *Les Paravents*; the artifice of the virtual, its impossibility, its ashes, a hilarious decay of its ambition. The play cannot purge itself of its place in theatre or as theatre and nor does it seek to. And yet the shameless looseness of 'des milliers de Parisiens' as a notion provides some form of resistance to the placing, fixing and stereotyping of the audiences, as well as by the audiences; a resistance that vaunts its own ineptitude and depends on it.

Moreover, Genet rejoices in the performance of his own identity in relation to that same conceptually flabby yet easily ignitable image of an audience – 'des milliers de Parisiens'. The play's first performance took place in 1966. Its response to the Algerian war and to the trauma it produced within the political and cultural life of France is notorious. If filth or the abject are somehow to be turned into positive effects – as they are in *Les Otages* and indeed in *Les Fleurs du mal* – then *Les Paravents* would seem to fit that bill. Resplendent in his abject roles as convict and homosexual, Genet now strikes at the heart of bourgeois self-righteousness. Articles appeared in *Le Monde* and elsewhere which openly cast him as traitor. There were right-wing demonstrations outside the Théâtre de L'Odéon where the play was being performed. The play was treated as a tract against France and provoked hate-filled and venomous responses.

And yet, though steeped in the politics of colonialism, this work asserts its right not to play out those scenarios, not to become involved, but rather to project images back at audience and readers. This is not to deny responsibility, but to assume it, to display the collusion of theatre in the dominance of the stereotype. The content of the play is indicated by its title. The staging of the play is populated by screens, each scene with a new set of screens, each screen representing and projecting an idea, the image which the characters before the screen identify with. The screen dominates, and on the screens, in turn, the image dominates. Such images include prison, army, Arab worker, white boss, abject poverty, vagabondage, traitor, whore, revolt, flames, machine-gun fire, an array of cultural and historical allusions and emblems paraded magnificently on the various stages employed. A paradoxical magnificence, since it revels in the stereotype and the received idea. The stunning creativity of Genet's stage craft is absorbed in repetition and conformity. Equally, that conformity is now the stuff of a glorious formal resistance and even freedom.

But there would need to be more for this freedom not to ring very hollow. The screens allow the boundaries of identity to be drawn on – metaphorically and redeployed socially as well as calligraphically. But to discover the impetus for improvisation in the representations of identity and in its permissible allocations might only result in mimicking those emblems without miming, in adoring without betraying, in engaging with without troubling or destabilising. Perhaps such lack of ambition is in effect the only way of trying to say what Genet is attempting, a lovely and lonely approach to representation – 'afin que cet événement – la ou les représentations – sans trop troubler l'ordre du monde, impose là une déflagration poétique . . .': some lyrical fire germinating in the belly, keeping its own council and its own secrets as it cajoles and seduces its hosts into veering towards some new culture of gift. But to trouble, to destabilise might itself turn out as the ambition of the collaborator: think of Louis Malle's *Lacombe Lucien*, and the sad self-righteousness of the self-styled victim turned tyrant or ostentatious and ignorant rewriter of the rules of cultural engagement. Nonetheless Genet envisages 'une déflagration' implying a chemical or even geological explosion *the idea* of which might remove opposition and conflict from the Western culture of representation and infuse it instead with chaos and the absence of form.

But once again, and immediately, to impose chaos, to imagine it imposed or even just in place, is to call a halt to its potency and to transform it into the vehicle of mastery – the champion, say, of strategies such as divide and rule, or indeed of any strategy at any time. Some suspended chaos, then, is maybe what would be needed, active in its inactivity, chaotic precisely in the profusion and proliferation that characterises its effects. This would come in the guise of a spectacle suspended in the gazes that maintain it and in that sense produce it, a spectacle that promises but does not provide the refractions of the glance. A spectacle caught up in the paranoia it seeks to undo and which forms its adherence to the law – or, in Freudian terms, to the demands of the superego, those innumerable voices of training and guidance in the demands of social interaction.

For Kristeva, there is some possibility of finding some weapon, or at least some mode of resistance, or if not some signs of life from within this psychically implanted conservatism. There is an erotic charge, some barely sayable, dense and suffocating fascination with collapse, with the fluid, with the fluids of decay and corruption, with what makes you retch and recoil, with taboo and with horror. This is a fascination linked both to orgasm and to menstruation, a 'jouissance' of ending, of crumbling fortifications, of degenerative miasma. The power of horror consists in its appeal, then, the appeal of the power to see the back of power. It is a distant remnant, a pregnant vicissitude of the narcissistic retreat from desire, a vicissitude of a sense of another or others absorbed in the forms of the one body and captured there in fascination with surfaces, the visual impact of which is, in any case, already undermined in the infinite regress of sensation. After all, as Guy Rosolato reminds us, the self is already other[7] – but how is this collapse of boundary to be accepted, accepted as beyond arrest? And beyond also the safety of some reaffirmed place – the 'Car JE est un Autre',[8] of Rimbaud's early psychocultural democratic idealism? Certainly, Rimbaud himself might offer a way past such idealism, however circular, however tautological. To accept the other is, simply, to accept the other – 'la réalité rugueuse';[9] to accept it as gift offered and received, manufactured in metaphor, a metaphor that seeks to elude the castles in the air of its own making, a metaphor made literal, paradoxically. Rhetorical gesture – such as irony – combines with grammatical figuration – such as the pronoun 'il' in 'Génie', where 'he' is simply and not performatively not 'I', and allows for the 'not I' and the 'she'. We might imagine an uncircumscribed language produced in this way, one in pursuit of a 'destinataire' or receiver and collapsing in the absence of a stable one; a language with the self-emptying power to reach beyond fulfilment and beyond representations of it, if only assertively and affirmatively.

> Sachons [. . .] le héler et le voir, et le renvoyer, et sous les marées et au haut des déserts de neige, suivre ses vues, ses souffles, son corps, son jour.[10]

Perhaps this 'beyond' would be the loose 'now' of Genet's 'milliers de Parisiens' of which I am at this moment an imaginary one. But a now in reading is intransigently subject to the laws of exchange, of interaction and integration – to the dynamics of paranoia and knowledge, of knowledge and emulation. Kristeva's theorisation of the abject[11] deals simultaneously in representing the filthy and in representation *as* filthy, and in the collapsed state of *that* distinction among the multitude of others she indicates. Women really are represented as the hated Other in this writing, but rather than collaborating with this, Kristeva instead charts the collapse of this hatred in its own implication in or collusion with the mellifluous and seductive viscosity it abhors. Encouragingly but also devastatingly, it is *within* the framework of Oedipal organisation and within the dynamics of repression that Kristeva allows an oscillation to be born of the apparent and the obliterated. Laws and their fortifications tumble and cascade, but from within and only from within. The abject is born of experiences of the social – of others, of appropriation and of loss – and not of further intimations of utopia. And its figurehead is the traitor.

One orthodoxy is very much another in Genet's drama. Sex, gender, race and class each partake of the same banquet of hate and lust, dreaming spires or towering infernos of gluttony and excretion; you can take to the heart and rip from the bosom in the same moment. Orthodoxy and tradition:

> Par le fait de quels cheminements les mots tradition et trahison, s'ils ont la même origine, signifient-ils des idées si différentes ou si foncièrement – je veux dire radicalement – semblables? [. . .] C'est à cela que devra réfléchir le metteur en scène [. . .][12]

'Tradition/trahison',[13] – a phonetic platform for an imagined common root, an imagining all the more powerful for its lack of substance, and all the more dedicated to an unstable, shaky and shabby definition. Saïd drifts continuously in and out of the play like a threadbare leitmotif. He is down-trodden and self-down-grading, seeming on that basis to move inexorably through the play from the ordinary to the symbolic; from the messy oppression of race and class, familiar to both colonised and coloniser and by which both have been cauterised, to the dramatic, the magnetic and the dominant; from the plural, imperceptible qualities of lived and inequitable cultural jostling, to the synthetic, the projected, the impregnably represented.

But Saïd turns out to be an odd mascot, tenth-rate and abject not only in the eyes of his colonisers but also in the eyes of those who might have been his friends and his ethnic and political allies. Lumbered with Leïla as a wife, whose supposed ugliness is on such a scale that she wears a black hood to hide it and to advertise it still further, who comes without a dowry and in that way adds still more to the living humiliation which is his marriage to her – this same Saïd steals from the coat of another Arab agricultural worker, one of his own, you would think, in both racial and class terms. Genet emphasises this down-trodden and destitute status of Saïd and his family – mother as well as wife – in every aspect of the stagecraft of the play. The ninth tableau in particular, Genet notes in his 'commentaire', 'est écrite pour montrer l'avilissement de cette famille'.[14] And the particular degradation of Saïd is compounded by the paced intensification of the symbolic impact of Leïla and la Mère throughout the play, eclipsing Saïd still further from the place he might have called his own, even though or even *as* the expectation rises of a Saïd acceding to the full emblematic status of Traitor.

A competition begins to emerge in this way between affirmative and degenerative revolt. One of its dramatisations is the denial of the right of la Mère, as punishment for Saïd's thieving, to take her part as mourner and weeper at the funeral of Si Slimane.

> Mais les chiens, les chiens dans ton ventre, tu m'entends, j'aurais interrogé les chiens qui se préparent à nous mordre qu'ils auraient répondu non. Les chiens, les juments, les poules, les canards, le balai, la pelote de laine auraient dit non![15]

What *is* this fighting over the dead that goes on in this instance between La Mère and Kadidja, this vying for the right to represent them and to claim them? La Bouche – the mouth of the deceased Si Slimane, but beyond that the mouth of the long dead, a hilarious revisiting of Hugo's *La Bouche d'ombre* but any uncanny revisiting as well since it eludes any such reference – La Bouche calls the bluff of La Mère. Cast out by the living, La Mère would seek private council with the dead, a privileged refuge of acceptance and valida-tion.

> Les morts, bien sûr, sont le dernier recours. Les vivants vous crachent sur la gueule, mais les morts vous enveloppent de leurs grandes ailes noires, ou blanches. Et protégée par elles, les ailes, tu pourrais narguer ceux qui vont à pied? Mais ceux qui vont sur la terre, d'ici peu seront dedans. C'est les mêmes.[16]

But La Mère is unconvinced, heuristically unmoved by the lyrical dispersal – dispersal and not concentration – of the voice of Si Slimane which is in fact the paradoxical message or gift he has to offer. His hyperbolic impatience with her here remains uncontested: black or white, any quality at all, any affectation or costume or passing metaphor or living whim can become a spontaneously, arbitrarily, fleetingly held and defended platform for domi-nance, for the absorption of conflict and difference, for the pride of place of the performer and the blinkering of the spectator. To claim the dead is to

reach out for a dialogue of equals, but one in which there is only one partic-
ipant.

But in loudly proclaiming her exclusion zone, the ideological orchestrator extraordinaire that is Kadidja has in the same gesture let La Mère in and
exposed herself to her contamination. By invoking the future, by seeking to
catch up with it and in that way to establish also the round reign of all-involv-
ing hindsight, in performing the future perfect – 'qu'ils auraient répondu non'
– Kadidja becomes embroiled in a psychic and cultural unguent which comes
with that very dissolution of the future into the present that she so desires.
She articulates, even in her magnificent 'Non!', the decay of the future and
the future as decay – the only possible future for any sentient being born in
and borne on the incapacity to sustain not only existence, but identity and
cultural attitude. If I wondered a moment ago what this competitive vying
for the right to claim the dead consists of, now Genet makes me wonder what
is the game-playing – rather than competition – and what are this clowning-
around and this playing at an enmity that barely survives the tableaux that
perform it and project it.

> Quelle que soit l'intensité dramatique que l'on veuille donner à cette scène, les
> comédiennes devront la jouer d'une façon clownesque: je veux dire que,
> malgré le sérieux des malédictions prononcées par les femmes ou par la Mère,
> le public doit savoir qu'il s'agit d'une sorte de jeu.[17]

The claims made for invective really are a joke – a joke at the expense of invective itself, of its performance, and of the burial it anticipates of the enemy, of
others and of any *destinataire* at all. But a deadly serious joke, nonetheless, a
'jeu'[18] – now in the sense of stagecraft – that may after all at least sketch in
our minds the demise of antagonism, and etch in as well an acceptance of the
uncanny, of the future as unthinkable, carried away on its own death and on
ours. Significantly, Genet introduces the idea in terms of the *reader* of the play
and not purely in terms of the spectator, and encourages resistance and fight-
back by underscoring reading, the reading of notes on a play that in this way
is presented as being imagined rather than seen, and the performance of
which – the fervent brutality of which – are all the more actively and unsta-
bly affirmed.

> Mais le lecteur de ces notes ne doit pas oublier que le théâtre où se joue cette
> pièce, est construit dans un cimetière, qu'en ce moment il y fait nuit, et que,
> quelquepart, on deterre peut-être un mort pour l'enterrer ailleurs.[19]

The exuberance of performance in the play is not to be foreclosed, in the
imagination at least it extends beyond the limits of the stage and it cannot be

contained in its own performance. Exuberance will be deadly, it is a performative act in that sense. But this is textual acting as well, bound up in its own performing if only in that operatic futility and deadly hilarity that characterises the rhythms of the play's unfurling, its unwinding and its scattering.

> WARDA, *hautaine, même voix traînante, désenchantée*: Vingt-quatre ans! . . . Une putain ça ne s'improvise pas, ça se mûrit. J'ai mis vingt-quatre ans. Et je suis douée! Un homme, qu'est-ce que c'est? Un homme reste un homme. C'est lui devant nous qui se met nu comme une putain de Toul ou de Nancy.[20]

For Warda the performance of prostitution, the establishment of its required and predicted rites, allows tables to be turned on her clients and on the marketing of sexual and cultural manipulation. What could more pointedly be the arena of such manipulation and such play than the imagination itself, that spongy breeding ground of commodity appeal, as you might say thinking along the axis running from Balzac to Benjamin, whose astonishing malleability may yet be transformed into its own mirroring – into a miming that shadows detachment as much as fascination?

> WARDA, *irritée, et d'une voix plus vive*: Ce qu'elle a dit c'est pour la joie des paroles, le bonheur de la conversation, parce que nous, si par malheur on prenait au sérieux les malheurs de la patrie, adieu notre malheur et adieu vos plaisirs.[21]

The prostitute can play by fixing the game, keeping the game a game, keeping it predictable: a witness to its *un*predictability, to the need to *manufacture* her detachment from it, and to impersonate the obscurity of the rules to the clients fascinated by this game. By suppressing and supplanting any element of improvisation, Warda's performance seeks out the predictable, woos it and cajoles it before embracing it, before taking it on as she might an ally or a lover and manufacturing an unholy, tautological and potentially futile alliance of coercion and . . . its performance. Such is the dialogue of subjectivity and alienation.

> Une vraie putain doit pouvoir attirer par ce qu'elle est réduite à être. Moi, j'ai travaillé des années mon décrottage de dents avec une épingle à chapeau. Mon style![22]

Warda's ambition as a prostitute is certainly to make virtue out of vice, to transform coercion into a resplendent affirmation of her identity, of the power to perform it and, sequin by sequin, to inaugurate it. The French soldiers' expectations of her and fascination with her, their exaggerated sniffing around her, are the living proof of the power of her strategies, in which vision is inexorably privileged above the other senses, incorporating them in an increasingly untouchable impact: Warda's body, the body of her appeal, the lushness of its precedents.

And what a simultaneously glorious, grotesque, abundant and deadpan one-upmanship the appeal of Warda's costume has turned out to involve: unbearably heavy imitation-gold headdress, red beehive hair, absolutely white face, enormous red shoes. The whole effect is locked onto by the fascinated and stultified soldiers turned sniffer-dog, who are in fact hilariously deprived of any sense of smell, and who, we are told, in that way are locked into the mediated, symptom-laden, both unfathomable and directed sexuality of desire and resentment that forms the basis of Freud's vision of human society and its prospects, and which he traces back inexorably to the distant biological stage where the quadruped develops into the biped. The grand stage is certainly the one claimed by Warda, a stage where fascination is not just experienced but espoused, not only performed but intensified, not only exceeded but *confirmed*, repeated and redoubled even in flirting constantly with futility and oblivion. 'Fixe!',[23] Warda cries to the witless stalkers, using her gigantic hatpin as baton, wand and weapon combined, an implement turned standard-bearer that trips lightly over boundaries such as the ones of Occident and Orient, function and symbol, decoration and violence, appeal and revulsion. Rather than loosening the grip of, or giving some mobility to the ideas of implement and weapon, this signifying mobility in Warda's hatpin, this startling piece of dramatic invention gets its edge and its slap-in-the-face exhilaration from the ease – the paradoxical, ironic, futile, non-functional and dysfunctional, aesthetic and moral ease – with which it gives not only form but free rein to the idea of the implement turned instrument of force and to the appeal of *that*.

This is an appeal born of precedent, an elusive appeal grasped by Warda and turned into performance – with what hope of success? Her attempt to seek out the origins of this appeal, to travel 'à rebours' has the effect only of arrest, where 'Fixe!' ceases to be a command and now expresses a condition – not just as an epithet, but as some imperative to be as you are. At least Warda can relish this as an end in itself, the collapse of the distinction between travel and arrest immerses that 'self' of hers still further in the representation of it. The open-ended beginning of that distinction between identity and performance is now what is performed, and the performance of performance is made by Genet to oscillate continually between infinite regress, or an evasive and pseudo-radical open-endedness, and an increasingly desperate imaginary leap-frogging over distinctions, different levels and different moments in the dialogic construction of an 'I'. But failure is tantamount to success in such imaginary jubilation. Overreaching has taken the

form of reaching for the given and the already there. Not for Warda any abandoning of identification with role, nor any resentment at being identified by
her audience in her role as whore extraordinaire. And to that extent, dialogue
with others is desired and relished – but always with the last laugh in mind,
or an endlessly repeated sneer, embroiled as Warda is in modelling others into
the shapes of herself she sees in the mirror – the mirror made flesh of her
clients and her servants, that most desirable of all mirrors if also the most
treacherous and the most unfaithful. The Lacanian 'désir de l'autre'[24] finds
here a living and breathing corollary, floating on the ebbs and flows of perception and all the more ingrained for that. If I want you to be puppets
miming my expectations, and yours, and yours of me, then you are at once
the stuff of my dreams and the stuff of those cacophonic Freudian 'voices of
training' that make up our cultural as well as a subjective *now*, and the boundaries or choices it offers for consumption.[25]

Not for Warda, then, an abandoning of the dynamics of identification,
any more than for the 'légionnaire' whose face is painted as the tricolour. Still
less for the 'lieutenant' as he demands of his troops that they take each other
as model, as mirror reflection of each other as well as of themselves. In
seeking to direct the already directed in this way, the 'lieutenant' seeks the
tiniest margin of distinction, in fact minimizes the distinction needed for the
perpetuation of the image of class, and of military and cultural might which
he is psychically glued to, and which now has no articulation and no history
other than the forms of that image itself. The drama of this image is built on
the dwindling sands of the audience, the stifling and the burying of its effects
and of the life-blood it provides.

Along the way, Genet takes a passing tongue-in-cheek side-swipe at
Sartre's ubiquitous example of the waiter in *L'Etre et le néant*. Genet's moving
target at this moment seems to be the capacity attributed to aggressive 'pour-
soi' perception to transform the example into a representative example, to
have this example perform any type of significance as though it were an attitude or a costume to be put on or shed at will. But in the company of his 'lieutenant', Genet imagines again soldiers already dripping in the psycho-cultural
unguent of a colonialist army:

> Il n'y a pas de garçon de café dans l'armée. *(Il se tourne vers la coulisse.)* Que
> chaque homme pour n'importe quel autre soit un miroir. Deux jambes doivent
> se regarder et se voir dans les deux jambes en face, un torse dans le torse d'en
> face, la bouche dans une autre bouche, les yeux dans les yeux, le nez dans le
> nez, les dents dans les dents, les genoux dans les genoux, une boucle de cheveux
> dans . . . une autre ou si les cheveux dans face sont raides dans un accroche-
> cœur . . . *(Très lyrique.)* S'y regarder et s'y voir d'une parfaite beauté . . . *(Il fait
> un demi-tour réglementaire et parle face au public.)* d'une totale séduction.[26]

To find seductive the performance of a role that has already been doled out: such is the sadomasochism, the regressive and acquisitive narcissism of the 'lieutenant''s desperate pursuit of synthesis, which has now degenerated into his defensive acceptance of the idea of knowledge as its own perpetuation.

> Ce n'est pas d'intelligence qu'il s'agit: mais de perpétuer une image qui a plus de six siècles, qui va se fortifiant à mesure que ce qu'elle doit figurer s'effrite, qui vous conduit tous, vous le savez, à la mort[27]

asserts the 'lieutenant' plaintively to his sullen 'sergent'. And this is not some acute insight, some detached moment of awareness of the fragility of the white's aspiration – as Lévi-Strauss might have it – to dominate by means of technologically inspired intelligence. Nor would an appeal to Hegel do justice on its own to the psychic and sensuous qualities of Genet's satirical probing away here at colonialist culture. The 'lieutenant''s erratic lament is an expression of the fragility at the heart of his own inherited pursuit of dominance and which is the engine of that pursuit; an expression of intimations of otherness as they seep into assumptions of wholeness. Instability – not just at the heart of orthodoxy, but also instability solicited by revolutionary fervour – does not turn out as an antidote to autocratic force. On the contrary, it provides it with nutrition and sustenance.

Identification, equally, is not to be destabilised here either; performance and its ironies do not have that power. Or rather they cannot sustain that power. Or if they do, then only in the instant of confirming those paths of identification and their plural, multibuckelled, multiform, super-adherent, one-size-fits-all straitjackets. But what of ironic self-awareness, the awareness of dialogue as socialising and also mobilising? Certainly such an awareness is nurtured in time, but its temporality is continually under threat because of the threat that it poses: 'une image [. . .] qui va se fortifiant à mesure que ce qu'elle doit figurer s'effrite [. . .]'.[28] If the image seduces because of some atemporal supremacy associated with it, if it is mirage and lure, then the pursuit of it, then attempts to keep ahead of the game and of time, will keep coming thick and fast. Moreover, appeals to image will not capture the lures that propel it and which it imposes. And as a direct result, the crumbling paths of identification that seem to lead however endlessly and circuitously to this Mecca are trodden all the more tenaciously. The requirements of identification are adhered to all the more ferociously. Contingency is absorbed all the more unrelentingly – suicidally, complacently, obsessionally, hopelessly, comically, unpredictably, humanly, desperately . . .

As the soldiers go about their business – shoe laces, hair-combing, generally making sure of looking the part – the 'lieutenant', with that less and less attentive audience of his own troops, muses on the job ahead:

Peignez vos cheveux. *(Felton sort un peigne de sa poche revolver et se peigne.)* Il ne
s'agit pas de revenir vainqueurs. A quoi bon? *(Pendant qu'il parle, tout le monde
s'active, de sorte que le lieutenant semble parler dans le vide, le regard fixe. Pierre noue
ces lacets. Moralès se rase, Felton se peigne, Helmut nettoie sa baïonette, le Sergent se
lime les ongles.)* . . .La France a déjà vaincu, c'est-à-dire qu'elle a proposé une
image ineffaçable. Donc, pas vaincre, mais mourir. Ou mourir à demi, c'est-à-
dire renter éclopés, pattes en moins, reins perdus, couilles arrachées, nez
mangés, faces rôties . . . c'est aussi très bien. Douleureux mais très bien. Ainsi
dans l'image de ses guerriers qui pourrissent, La France pourra se regarder
pourrir . . .Mais vaincre? . . .Et vaincre quoi? Ou qui? Vous les avez vus se traîner
dans la boue, vivre d'épluchures . . . vaincre ça! *(Haussant les épaules et faisant,
avec les mains, paumes ouvertes, un geste de marchand levantin.)* C'est bon pour eux
de vaincre. *(En direction du Sergent.)* N'est-ce pas? *(A Felton:)* Le képi davantage
sur l'œil.[29]

Every detail of style is a matter of continual correction of a performance that
will never be perfect – whose perfection lies in the manifestation of the
running wound that comes from that: a wound that remains unhealed, a
symptom of the sorry state of the Hegelian Master, always on the defensive
faced with the Slave on whom he depends for the signs of his own class and
of his class and racial dominance. Through and beyond that, it is an ineradicable experience of a psychocultural legacy – the weight of legacy itself –
that troubles the 'lieutenant'. He dramatises a Freudian conception of civilisation along with the discontents which are its only offerings, which are
made up of a narcissism that is at once unstoppable and desperate, and that
allows for one step beyond its own forms and *no more*.

> When a love-relationship is at its height there is no room left for any interest
> in the environment; a pair of lovers are sufficient to themselves, and do not
> even need the child they have in common to make them happy. In no other case
> does Eros so clearly betray the core of his being, his purpose of making one
> out of more than one; but when he has achieved this in the proverbial way
> through the love of two human beings, he refuses to go further.[30]

Freudian or not in his erotic constitution, Hegelian or not in the sense
of his own demise, Lacanian or not in his embroilment in that treacle of the
specular, Genet's 'Lieutenant' is entangled in the indeterminately heterosexual and homosexual vicissitudes of *jouissance* – of the pursuit of a 'not I'
that, like Beckett's, is barely, barely tolerably, intolerably different from I.

Genet locks into the scenarios of war and manipulates them with equal ease
at the levels of psychology, ideology and psychoanalysis. And once again,
Genet seems to 'lock into' only if that involves missing by a mile – or at least
the promise of missing, or if targets are not to be missed, then the artifice of

missing them. 'J'aurais beaucoup déconné . . .',[31] Genet writes of his play to
his reader, or his imaginary spectator, but certainly not an actual spectator,
since she or he would not be reading these comments but rather caught up
in the spectacle, the continual interplay of screens and projections, and subsequently would either never read the comments or could only do so after the
event. This is a kind of Stendhalian shadow-boxing with different readings
and positions, each provoking others and excluding them at the same time,
complete with feinted appeals to ignorance and orchestrated rehearsals of
the unpredictable. The imagination is given nothing but the most insecure
grasp on the play and on the ways it submerges us in the fake and the manufactured. The power experienced by, and then *claimed* by the imagination to
manipulate perceptions and the codes that give them form is both invoked
and exposed by the screens. Creative possibility and coercive asphyxia feed off
each other continually, and the gap between representation troubled and
representation affirmed is made increasingly narrow, increasingly hysterical
in the mind of anyone who might still care, and by the same token increasingly pliant. The magnetic appeal of power criss-crosses borders and boundaries and runs disturbingly free. The vibration of discontented intimations of
otherness and their quasi-immediate suffocation produces attitudes that are
shown to be psychic only in so far as they are ideological, ideological in so far
as they are cultural, cultural in so far as they are textual, textual in so far as
they are combative, combative in so far as they are ephemeral, ephemeral in
so far as they are codified, codified in so far as they are engrossing, engrossing in so far as they are entrapping, entrapping only in so far as they are enigmatic, alluring in so far as . . .

The 'Lieutenant' is placed in a spiral that also involves Sir Harold who
is desperate to leave his paradisiac orange-groves, his colonised little piece of
sun and luxury to his son, or at least the *picture* of his orange-trees painted on
one of the screens.[32] It is no secret either to Sir Harold or to the 'Lieutenant',
nor even to the increasingly self-assured 'Sergeant' and one-time Slave that
the image offers release from contingency, that it affirms a synthetic grace
born in a free-wheeling, free-floating decorativeness that now glides around
on the screens themselves. But this grace is tautological and circular rather
than endless or boundless – and needs to be, moreover, if the dream of the
self-affirming image is to be perpetuated, consuming those psychic, cultural,
enigmatic . . . relations I mentioned a moment ago, and removing them from
the unpredictable hurly-burly of bodily interaction and impulsive friction
which feeds them as well as that very dream of absorbing them. The investment in the image, in the powers of synthesis we depend on to construct
models of experience and to pass beyond them, is appropriative and acquisitive to the extent of allowing not only the future to emerge but also the multiple blinks and glances of present spectatorship – to emerge as an image of

their own life and half-life. A special absence emerges – 'une absence du monde' – and emanates from the performers of the play in Genet's description of how he would have them be and extends to the spectating of the play as well. This is the familiar absence produced by the ambivalent enticement 'love but do not touch'. In Genet's hands, this absence is able not only to solicit but also to mime identification in all its variety, its diversity of context, source and outcome. Suddenly in the play a massive glove appears dominating from above whites and Arabs alike, the colonisers and the colonised, it is equally and flagrantly inappropriate to both, remaining clearly beyond the reach and the minds both of those on the stage and of their counterparts in the audience, and *because of that* signalling the loose community of those recognising its power. This is a power to represent authority, a power perpetuated in the identification of it, in the imagining of it at work in any context, in the imagining of it absorbent and whole and at last impregnable to the indifference of others, able to command their love, or if not that, then their adoration, or if not that then their fear and their immobility.

Imagine a cathedral in which scaffolding is being put up or taken down for repairs to the vaults. Any sense of history or of possible occasion is dispelled by the loud and rhythmless clangs of the poles. And yet through the echoes, the space of the building – the subjective sense there of labour, craft, rite and grandeur – emerges in the very suspension of its undertaking, in the looseness of that subjective hold on the reverberations of the place and the picturings of past and future that are sited there. Scaffolding teams, tourists, cathedral officials, neighbourhood church-goers and passing critics, the leisured as well as those with lost goals to pursue, these and any others can all be taken up and assumed, but also given back some un-magnetic singularity in this haphazard and yet built intermezzo, this passing intimation of a breathing and consuming I. Such is the paradoxical, mobile, living and yet unforgiving stuff of which Genet's theatricalised glove and its clamp-down are made. 'Des milliers de Parisiens' – Genet's effortlessly loose imagining of the play's audience – carries with it the prospect of self-renewal, of constant mobility in any terms you care to imagine: racial? ideological? gendered? And such a prospect is propelled forward by this vast false glove suspended over the painted orange-groves, over Sir Harold, his corset and other body upholstery, and over the trembling but explosive Arabs whom he is attempting to subordinate.

But once again, textual and stage-crafted mobility does *stage* structures and their pathways, the backwards and forwards projections induced by cultural and political warfare of all kinds – stages them and confirms their glittering and astonishing effervescence, their rootedness in the micro-life of context, and their consequent power to elude not only boundary but premeditated resistance. 'Des milliers de Parisiens' are Parisiens after all, carrying with them, not just potentially shedding, the qualities of degenerate or hypersophisticated theatre-goers that can so easily be attributed to them, however unthinkingly and automatically. Genet allows and even encourages them to carry forward constructions of otherness particular to them, even in such a moment of cultural critique as this one of the painted orange-groves and the suspended glove. Arabs here remain nameless. This is a highly charged rhetorical manoeuvre that is handed down, as it were, from *L'Etranger*,[33] and deftly exploded sky-high elsewhere in *Les Paravents* through the panoply of roles exchanged among the actors involved – the policeman is played by the jailor, etc. – and through the exuberant array of mask and costume on display. But in the end masks themselves, to the clear and *simultaneous* delight and despair of Genet, do not just highlight or expose projections, they mirror them and perpetuate them.

In a manner reminiscent of the psychoanalytic situation particularly as reaffirmed by Lacan, the audience of *Les Paravents* brings with it constructions and confirmations, syntheses and self-fulfilling prophecies of all kinds that theatre might welcome with open arms just as powerfully as the figure of the analyst can be thought to by the analysand. What hope of a theatrical counter-transference of the image? Appeals to notions of a plural or composite audience, whether in the theatre or in the consulting room, might so easily appear as so many straws in the wind in the attempt to counter the effects of image-making – which seems to be precisely why Genet's definition of any audience of the play *is* so hilariously and resolutely shabby. Certainly Warda has no confidence in any spectator at all. At the beginning of the play, she is shown stoutly defending the cause of orthodoxy and is recognised as doing that by her colleagues in prostitution, artists every one in transposing the imposed into performances not only of itself but even perhaps of its transcendence, but artists nonetheless who can never rely on their audience, servile as it always is, always ready to confuse admiration with worship. And the stakes are high:

> Elle a raison, Warda: à qui offrir notre vie et nos progrès dans notre art, à qui sinon à Dieu? Comme les flics, en somme. On se perfectionne pour Dieu.[34]

The attempt to keep a step ahead of coercion results only in increasingly sophisticated, complex, fascinating, alluring, astonishing and *consumable* emulations of it. Here is the problem of the Sartrean *imaginaire* staged in acute cultural and psychic form – a form where it interacts in the most dynamic ways with the intellectual trajectories of Barthes and of Lacan. To seek a beyond to knowledge is to become further embroiled in the already known; and that embroilment takes the form of a further enacting and performing of it, with little hope of detachment or of any ironic undermining. What are the sorts of outcome to this that are envisaged in the play?

One is Warda's 'style', references to which have inched my digressive argument forward at various points – those years of practice spanning imaginary generations of transference and counter-transference and involving finger-nails, dress, hatpin, toothpick: reduced ingredients all of sexual acquisitiveness and armour-plated sexual shrubbery. This is generation in that other sense of energy and propulsion. Warda is at the centrifugal centre of ephemeral and atomistic models, psychic targets and lures of all kinds whirlpooling in the mind, models anticipated and adored, infantilising models weaving a kind of psychic skin that will stretch only so much, a signed identity turned quasi-biological but still susceptible to the possessive impulse: 'Mon style!'.

But is there anything else? Will the figure of Warda show a break in her style, a capacity to give up the bargain that gives her predictability at the cost of her endless repeat performance? Or can Genet see in her 'Mon style!' intimations of the sort of deadpan irony that Rimbaud uses in 'Alchimie du verbe'[35] to evoke and bury his former poetic glories? This is a desperately performed attempt by Rimbaud to propel his writerly persona into the next idiom, the next level of detachment, even if the destiny of this is again to be instantly transformed and reabsorbed. 'Mon style!' – the more plaudits it attracts, the worse the joke, and the more strongly Warda is tied to the post. A complex kind of cultural agility would be needed for Warda to disrobe – a panache that anyone might be free to imagine at this point here, or at any point of an engagement with *Les Paravents*. It would have something to do with the abandoning of the project Warda, with abandoning trying to please God and with giving up on the police – 'Dieu et les flics'; but this is an abandoning which no programme of action seems likely to ensure.

It is in this spirit that an appeal to the notion of superego might help here in discovering the mobility, if any, of Genet's representation of a colonialist culture, a representation that seems merely to oscillate between improvisation and repetition or replification. We cannot do without the Freudian superego, since civilisation itself depends on its effects and demands its activity. And since we cannot do without the superego, exactly in so far as we accept that implacable imposition, it becomes worthwhile imagining doing without it. We cannot live without the voices of conscience that make a society possible, nor without a commitment to the survival of society, nor yet without submitting to the orthodoxies of all kinds that result from this, nor finally without the imaginary dominance that is fed to us in compensation for this subjugation to the law. For this very reason we might bother trying to live without the superego. If violence is transformed only into civilisation and no further, only into implacably structural – gendered and economic – codifications of sex, then the imagining of a 'further' comes into its own at that very point, an imagining emerging from the blocking of any notion of its fulfilment and of any programme that might support it. An imagining, by the same token, that would have nothing to do with any psychic mindspin or freewheeling, any centrifugal dissolution of difference and opposition such as develops in observing – in both senses – the battlelines of superego and ego, where suddenly instead of policing there is collaboration, and the ego bathes again in a quasi-universal, wrap-around sound and fury of attention. Down with all that masochism and paranoia, Genet seems to proclaim in a fit of the giggles, and down with the gesture of saying *that*. And down also with this snapshot of a tired theoretical account of human relations and their prognosis. For Genet, the 'signifying nothing' part needs to go well beyond Macbeth's lament, and well beyond any Utopian recipe or dream of a society unburdened of signifying coercion – a dream that Barthes entertains, seemingly, with the one intention of interrogating it. For Genet, 'signifying nothing', imagining, involves letting go of that everything and of anything that we cannot do without.

It means doing without plans, any number of programmatic lassooings of the future, it means living without projects and the forlorn hope of projects being fulfilled or just bounced back as projections, as (purely) psychic reformations of our interaction with others and with the invasive and invaded environment each of us inhabits. To break from what Leo Bersani magnificently encapsulates as the 'culture of redemption'[36] – the culture of compensation spanning the aesthetic, the gendered, the ideological – involves abandoning transitive thought, synthetic thought at large, the motivated revolution, the theorised anarchy, even the fantasy of spontaneous combustion and dissolution. There is no saving the body here, neither the one we sense we have, nor the body-politic, there is no salvation from the indefinite and the incomplete, no shoring up against any ruins that ruins themselves would not beat hands down for mobility and erotic pleasure. But neither is there any saving *from* the body or the body-politic, even at the moment when the eruption of Erotic pleasure feeds that ambition, that same egoistic ambition of asphyxiation by any means including the ego's own immobilisation. Abandoning Redemption – abandoning anything – might so easily turn into another feather in the cap of that archaic narcissism that survives at all levels of the Freudian conception of the psyche and *as a consequence* of that conception as well.

Perhaps at such a point, where theory is seen continuously to impose limits on its own development, Sartre's early refutation of the psychoanalytic model of the mind still carries some weight. And yet as part of the interaction of psychoanalysis and existential biography that Rhiannon Goldthorpe in particular has investigated so probingly,[37] Sartre, in his discussion of

Mallarmé,[38] develops the notion of 'pro-jet' – of some broken project for poetry indicated with such force here in the signifier, the broken project of consciousness leap-frogging ahead of itself in pursuit of some sort of naming, some sort of circumscription of the responsibility that defines it. A project projected forward – 'pro-jet' – on the basis of the collapse of this project turned ejaculation, dissemination, diffusion and defusion. And certainly, Genet's project to defeat the project here in *Les Paravents* has just as much and more to do with the flaccid as the erect, the formless as the formed, with degradation as with propulsion. The play's play has moved on from that of *Haute surveillance* and from the shadowing or the strangulation of *Huis clos* that goes on there, and it has also moved on from the immolation of the cultural self imagined and performed in *Les Bonnes* and in *Le Balcon*. And yet any simple or unfaceted prospect of *generosity* emerging from ruin is not apparent in the play – the capacity to give is nowhere apparent in the play, at no point does it emerge from the hall of mirrors and the parade of screens and improvised projections that is the play of the play. In fact, improvisation can become embroiled in a further clinging to orthodoxy. I indicated earlier the alarming cohabitation in the play of agile stagecraft and the performance of emulation. Genet's inventiveness seems to have the quasi-Baudelairean effect of underscoring or understudying the clouds and shrouds formed by the obstacles in its way. Nowhere in the play is this made more shocking and more enlivening than in the twelfth tableau where the Mannequin makes its first appearance.

The tableau as a whole is a testimony to the mimetic principle, to some ineradicable sense that art should imitate life. What is recognition if not both climactic and deadening, releasing and imprisoning? Such questions might also have something to say about Genet's loose representation of the relation of revolt to revolution in the play. In any event, the twelfth tableau is one of many in the play displaying a diversity of attitudes, perceptions and glimpses of the colonial situation – if it can be called that, if that situation survives with its name intact amidst the range of soapboxes, grand gestures and enveloping rhetorics that populate the various stages used in this tableau, each one visually and verbally distinct from the others, but also visually swimming or sinking in the same scenic fluid.

The emblematic and trivial 'notable', the notary representing the laws of orthodoxy, kicks off with an operatic little confrontation with Kadidja, previously seen competing with 'la Mère' for the right of access to the dead, and seen here representing the rights of all women in a language that ironically – troublingly, hilariously – is both unique to her and, in its ludic fury and sexualised messiness, common to a host of others in the play at one point or another:

Sans les femmes tu serais quoi? Une tache de sperme sur le pantalon de ton père, et que trois mouches auraient bue. C'est mon jour. Ils nous accusent et nous menacent, et vous pensez à être prudents. Et dociles. Et humbles. Et soumis. Et demoiselle. Et pain blanc. Et bonne pâte. Et voile de soie. Et pale cigarette. Et doux baiser et douce langue. Et poussière tendre sur leurs bottes rouges![39]

But Kadidja is silenced, performatively, assertively, parodically silenced: she spends much of the rest of the tableau, until her triumphal return centre stage, standing with the fist of an Arab in her mouth, a gag she actually demands later by grabbing the man's arm and stuffing his fist back in: revolt and collaboration, terrorism and assimilation are hand in glove in a grand gesture of localised disgust and generalised futility.

And terrorism there certainly is – the shooting of 'la communiante'[40] at the point of her saying:

Moi aussi j'ai mon mot à dire: j'ai gardé un morceau de pain béni dans mon aumônière. Je veux l'émietter pour les oiseaux du désert, les pauvres choux.[41]

Not even the perfection of her performance and of its conformity to type, nor the perfume of ironic detachment that drifts off the little scene and that is an integral, active ingredient of the cultural associations and mnemonic chords that it reactivates – none of all that, predictably enough, is sufficient to sustain the pity of Kadidja. Though initially silenced by the sight and sound of this shooting, she will take the fist back into her face in a resumption of uncompromising defiance when Sir Harold takes up the space again with his discourse of orange-groves and tulips.

The vacuous Sir Harold and his dated gestures of mastery are a magnificently reduced account of cultural importation and imposition in which decorativeness, as so often in Genet, acts as a metonymic, 'explosante-fixe' (to borrow Breton's expression)[42] account of the social persona, of an unending but also losing battle with the superego for something like *a voice*. The coloniser is emblematic of more than just his own status. Obsessed with leaving a legacy of colonised paradise to his son, to an image of future generations absorbed in his own sense of himself, Sir Harold forms part of a gaggle of what are not only bourgeois stereotypes, but beyond that also fantasms, bits and bobs of the bourgeois imaginary and sense of lost cohesion: 'académicien', 'soldat', 'vamp avec son fume-cigarette', 'un reporteur-photographe', 'un juge', the whole mass seething around to the fanfare of the Marseillaise. And here, in the echo of the shot that kills the 'petite communiante', appears the mannequin, two and a half metres high, covered with medals and decorations of all kinds, dispelling and absorbing at a stroke that gaggle of its colleagues and potential admirers. An enormous figure – of what? In any event, Genet gleefully puts a telescope on a tripod next to it: what is it? where is it? will we ever see it properly or know it?

It is hard to know what is best: to imagine, as I did a little earlier, that Kadidja's jaw drops and lets the Arab's fist fall out of it in horror and empathy at the death of 'la petite communiante'; or to imagine that it drops in wonder at the anticipated appearance of this totem-pole, as Genet calls it in his stage direction, a totem that is 'un peu terrifiant',[43] on the fringe of the horrific but at the same time appealing or at least playful – 'les décorations sont très visibles'.[44] But what do these 'décorations' amount to beyond that very visible visibility, and beyond the fact that adorers are continually pinning still further decorative military medals to this totem? The impact of this appearance is powerful enough to dispel any particular answer, we may all be relieved to know, even at the armchair level. But equally, a simple appeal to pluralism quickly loses stamina here. Programmatic definition does seep in continually, and it is here that the idea of improvised, 'clean-slate' stagecraft betrays its roots in what it seeks to detach itself from, or in what it seeks to represent, or quite simply its roots *in* . . .What would be its point otherwise?

Clearly, the mannequin is circumscribed by the interests and the history of those performing the ritual of pinning on the decorations. To accept that is also to accept that performance of performance does not produce some free-wheeling play of forms, precisely, but on the contrary bears witness to successive failures of the mimetic process to produce either detachment or novelty. Instead it encourages capture, affirmative acquisition and absorption of all the familiar and desperate kinds. A chief decorator is Madame Blankensee, predictably one of the bourgeois gaggle that flocked in earlier on the wings of the Marseillaise. The circle of reference is continually closing in. But it still does not focus or stabilise. Obsessions here seep out of their channels. Their history and their future are as far beyond mental grasp as their force and effects are static.

The Blankensees and other couples compete to produce the best totem – but Genet does not give the audience any of these further totems to see. Spectators only see the telescope being used to get a sight of and a hold on the optimum totem, the most powerful one, the perfect one. In the ineffable and also shrink-wrapped presence of its own class, the bourgeois and colonialist supremacy is never established, the proliferation of its representations, associations, imprints and implants prevents it. And to represent the colonialist project is then also to display its own incapacity to reach beyond it and to establish any sort of out-post. Project abandonment is then no easy task, and may never get beyond refractive performances of it. To abandon the bourgeois project may produce understudies rather than overturners of the 'lieutenant', himself disgusted with his role as I indicated earlier, but increasingly awe-struck by his 'sergeant' and vulnerable to him.

Stagecraft alone, for all the parodic, seductive but also *seduced* mobility that Genet accords it, for all its loudness, its gleefully exhibitionist, slap-in-the-eye encounters with the audience, is yet still not enough to bring about the project of abandonment that the play seems to promise. What of that ambitious claim that humanity – or at least that loose conglomerate 'des milliers de Parisiens', that acts for Genet as an agent collapsing any such vapid notion – might be able to live *without* everything it relies on so tenaciously, so retrogressively and with such desperate conservatism? Perhaps it is in continuing recognition of the chameleon-like, multi-tentacled labyrinth that he is involved with of overtheorised psychic lures, or just plain banal culturalised carrots and sticks, that Genet makes a plea for his actors to acquire an empty, self-emptying form of stage presence:

> Les acteurs, pour jouer, – mais ce que j'écris vaut pour toute la pièce, – doivent essayer de rentrer en eux-mêmes, d'être 'absents à la salle' comme on est absent du monde. Je crois, finalement, que c'est l'absence d'éclats de leurs regards qui rendra compte de cette concentration en eux-mêmes, sur laquelle je compte. Encore plus qu'ailleurs, dans cette scène [neuvième tableau], les acteurs ne doivent pas jouer avec le public.
>
> Mais durant toute la pièce, 'leur absence à la salle' doit être sensible, presque offensante pour le public.[45]

Genet seems to imagine a spiritual type of self-emptying, a concentration on the inner self and a withdrawal from material or social exchange. But this is from the outset a highly heuristic, strategically minded sort of spiritualism, since no sooner is it announced than Genet stipulates its offensiveness and its rudeness. Withdrawal from exchange is here a sketchy but still potent little platform from which to embark on a shift in social interchange and its centres of gravity. The Brechtian alienation effects have been lodged in a further hall of mirrors – perhaps they were never anywhere else. Where before Brecht might have held up colourful theatrical disruptions of all kinds, each a challenge, or if not then at least a counterpoint to the habits and coercions of identification, for Genet the screens reflect back the hubris of even that modest 'challenge'; the empty acting would seek to take with Brecht a step beyond it – or at least to perform such a step. And Kadidja gives a magnificent initial lead.

Certainly she could not be more 'offensante' and rude. In the final, climactic evolution of the twelfth tableau, Kadidja is shot dead by the son of Sir

Harold, the voice of rebellion is silenced once more by the interests of inheritance and by the image of a long-term, colonised future. But she will not lie down. Earlier, the theatricality of stuffing the presumed fist of the oppressor or the collaborator into her own mouth with her own hand magnifies and pluralises the harmonics of her resistance, the slipperiness of its adversaries, the possible entries and imaginary accesses to it. Audiences and readers are given a glimpse of the mobility that might be planted at the heart of what is still the stoicism and the stasis of the attitude of resistance, its willed absence from the world of possibility and the spectres of assimilation. Now Genet goes further with her, she absorbs death and the Idea of it into her own project to 'overcome' on behalf of her people and her class:

> Je suis morte? C'est vrai. Eh bien, pas encore! Je n'ai pas terminé mon travail, alors, à nous deux, la Mort! Saïd, Leïla, mes bien-aimés! Vous aussi le soir vous vous racontiez le mal de la journée. Vous aviez compris qu'il n'y avait plus d'espoir qu'en lui. Mal, merveilleux mal, toi qui nous restes quand tout a foutu le camp, mal miraculeux tu vas nous aider. Je t'en prie, je t'en prie debout, mal, viens nous féconder notre peuple. Et qu'il ne chôme pas![46]

The build-up of resentment is weighing down. The oral and lyrical tradition combines with a fist-shaking Ode to Evil, and on the platform of this mercurial, deadly earnest linguistic hilarity, Kadidja manufactures her Orphic power to deal in death and dance with demise.

She orchestrates a performance at the end of which she lies in a bath that is also a bier, attended to by those flies handed down to us from Aeschylus through Sartre:

> Couchez-moi et lavez-moi bien. Sans bavardages idiots. Non, ne chassez pas les mouches. Je les connais déjà par leurs noms.[47]

In Aeschylus, the flies merge with the chorus producing a fickle mix of encouragement to the just matricide of Clytemnestra, and the opprobrium generated by the smashing of taboo that this event involves. In *Les Mouches*, Sartre's early play steeped in the philosophy as well as the practice of the Resistance, that other rearguard action against Empire, the flies threaten to engulf actors in remorse for the fragility of their own projects and for their own vulnerability to an agglutinous, seductive miasma made of circumstance and nostalgia. Here as everywhere, *Les Paravents* sides with the fickle. It then here seems to take issue with the defensiveness of the Sartrean notion of a project, or rather to exploit the vulnerability of *any* project as well as Sartre's own profoundly observed hypersensitivity to that, and to transform this defensiveness into a filthy object of erotic desire whose very paucity and insignificance makes it open to being trashed and vaporised. It is not that the potentially static or predictable Sartrean antagonism of *en-soi* and *pour-soi* must be cast aside if some initiative of Genet's is to be followed; but that the very defeatism of this structure gives us the opportunity to do that, to put it aside, and to invent in the resulting vacuum or in any other.

As dead, as imagining death, but as still coarsely and insolently dead, as both dead and floating on the idea of death and the scum of it, in both resisting death and anticipating it, Kadidja opens the stage out to its own shabbily defined uniqueness. Inventiveness on the stage is now performative, with all the tautotology that implies – here an insolent 'je m'enfoutiste' circularity: to be inventive is to be inventive. Equally, a performance of invention is invented.

KADIDJA: Kaddour! Pour que le mal l'emporte, qu'est-ce que tu as fait?
> *Toute la scène qui va suivre se déroulera très vite – paroles et gestes – presque comme une bousculade organisée.*
KADDOUR: *(d'une voix sourde mais fière):* Leur gueule est encore chaude – mais ta main dessus – regarde: j'ai ramassé deux revolvers.
KADIDJA: *(sèche):* Pose-les là! . . . le canon fumant . . . l'œil féroce et farceur . . .
> *Kaddour, très vite, avec un fusain, dessine les revolers sur le paravent. Puis il se place à gauche de la scène. Les dessins doivent représenter les objets monstrueusement agrandis.*[48]

A whole other gaggle, a just about controlled rush, a barely rehearsed chorus of narrative, allusion, command and improvised sketching now takes over the stage, even a second large screen is needed when room runs out on the first, much bigger this time and covered in flags, and the by then large crowd of Arabs rushes to cover it with more drawings of their exploits and of their revolutionary and violent booty.

> Des yeux bleus à la demoiselle. Sous les orangers, violé une de leurs filles, je t'apporte la tâche de sang. *(Il dessine en rouge la tache sur le paravent et sort. Maintenant les Arabes entrent à un rhythme plus rapide. Ils attendent à droite, pressés d'entrer.)*
KADIDJA: *(sévère):* Ça, c'est ta jouissance et la sienne. Mais le crime qui nous sert.[49]

Drawing, sketching, painting the rewards of revolt and violent conflict – even of the Eldridge Cleaver-type injunction to the Black Panthers to rape white women – this energised, mad dash to the scribble-pads of the screens has the effect of purifying those rewards and the pursuit of them. By purifying I mean removing quality from those rewards, removing moral or political targets from them, removing their context and their decipherability, removing their limits and their point. This is now a carnivalesque, centrifugal dissolution of any working distinction between desire and fulfilment, oppression and freedom of movement, restriction and agility, creativity and emulation, novelty and novel-mongering, heroism and the bums-rush.

A shabbily defined, dilapidated community emerges, a community made of images and image-*making*, made of an ability to draw on and in and around models of fulfilment, agility, race, revolution and the rest. Projection comes home or bounces back and around as the medium of invention, a *staged* invention. Echoing Barthes's Brecht-inspired *mise-en-scène*, this staged invention is now devoid of the aspiration to 'signer l'imaginaire',[50] as Barthes would have it, in the sense of personalising cultural or psychic textures and the body in which they are inscribed. But this *is* 'signer' – in the other sense implied by Barthes that I discussed in chapter 2, the sense of to mime, to speak in sign language, and in *Les Paravents* this is sign language without the voices of orthodoxy and authority – which are signed here nonetheless. The 'signer l'imaginaire' that Genet offers – if we can still imagine a Genet in amongst the crowd – is one that performs image-making; it complicates and also mobilises the spectators' imaginative engagement – with what? With screens, with projections, with anticipated breakthroughs and failures, turmoils and utopias, orgasms and flaccidness, exuberant heroism and equally exuberant cowardice, with improvisation and with command, each with every chance of being enacted and also abandoned at any and every juncture. All this is contained in the leaky screens that are pictorially manhandled, balletically shoved around during the play and which give it its title, its mobile, collapsing and humble claim to a point.

But it is not enough. Kadidja remains in command. Despite espousing death, the imaginary capacity to talk from the beyond, to wrap herself in opprobrium and in a Baudelairean oxygen made of decay, Kadidja remains in the rhetorical driving seat of the *dispositio*. To espouse crime and evil is simply to conform to the scenarios that they map out – and to rehearse this tired old critique fares no better. Nor is some carnivalesque mix of cliché and energy anything but an inadequate bulwark against megalomania or the living death of racial cruelty, ignorance and class violence which it is the mission of the play to confront and resist. So many failures are charted in the play – many of them with delight. 'La Mère', for so long in the play the arch-competitor of Kadidja, sees clearly that Kadidja's eulogising of evil and betrayal is simply another totalising attempt to 'aller jusqu'au bout', to smash compromise and a corrupted social relation. With a paradoxical stoicism reminiscent of Sartre, 'la Mère' recognises that 'aller jusqu'au bout'[51] is already where Saïd and Leïla are – reviled traitors to the practices and interests of their race, the one stealing from his 'comrade', the other arriving without a dowry. This is a 'jusqu'au bout' of the status quo, from which there is no liberation and of which there is no loathing without entrapment. And no bad thing either, Genet seems to suggest. 'La frousse'[52] that Kadidja asks one of her number to draw is the trembling foundation of any project, of any project 'pour-soi', the destiny of which is to collapse and to bear witness to the Passion of intent. Perhaps this is what the speed of the drawings and the rush to accomplish them anticipate: the living breath of the transient injected into that seductive integrity, that flesh-made-mine of the image. But anticipation is also not enough. The pleasures of the image, the gesture and the language that perform their collapse are not enough to reform a community.

Take the Gendarme. Here is a stereotype born, overturned and confirmed in the idiom appropriate to its image. Genet imagines him this time as troubling himself over whether to address the colonised Arabs as 'tu' or as 'vous'. In the ninth tableau, the situation is treated comically as the Gendarme discusses his problem with 'la Mère', the archetypally colonised Mother born in cruelty, hypocrisy and evil: '. . . ma cruauté, ma méchanceté hypocrite que je gardais, une main derrière mon dos pour blesser le monde'.[53] In a rather obvious way, habits of dominance are inscribed in habits of address, but the ins and outs of this are too much for our 'flic':

> Heureusement qu'on vous a et que comme ça y a plus petit que nous, mais si on nous oblige à vous dire vous on sera bientôt plus petit que vous.[54]

The confusion of various grammatical functions covered by 'vous' – subject, vocative, direct and indirect object, compounded by a 'vous' that *refers* to its function as vocative – this seems very clearly to mechanise address and to transform dominance and its abuse into the comedy of the dwarf in Emperor's clothing, the 'bourgeois gentilhomme' with his little bit of instruction.

The clockwork is kept well-oiled by the interventions of 'la Mère', intent on her satire, sticking obdurately to the niceties of conversation. Perhaps an occasional 'tu' might help shore up against the erosion of differentials?

> De temps en temps vous pourrez oubliez le vous et nous dire le tu.[55]

This couple of well-heeled cultural hermeneuticians debate the finer points of this very fine distinction, watching all the while the erosion of the power lines that just now divided them.

LE GENDARME: Surtout que vous aimez mieux ça, hein? Le tu es plus chaux que le vous et le tu protège mieux que le vous. Quoique si le tu protège, le vous de temps en temps fait du bien, ça je m'en doute.

LA MÈRE: Un peu de vous, un jour sur quatre, et le tu le reste du temps.

LE GENDARME: C'est mon avis. Le tu comme base et du vous goutte à goutte. Pour vous habituer. Nous et vous on y gagne, mais le vous tout à coup, à qui dire le tu? Entre nous le tu est le tu de copain, entre nous et vous le tu qui vient de nous est tu plus mou.

LA MÈRE: Juste. Le vous pour vous ça vous éloigne de nous. Le tu nous plaît, le s'il vous plaît n'est pas pour nous.[56]

The stock-in-trade of the signifier – acoustic difference – is made to perform its own instability in a manner reminiscent of Desnos's wordplay that I discuss in chapter 3. 'Nous' and 'vous' appear in the nominative, the accusative, the genitive and the dative, and adverbially. This ludic dissipation of the relationships that 'tu' and 'vous' articulate, this hilarity now turned phonic carries the Gendarme ultimately to the recollection of further carnivalesque wordplay and play and some wholly unexpected cross-dressing:

> Les musulmans! Si je les connais, vos astuces! Un jour – ah! le Morbihan, ce qu'on rigole! – un jour de carnaval, avec un drap et un torchon, je m'étais déguisé en moukère, en fatma; d'un coup, d'un seul, j'ai compris votre mentalité. Tout dans l'œil. Et si les circonstances m'y obligent, malgré ma blessure et mes deux filles, je prends le voile.[57]

'Tout dans l'oeil' – image has the power to capture costume and its history as well as the gestures which animate them, the prejudices that inhabit them and the projects that propel them. And good as his word, the Gendarme wraps himself in Leïla's magic blanket – redolent of her power to have objects move independently in space, independently of gesture and word, and of her power to carry herself in and out of many places – and drifts obliquely off stage, into another zone where Gendarmes and the idea of them have lost face, costume and profile:

> Dans la couverture il s'enroule et [. . .] il traverse à reculons et obliquement la scène, pour sortir dans le fond, à droite.[58]

But it is not enough. It is a speck in the controlled chaotic rush to the screens orchestrated by Kadidja, itself not enough. La Mère has already seen through the hilarity at the level of the signifier to the immutability of the class and cast relations it barely troubles:

> Le vous pour vous ça vous éloigne de nous.

Grammar distinctions articulate unbridgeable cultural gaps and fissures in the collectivity. Guarded and nurtured barricades re-emerge instantly, layer upon layer of workaday suspicion, of almost indispensable defensiveness and recoil, of which la Mère's homophonic tautology is not only a parody but a sort of aural miming, testimony and reinforcement. Linguistic irreverence, the hilarity of manners, and the ludic, quasi-digestive confusion of utterances and of codes, all together simply add to that *absence* from the stage that is so important to Genet, that projected sense of dull or sullen alienation from utterance and the sense of the communal that it might produce . . . And all to the good if it did, clearly, if community is made simply of precedence and coercion. Perhaps something less aware of its opposite, less dialogic and in that way less scripted, is needed here to push past alienation, parody and cross-dressing – or to push further in, perhaps; perhaps it is asphyxia and only asphyxia that knows no limits and therefore holds out a promise of excess.

A motif on wings in the play, or a shroud, is the slow passage towards each other, never completed, of Saïd and Leïla. From within their respective cells of unconditional recrimination, loathing and self-loathing, and unconditional adoration and loyalty, Saïd and Leïla reach out and never meet, just as Saïd himself, as Genet asserts again with a kind of Stendhalien narrative untrustworthiness, will never make it to being a traitor. Once again, 'aller jusqu'au bout', the fulfilment of a destiny, the logics of attitude or situation, all this would only confirm a community made of the face-off, each side of many colluding with the others in maintaining powerful images of *itself*. It is more the creeping, mole-like tentativeness of the passage of Saïd and Leïla – towards what? – that begins to seep both intermittently and firmly into the fabrics and textures of the play. At the beginning of the eleventh tableau, Leïla and Saïd are shown in separate cells, they communicate impossibly through the walls in a way reminiscent of Genet's own *Un Chant d'amour* or of Fabrice and Clélia in 'La tour Farnèse' in *La Chartreuse de Parme*.[59] The 'douceur' of their respective tones and its anticipation (both intense and lacklustre) of ecstasy takes over the content of this interchange, and this tumescence in the signifier performs the opposite of what theoretically minded readers such as this one might expect – an oddly *increased* intensity in the lyrical I, an Orphic embrace of past and future, of precedent and desire, of the entrails of the soul and improvisation on the airs of the model:

LEÏLA, *d'une voix très douce*: . . .en marchant vite, et les reins courbés, mais surtout la veste pas boutonnée, personne n'aurait remarqué la bosse que faisaient les boîtes de conserves sous ta chemise.

SAÏD, *même douceur*: Si tu as raison, c'est encore pire, puisque tu me montres le moyen de m'échapper une fois que c'est rendu impossible. Il fallait me prévenir avant . . .

LEÏLA: J'étais déjà bouclée. Dans ce cachot enfermée. Je ne pouvais plus te conseiller.

SAÏD: Je ne veux pas de conseils, mais tu peux me guider puisque tu es invisible et lointaine, derrière les murs épais . . .Et blancs . . .Et lisses . . .Et inaccessibles . . . Lointaine, inaccessible tu pouvais me guider. *(Un temps.)* Chez toi, où c'est que c'est que ça pue le plus?

LEÏLA, *extasiée*: Oh moi! Qui, à mon approche, ne tombe foudroyée? Quand j'arrive, la nuit se replie . . .

SAÏD, *extasié*: En déroute?

LEÏLA: Elle se fait petite . . . petite . . . petite . . .[60]

This is the 'extase' of the religious rite, perhaps, so central to Genet's attachments and to the irony with which he fondles them. Or iconoclasm, on occasion, rather than irony: a Baudelairean or other metaphysics of collapse so easily combines with a eulogy of stink and the predictable antagonism that that implies. Certainly, Leïla's and Saïd's Odyssey of the mind, of projected and decaying sensation, is after all foreclosed and enclosed, brutally disrupted by the yelling of the legionnaires at prayer, in a movement in the play which yet again embroils ecstasy with orthodoxy and which produces again the implacable rhetoric of command:

> UNE VOIX, *très forte, dans la coulisse*: Les hosties et le latin à peine avalés . . . qu'on serve un café bouillant.[61]

That voice is that of the Lieutenant, we learn, intoning in the direction of a further screen that appears and which shows behind it the obscured symbolism of soldiers at prayer to their defensive and unforgiving gods.

And throughout her travels in the play, Leïla seems constantly to be threatened with her Orphic burrowing turning into finality, confirmation and conformity. With her drawing on the screens early in the play she claims power to move around objects beyond her reach, and continues at intervals to perform or sketch a shattering of the signifier and its power to position. With her implorings and exhortations to Saïd, she can mime in advance the incantations of the 'condamné à mort'; his psalm of violence that acts as a visceral, uncluttered, but contemptible and sickening aspiration to the purity of a role turned identity, of imposition turned invention.

> LA VOIX DU CONDAMNÉ À MORT, *très virile et décidée*: Non. Si c'était à refaire: je m'approcherais de face, en souriant, et je lui offrirais une fleur artificielle, comme elle les aimait. Un iris en satin violet. Elle me remerciait. Aucune poupée blonde comme celles des films n'aurait écouté de pareilles foutaises que les miennes, et dites avec un si câlin sourire. C'est seulement [. . .] quand mon discours aurait été fini, qu'elle aurait respiré la rose et qu'elle l'aurait piquée dans ses cheveux gris, que je lui aurais . . . *(A mesure la Voix s'exalte, et vers la fin elle psalmodiera et chantera.)* délicatement ouvert le bide. Délicatement, j'aurais soulevé les rideaux du jupon pour mieux regarder couler les boyaux, et j'aurais joué avec comme les doigts jouent avec les joyaux. Et la joie mon œil l'aurait redite à l'œil égaré de ma mère![62]

This is an abject incantation attempting to force a way out of precedent – in the form of allusions to *Bois dormant*[63] – out of its psychocultural sediment, out of the lures and appeals of known desire and its representations: all that sense of a hopeless and ludicrous, mechanistic funelling of the indefinite into the origined, the plural into parameters of the plural, revolt into the magnetic and adorable forms of its targets: 'la mère' . . . But it is not *that* mechanism that cuts this incantation short, but the guillotine; and the Camusian inevitability of it is carried, as ever, in *'la parole'*, it takes over the power of the word to transform itself into song, takes over the incantation and gives it back as a script:

LE GARDIEN, *brutal*: Au point où il *doit* chanter. Et vous autres, les apprentis, vos gueules![64]

But Leïla with Saïd continues her contrapuntal psalm with the 'condamné'. Leïla and Saïd seem still to invent as they go mythifications of detritus and the morally abject, as well as their roles as avatars of that. In this they pick up echoes of Le Cadi,[65] the folkloric judge or dilapidated Solomon who in the seventh tableau declares that truth and judgement are now to be found in the air, in the dust of the road, in someone *else's* imagination or in a wasp's somnolent buzzing:

> Dieu a foutu le camp. Si tu veux être jugée par lui, donc avec un reste de bonté, aide-moi. Dis-moi quel jugement tu veux, mais dis-le vite. [. . .] Dieu s'est cassé, tiré, taillé. Dieu s'en est allé. [. . .] Il vient, il s'en va, je me demande où? Dans une autre tête? Dans une guêpe au soleil? Dans la courbe d'un chemin?[66]

More than a dissatisfaction with the ramshackle Master/Slave exchange of truth and value, Le Cadi both admires and bemoans its collapse, which is now the platform for his erratic musing on precedent, on script, and on some archaic but also unmediated release from them. Leïla's own poetry, and her odes to Saïd in particular, also combine lyricism with arbitrariness; hers is a lyricism built in the familiar arbitrariness of signification as well as contingency. It is a lyricism that has become still more rampant than Le Cadi's, this is the non-specialised stuff of a blink or a passing sensation, and makes the most of countering purpose with futility:

LEÏLA, *d'une voix gutturale, et appelant comme à la foire on appelle les badaux*: Qui . . . qui?
    Et qui encore n'a pas vu passer Saïd désossé, disloqué quand les flics lui filent son avoine? Et qu'il bave du sang, saigne de la morve, suinte par tous les trous, qui n'a pas vu? . . .
    [. . .]
    mon homme autour des vestes
    [. . .]
    rôder, s'amener à quatre pattes dans l'herbe, son ventre ramassant tout . . .
    [. . .]
    si prudent, si vif, si vert qu'il est le carré de poireaux, si gris qu'il est ma peau sèche . . .[67]

This Brechtian, carnivalesque advertising of the figure of the robber and the traitor is opened out like a dancer's dress in Leïla's vocal assemblage, in her 'bricoleuse',[68] on-the-hoof myth-making in which Saïd being treated like an animal is both revered and raised to the ground; such is the linguistic, performative magic that is Leïla, the apparent forms of her adoring. It is part of the same theatrical magic that allows her elsewhere in the play not only to bypass the signifer but also to move objects spatially, or literally, with the force of gesture and word alone. Her songs of devotion move; they are made of remnants of expression, the gestures of persuasion and empathy, they move and are on the move with the renewed vigour that comes from severing the umbilical cord of reference.

But her song is also a shouting match. My quotation, though emphasising the circus and its crowds, has excluded the yelled descant of Saïd; vocalisation, rhythmed, multi-layered, multi-signed semaphorings of devotion, I mean *even* of devotion, and still more of abjection and filth, are carried on the bones of yet another, still more primeval empire. Leïla's magic with reference is refracted perversely in M. Blankensee's sense of the linguistic foundations of imperialism:

> Nous sommes les maîtres du langage. Toucher aux choses, c'est toucher à la langue.[69]

Wordplay, ultimately, confirms the Word, improvisation echoes confirmation and carries it forward. And this little juxtaposition I have manufactured of Leïla and Sir Harold raises another curtain on the part played in this by the superego, on the performances in the play of the polymorphous (manifest, visual, social, impulsive) and intestinal (absorbed, ingrained, and equally impulsive) boundaries of identification, of the permissible and the known.

> C'est ce que je vaux. C'est ce que je veux.[70]

Leïla says at one point with a simplicity that binds stoicism to affirmation. I want the abject role of detritus and scapegoat that I am worth. Revolt or even simple assertion conflates desire with value, and once again we are what we are told we are. Here, vowelplay sets reference and position in stone, rather than erasing or fragmenting them or anything else as grand. And however much the Gendarme in the same tableau may cross-dress and leapfrog over boundaries of race and gender, this moment of recalled imaginary play casts him and his verbal-gestural jocularity in the retentive attitudinising of his cast, and the relentless narcissism of his uniform re-emerges intact. And Leïla's wordplay and play with reference is inevitably in dialogue with that –

> Et si les circonstances m'y obligent, malgré ma blessure et mes deux filles, je reprends le voile.

The face-off continues, Leïla's culture of the tattered blanket and other broken bits and bobs remains in stultifying conflict with the coloniser's value of value, property, assimilation and synthesis:

> On est venu chez vous avec la civilisation et vous continuez à vivre en vagabonds.[71]

An interminable satirical jostling seems to lie ahead, consisting in an ever more desperate search for an ever more adjustable rhetoric to hurl at the others.

No. Something slower. Something without direction. Something without dialogue. A community made at least of that. La Mère senses it, smelling a rat in Kadidja's extolling of the 'aller jusqu'au bout' in the twelfth tableau, that supreme moment of Kadidja's as the orchestrator of all forms of revolt that I discussed earlier. She damns with ironic praise in her own adulation of the hero:

> Ainsi, ma belle Kadidja, tu es morte! héroïquement crevée. Et si je voulais te parler il me faudrait encore utiliser la vieille bouche des morts? mais . . . tu es morte en faisant quoi? En excitant les hommes et même les femmes à aller jusqu'au bout? ils iront jusqu'au bout de ce qu'ils font, et de ce qu'ils sont devenus![72]

People are already 'jusqu'au bout' of their being and of their becoming in the stand-off of Sartrean antogonism and Freudian psychic determinism that is one of the ways I have been trying to site *Les Paravents* – this would be a dynamic site made of perception and the imaginary, on the one hand, and of symptom and structure on the other. 'Jusqu'au bout' – and then what? La Mère's somnolent recitative gives no clue here. But its stark lack of direction, its associative crawling or leaping from notions of Saïd's and Leïla's journey and its indistinctness, to the beauty of Saïd's dead father, to the miscarriages that had preceded his birth, to fantasies of death and destruction, to an inkling that fantasmagorias and nightmares of this kind serve only to reproduce themselves . . . – all this acts as an engagement with precedence, with antecedence at large, pressure, pressure and more pressure. It is pressure of this kind that builds up behind the screens. A pressure that keeps Leïla's Orphic burrowing alive in its diffuseness, deflections and refractions. A pressure whose explosiveness opens out onto the fraternal and takes it in, a pressure produced in an ostrich-like burying not of the head but of all reference in the sand, a willed invocation of the dark side of ignorance along the lines imagined by Cixous more recently.[73] It is the pressure of the dead from both or all sides in the war, each laying its claim to supremacy in the psychic soil of the living, to the totemic status of being fought for to the death, to more death and still more, each death cast in the image of a living victory, a living and breathing image that is now only ever a chronicle foretold and only ever without destination. When and where is that absence of destination to be given back to dialogue and to a community that would then be able to speak without imprisoning? More magnificent still than a screen allowing you to display your obsessions, fantasies and ambitions is a screen that is divested of them – that is blank – which you do not paint on or draw on or write on or pour directly or psychically onto – but which you step through.

Genet introduces gradually this further set of screens. The blank screens are announced as separating the living from the dead. The dead in the war pile up behind them, as competition between the living and the dead continues to intensify, each vying for precedence and authority. Eventually the dead burst through, French and Arab alike, stunned by the ease of it, by the ease of shattering the image and the stultifying synthetic, ideological warfare that the image allows to go on around it. This astonishing dramatic moment has nothing of the supernatural or the redemptive about it. It is supported by the imagination of the audience, of you as you read and I as I try to stop. On the stage as the play is watched or read, a space is imagined, in fact it can only be imagined, but it is a generous space nevertheless, a space of a noisy community of images and their collapse, of purpose and futility, and any other amorphous but also giggly combination of the living and the dead that you might care to imagine now.

Picking at random a feature of this noise might be an appropriate way to say farewell to the play – of acting as a member of that loose conglomeration of an audience that Genet imagines for the play and which gave me a way to set this piece off. This community past the blank screens, made of the blank screens and the capacity to step past our identifications, is one in which competition has dissolved. Kadidja, who has 'died' earlier in the play as an overture to her great moment of revolutionary apotheosis, now is the first to appear through the blank screen –

Et on fait tant d'histoires![74]

Staying ahead of the game and of time is an approach that has lost its footing –

NEDJMA: Rien. Rien à faire. D'habitude, le temps est comme le café, il passe, et dans le filtre il retient les accidents: maintenant il ne passe plus.[75]

La Mère finds her way through the forest of metaphors and pronouncements and other linguistic smokescreens and tactics –

De rubis, vous traînez sous vos couronnes de rubis un chariot d'épluchures
[. . .]⁷⁶

only to find that the endless bickering between her and Kadidja seems for a
moment to be endless:

KADIDJA, *souriant*: Je suis morte la première.
LA MÈRE: Ça t'avance à quoi? Moi, je suis morte d'épuisement.⁷⁷

Ultimately, exhaustion has replaced one-upmanship, the place of competition
is dissolving, or rotting; vying for supremacy has been taken over by coming
together, but this has now nothing of an imaginary wielding of forms or a
narcissistic fondling of the one. Spectators, audiences, 'des milliers' of unpre-
dicted participants or passing fanciers are included in this new community
rather than taking their turn to be silenced.

KADIDJA: L'image de moi que j'ai laissée . . .Est-ce que je peux la voir?
SI SLIMANE: Tu veux savoir s'ils ont découvert que pendant vingt ans tu te vendais
    aux soldats? Tout le monde l'a su au bout du premier mois.⁷⁸

Amour-propre, the metaphysics of self and other, the scar-tissues of the ego –
all this and more is set aside by the amorphous mobility of the dead crowd
and its power to set aside the mirror. Le Cadi re-emerges to remind us of the
magic of the colonised, the imposed magic turned emblem of the power to
dissolve reference and position:

LE CADI, *riant*: Plus à moi. Les choses cessent d'appartenir à ceux qui ont su
    les rendre plus belles. Libérées, délivrées, agiles, elles s'échappent et vont vivre
    ailleurs, sur qui, sur quoi, vivre comment, je m'en torche, je m'en branle *(Les
    femmes rient aux éclats.)* . . . meilleures et plus belles, agiles, ailées, elles aban-
    donnent avec gratitude celui qui les a rendues meilleures. Elles parties, plus
    rien, que dale, zéro, foutu!⁷⁹

And for Leïla, the process of her becoming and of her becoming Leïla is
impregnated with this collapsing reference, hers is an Orphic journey that has
no end, no return, no looking back into some mirror made of the past that
will fix her as Leïla, but only a drowning in the threadbare blanket of possibility that has now become her shroud. The mascot, the guiding principle or
lyrical voice of non-conflict and decay that is Leïla is not formed but an idea
that we inspire, breathe and scatter.

Vous voyez . . . Je remonte . . . roulis . . .Tiens, plus rien. C'est le fond? . . . Je
remonte . . .et je reflotte à la surf . . . non? Non. Bon, si vous le dites, c'est que
c'est vrai puisque tout commence à être vrai . . . bien . . .Voilà. Enfonçons
encore avec les deux épaules.

Elle s'enfonçe définitivement dans sa robe qui était faite de façon – sorte de crino-line – qu'elle puisse, vers la fin, s'y noyer. La lumière revient en scène.[80]

Being and being told to be and what to be can now coexist in the confusion or the avalanche of naming and valuing that is the space of the dead and the cyphering of Leïla. But can we accept this healing by the music of decay, by decomposition, a manufactured generosity whose gifts have no trails any more than do the naming and the renaming and the valuing of them? Can we accept being bathed in this staged, balletic light of generosity, of a society made of an openness that comes only from the acceptance of mortality?

As a critic, I can accept this gift by trying to prevent my own idiom from taking over the language of the play, and in that way I can try to enact tolerance of otherness on the heuristic basis of not-understanding and of non-appropriation. Perhaps this might act as a reflection of that absence from the stage and from the audience that Genet prescribes as the crucial feature his actors should aim at achieving. But this would be small, liberal-minded beer, perhaps.

And in any event, Warda, when in the situation with Kadidja and La Mère and Malika and the others of divesting herself of her robes, of the image that will purify her of contingency and free her from that continual pulling and tugging at her integrity, can enact only lament, that faded, age-old, repetitious lament of a lost voice, lost continuity, a lost past and lost domains:

WARDA, *seule*: Pute! Moi, Warda qui devais de plus en plus m'effacer pour ne laisser à ma place qu'une pute parfaite, simple squelette soutenant des robes dorées et me voici à fond de train redevenir Warda.

> *Elle commence à déchirer sa jupe, si bien qu'à l'arrivée de Malika elle sera en guenilles, cependant qu'elle pousse une longue plainte.*[81]

Far from developing 'mon style!' with the prospect I evoked earlier of a Rimbaldian irony allowing rhetorical attitudinising and the fetishisms that accompany it to dissolve rhetorically, but also poetically and bodily, Warda by the end of the tableau of blank, crossed-through screens has become 'un véritable monstre, de haine et de tristesse'.[82] So much for some capacity to interact without silencing, to abandon capture in favour of invasion, position in favour of its collapse, identification in favour of . . . But then again, in the next tableau, Warda is given that which escaped Kadidja, which is to see herself, that is to see her image as she would have had it or imagined it amongst the living – to see that from the 'place' of the dead.[83] It can be done, that detachment can be made. From what? Detachment from dominance bought with asphyxia, from identification with the boundlessly coerced, from the victim turned totem, from stability made of immobility, from desire made of adoration, from the astonishing power of the image to make the needs of the group, or of class, race or gender indistinguishable from those of the ego and then also to make the ego indistinguishable from its articulations as the speaking I. Detachment can be manufactured from a synthetic, self-fulfilling prophecy of achievement of the kind that the Lieutenant earlier had despaired of ever being rid of, and had seemed to congratulate his cast on, for the *same* reason:

La France a déjà vaincu, c'est-à-dire qu'elle a proposé une image ineffaçable.[84]

It is not this theory of the image, or its history, that I am seeking to convince my readers of – or not particularly – though this book is certainly the product of a fascination with it and its potency. And I seem also to have got beyond making pronouncements about the disappointments of that theory, the education in disappointment that it can provide; and certainly past warnings of the potentially reductive pincer movements that any theory can exercise on the plural and the lived. It is now a matter of disappointment in that education itself, and the potency of that. Genet comments on the end of his enormous play with a farewell that is both grief-stricken and loving – 'la scène est vide. C'est fini.'[85] Not a Freudian mourning this, one that secretively bathes in a return to immobility. This is more a scattering of investment, in fact a divestment, a stripping away of the vocabulary of forms, of imaged obsessions and their remnants, the swathes of mobility in the perusals of our culture that not only leave comet-like trails but impose them, each speck like a pore in our psychic skin. A farewell to the dimensions of known conflict, the boundaries of resentment and of a civilisation of discontent.

But once again, perhaps this is a gift of no-return and of non-redemption that cannot be accepted or even made. Very much a clothed nakedness is on offer. The fate of Leïla's burrowing and of Saïd's non-arrival either this side or that of the blank screens is to be transformed into a song – some vehicle or vessel or voice or form in which the familiar and the desired, the resisted and the adored coalesce:

LA MÈRE: Saïd! . . .Il n'y a plus qu'à l'attendre . . .
KADIDJA, *riant*: Pas la peine. Pas plus que Leïla il ne reviendra.
LA MÈRE: Alors, où est-il? Dans une chanson?
Kadidja répond par un air dubitatif.[86]

Perhaps the song will float away on the air, on a gesture, on the volatility of language itself as it is lived and breathed in the tatters of a psychocultural subjectivity that make up a speaking I, and which is paid such a mobile homage to by Leïla's torn and magic blanket. But perhaps not. Perhaps that popular song still in the making will signal the funnelling of those distant intimations of hope, of a self yet to be born, of a dialogue made flesh with silence or with invented voices – the funnelling of all such things into the idea of them: an outcome that takes over the revolutionary ambition of Chantal in *Le Balcon*. An idea made image, producing and inducing those wrap-around sensations of intimacy combined with inevitability, of a self both indulged and coerced. An idea made image such as the one incarnated in the Prussian Eagle:

> L'Aigle de Prusse. L'emblème veut imposer – et le réussit – une idée de force irrépressible, une idée aussi de violence et de cruauté[87]

muses Genet in his 'commentaires du treizième tableau'. A reading of this emblem, an engagement over time with its stylistic features and the resulting immersion in their invasive powers – this is the stuff of which the adoration of Prussia is made, or the adoration of any other dominant idea, however temporalised and volatile this idea may still remain. Adoration loses its impulsiveness and is slowly, without trace or endgame, transformed into emulation. Textual features of the emblem that holds Genet's attention here are the agents of violence and cruelty and of their passing into orthodoxy. The pluralisation of sense fails once again to break the codes of identification, the gendered and racial elements of which may be so clearly drawn at the ideological level. The textures of ideology bear witness to its intransigence and confirm it.

Perhaps this is the essence of that 'blessure' that gathers such insidious but moving weight as the play develops – the failure of theatre, of language, of either spontaneous or performed social interaction to undo their adherence to the roles and positions, the psychic vistas and anteriority they embrace.

Madame BLANKENSEE. [. . .] Que l'amour commençât par une trahison se perpétuait comme la secrète blessure d'un ordre qu'on respecte encore.[88]

That failure, that continuing adoration of an order of things that by its existence can only speak violence, opens the book on yet another chapter in the performance of subjectivity, its status as performance and as representation. It is also that sign of intimacy, of that signed intimacy we call our own:

> C'est bien mal dire qu'autour d'une invisible blessure un homme amoncelle ce qui cachera la blessure cependant qu'il la montre du doigt. Il me semble donc que chaque personnage n'est qu'une blessure disparaissant sous les ornements et apparaissant par eux.[89]

For colonised and coloniser alike, will offers no alternative to wish. Wish envelops will in the endless veils of its appeal and of its imagined or projected reception. The pain of sense, of subjectivity made into sense, can only be shown in gestures and images that depend on it. Here, the play takes its place in postwar Parisian culture and thought, the highways and byways of the image and the sign of which it is so much a product and a child. And it is in that place of circumstance and of decay even now still to be imagined that Genet discovers the humility and the generosity that he invites us to share and to imagine accepting.

Epilogue

Pursuit and decay – the one concerned with fulfilment, the other dissolution. This apparent antinomy speaks about the nature of the problems that I have engaged with in the essays here: the mutual dependency of orthodoxy and subversion; of celebration and revolt; of creativity and mortality.

Books by definition come to an end, and I would like to find a farewell appropriate to the gifts of the artists and writers I have discussed, and who have produced in me the critical passion and perhaps the critical humility that I have tried to communicate here. But I cannot think beyond the conventional way of concluding which consists in reviewing the intellectual kernels that I have nurtured and which have formed my critical orientation and my critical idiom. Still, in that way I might succeed in emulating those great conclusions in literature and in film which effect a kind of letting go, a dispelling of obsession, or rather a returning of perennial inwardness to some public domain, anonymous but also *noisy*. As Stendhal's grief-stricken narrator puts it so ambivalently at the conclusion of *La Chartreuse de Parme*, all the jails are empty at the moment of farewell and dissolution.

There has been much talk here of form and of various investments in that idea. The manipulation of form provides an obvious starting-point for a definition of the aesthetic. Rapidly, though, the magnificence of such manipulation testifies to an equally magnificent overestimation of the powers of hand and eye, of fantasy and mentality at large to redirect the terms of life and of any interaction with the material, the social, the sexual, the racial . . . But this spectacular and specular juggling with the dimensions of life might still reach past the nostalgic play of matching sensation, association and thought to the environment that prompts them. Such nostalgia is the harbinger of its own temporality and its own falling away. In the texts I have been involved with, grabbing a hold of the world in the mind, assigning it shapes and codes and models is a sensual response and a response to the senses, those very sensations that have decay and mortality as their unspoken word. In *L'Etreinte* that preoccupied me in chapter 1, Picasso brings a life-time working with what the body's appearance disguises back to the body itself – that is, inevitably, to further surface representations of the body's mnemonics and its elusiveness. But this 'further surface' punctures the obsession of art with itself, it is a place where the indomitable pursuit of a mirror-matching of one body to another can be shown to collapse in an orgasmic mess. Participants in this art might be detached from their governing sexualities, let loose rather than shaped and quantified; time may say this, Picasso suggests, or its passing, or ageing might.

So there is a humanity of form that takes it beyond arid formalism: perhaps we might at least imagine forms of exchange that do more than confirm the terms of any transaction past and future. Luce Irigaray has done more than many to move symbolic exchange on from method-inspired narcissism and towards sites where a range of positions, perspectives and subjective histories might interact. Such is the notion of form I have tried to present here: various ways of telling the story of French, or rather Paris-centred, twentieth-century practitioners' investments in reading, in the capacity of readers to imagine differently the boundaries that allow movement and rebirth.

Irigaray's method is to inhabit the philosophical both in the feminine and in the poetic. My own is self-evidently more humble – and has had to be, since it works with that crumbling structure which is the aesthetic and the textual, a structure that provokes an indefinite range of readings, and which is for that very reason deprived of a secure place where its effects might be legitimized. (What *is* the point of an Opera House? or the street-art in front of one?) Its only power is to stage the absence of its own supremacy, and in that way to suspend itself between disruption of a rich, but escape-proof past and suspicion of such an exhibitionist pretension to the *tabula rasa*.

A humanity of forms, then: speculative, but resigned. A manufactured one as well, closely guarding, rhetorically re-inventing its immunity to place and position. But what might be thought of as a purely symptomatic type of resistance allows various other effects to be staged, and an active resistance to them to be constructed. I am thinking among others of the effects of gender, race, ideology – all loves that in my idiom in this book have scarcely dared breathe their name. But a textualised approach to these issues characteristic of writers from Breton to Cixous and from Benjamin to Barthes reveals at the very least the all-pervasiveness and the insidiousness of the implications involved. That is the open but unspoken secret of plurality, a secret, lost in its speaking, of an elusive signified which the notional primacy of the signifier fails to see beyond. The signifier is a vulnerable indicator, colluding with the silencing of its own messages of signifying dismemberment and discursive relativity. For any sensation or fleeting perception is, after all, also the idea of it. Plurality, the assumption of a range of readings attached to any artefact tagged as text, is made of such collusion. And yet on the basis of its own vulnerability, the signifier showers readers with further indicators of the high-stake dramas in which it is involved, and which might produce still further ways of staging this rather sickeningly familiar set of questions. Does sense merely engulf? Are forms merely imaginary? Do art and thought have the power only to oil the wheels of permissable symbolic dialogue and the domination that lurks there? Does the capacity to think form, to think the relative, to rediscover the other words breathing in every word undermine itself at every turn?

A textual approach to such questions is volatile, humble and humbling. I have tried to show Barthes's admiring disquiet, his horrified fascination with unpredictable passages from signifying bittiness to imaginary completion and impregnability. Reading the effects of the signifier in Surrealist practice has allowed me to show its place in the history of the ways this anxiety has been engaged with in writing and painting this century in France. Surrealist interference in signifying relations and the other relations they involve – gendered as well as ideological ones – is suspended between an imaginary, magical mobility and a staging of this specious magic. The scope of the signifier seems to narrow to two options at the hands of Desnos and Magritte: alienation and fantasies of escape. Signifying potential is taken over by the equally protean activity of the symptom; a sense of the plural in perceptual or affective response gives way to an implacable determinism; the reign of the mirror is reaffirmed, tyranny and the asphyxiation of difference find new homes.

For the unconscious which Magritte 'knows' is not the one of surface shocks or the alarming bizarreness of the dream narrative, nor its alternately ludic and horrifying free play with material conditions; nor even the unconscious of trap-doors and abysses opened out in the floor boards of language. But the indefinite, multiform, protean, malleable, insidious, deceptive, omnipotent and impotent, energised and victimised, sterile, kaleidoscopic and violent energy with which the ego protects its domains. This is where Magritte reinvents invention, its limitations and its honesty.

Elsewhere, in a parallel space to that of Surrealism, Kafka's figure of Josef K and then of K exemplifies with special poignancy the collusion of the desire for a place in a mechanism with the resistance to being allotted such a place. The pleasures of meaning, it would seem, will always win through over the pleasures of excess, which in that way at least are displayed for the pointless utopia they offer. If not transgression, then a more resigned pursuit of mobility within the tense places of sense and sensation, orthodoxy and improvisation returns to the critical encounter. Tentatively, for the sake of argument almost, or of a relationship with you, I have sought with many others to turn involvement with texts into a site where narcissism might be transformed into generosity.

In the readings I have journeyed through here, the social encounter is presented as already absorbed, embodied without being accepted. Sexual and cultural identity would be complacent and enclosed if not for the battles that articulate them – those war zones written in the minutiae of habit and impulse just as much as in public conflict and spectacle. Breath-taking in their magnificence but also in their violence, I have found that these impulses turned spectacle are not just static but temporal, not entrenched but collapsing, not transcendent but decaying. But there is no alternative space either to the abject tyranny depicted, say, in Fautrier's *Les Otages*. A beyond to violence is pursued from within and not without; neither in resignation to corruption and corruptibility nor in a suppression of them.

Les Paravents, like *Les Otages* and Duras's *Les Yeux bleus cheveux noirs*, exudes the traces of unhealing, mobile wounds made in words and the dire effects of racial and sexual exclusion. Duras's text is uncompromisingly intimate, ingraining the private with public marks of sexual – and in other texts, racial – resentment and violence. Perhaps this is the source of the notorious popularity of Duras's writing – its ability to steep its readers in ancestral ghosts, attractions and models, in unguent and treacherous forms that indicate what we are and cannot have, that tell the stories of our silences, and then flip over and place us in the public space of other ideas, shapes and bodies.

The idiom of *Les Paravents*, written some twenty years earlier, is a noisier one. It is made of continual disappointment, of intimate longing or ambition for bodies and wrap-around sensations rapidly returned to the common spaces of consumption and exploitation. Alienation and attraction speak in the same forked tongues, creativity and despair meet in the same dark corners and shriek the same guffaws. Colonialist oppression prolonged by the Algerian war appears none the less violent for being represented, painted, acted out, performed and decorated: the wounds it inflicts on both perpetrators and victims form a language that is boundless and shaped, orgasmic and sterile, historical, subjective, unpredictable. Might such a language suggest the language of community, or the language of its disintegration – or both in the same breath, or in the same image, either side of a dissolving screen?

But if democracy is to be given back its space in the mind and in the senses, this cannot be at the expense of society, of place and context, of all the codes, idiolects and the other legion specificities that demand the right to voice and form at any one moment. The image and its imaginary forces cannot take us beyond place; but then neither can the signifier keep us securely within it, comfortably within the embrace of others and the unlevel playing fields of exchange. If the image would have us whole and dominant, its decay would immerse us in the acceptance of others and of our place in others, and in mortality. Such is the history I have tried to bear witness to in this book of the development of modernist or avant-gardist forms in twenti-eth-century France. More than an orthodox downgrading of the image at the hands of a self-validating, all-validating anti-illusionism, this history has offered me an education in the unlearnable: in the relativity in which Narcissus is immersed in exchange for a body; in the grandness of the aspira-tion to set violence aside; and in the humility provoked by the repeated, multi-levelled failures of this ambition. A lesson in the equality of collapse, a willed collapse, or if not willed then imagined, but not a pessimistic one. This is not a history that can be unearthed in terms of a strict chronology; it folds and unfurls in the recesses of emotion and memory as much as in the grand or catastrophic gestures of public life, conflict and discourse. It is this *imag-ined* sense of a culturalised, specified, intimate and dispersed temporality that I have tried in this book both to revere and to foster.

Two final farewell gestures. The first to Baudelaire, whose writing con-tinues to dominate my own and many others' understanding of modernisms high and low; and 'La Mort des amants' in particular, the death of the lovers. Orgasm has passed, the lovers have separated, only an Angel remains, an indulgently and inveterately material one. 'He' is now the only being able to imagine what is now not there. For this very reason, he needs us to imagine with him, to live with the impossibility of his being there, and to imagine him visualising what is not there. There *is* nothing there. Something may begin.

My last allegorical farewell is addressed at a film: *Trois couleurs: rouge*, the last in Kieślowski's trilogy, his testimony to the idea of revolution, *Bleu, blanc, rouge*. A man at a red traffic light is captivated by an enormous red poster with the profile of a woman's face. The advertised product is irrelevant to the impact produced both on that viewer and on me, the viewer of the video. Mythical, symbolic, subjective constructions mingle with each other and with others, are lost in the imagining of the new, and of an arrested past in the form on an arresting present.

But the image is not free from the advertised product, which is chewing gum – pointless in the extreme, at one level; and it remains that, but also becomes sinister as viewers learn that someone has used chewing gum to block up the key-hole to the model's flat. Voyeurism emerges as nonetheless all-pervasive or violent for being frustrated. Moreover, viewer and model are in fact known to each other; the painfully slow awareness I, at least, come to of this relation signals implacable legality, systematic exchange for profit, the herding of reading into ownership. But that system is shown, is imagined col-lapsing in a catastrophe familiar to all, in a language of catastrophe that all share and are horrified by: the sinking of the Zeebrugge ferry in 1993. The small group of heroes and heroines of Kieślowski's trilogy, victims and per-petrators all of sexual violence and Oedipal capitalism, are the sole survivors of this decay in the edifice that has produced them – filmic cyphers all, made of life, love and pain. What we have of ourselves is given to us and taken away in reading, that inadequate measure of events and of the subjectivities that are swamped by them. But still, in our minds, something may now begin.

Notes

1 Looking and loving: Harlequins in Apollinaire and Picasso

1 *Soldes, poèmes inédits de Guillaume Apollinaire*, ed. Pierre Caizergues (Fontfroide: G. Boudar et Fata Morgana, Bibliothèque artistique et littéraire, 1985), n.p.
2 Harold Bloom, *The Anxiety of Influence* (Oxford: Oxford University Press, 1973), p. 26.
3 '[Satan's poetic] heroism is exactly on the border of solipsism, neither within it nor beyond it.' Ibid., p. 22.
4 Guillaume Apollinaire, 'Les Fiançailles', *Alcools*, in *Œuvres poétiques*, ed. Marcel Adéma and Michel Décaudin (Paris: Gallimard, Editions de la Pléïade, 1965), pp. 128–36.

5   'Forgive my ignorance
      Forgive me for no longer knowing the ancient play of verse
      I know nothing anymore and I can only love'

   Guillaume Apollinaire, 'Les Fiançailles'/'The Betrothal', *Selected Writings of Guillaume Apollinaire*, trans. Roger Shattuck (New York: New Directions, 1971), p. 69; 'Les Fiançailles', *Alcools*, in *Œuvres poétiques*, p. 132.
6 'From my ancestors the Gauls I inherit pale blue eyes, a narrow skull and a lack of skill in fighting [. . .] from them I inherit: idolatry and love of sacrilege.' Arthur Rimbaud, 'Bad Blood', *A Season in Hell and Illuminations*, trans. Mark Treharne (London: J. M. Dent, 1998), p. 5; 'Mauvais Sang', *Une saison en enfer*, in *Œuvres*, ed. Suzanne Bernard (Paris: Garnier, 1960), pp. 213–19.
7 'I've got mine and it's all the same to me.' Rimbaud, 'Bad Blood', *A Season in Hell and Illuminations*, p. 5; 'Mauvais Sang', *Une Saison en enfer*, in *Œuvres*, p. 213.
8 Nathaniel Wing, *The Limits of Narrative* (Cambridge: Cambridge University Press, 1986), p. 83.
9 'If only I had antecedents at some point or other in the history of France!
      But no. Nothing.'
   Rimbaud, 'Bad Blood', *A Season in Hell and Illuminations*, p. 5; 'Mauvais Sang', *Une Saison en Enfer*, in *Œuvres*, p. 213.
10 'Utterly in the present', Rimbaud, 'Adieu', *A Season in Hell and Illuminations*, p. 53; 'Adieu', *Une Saison en enfer*, in *Œuvres*, p. 241.

11 'I smile at beings which I have not created', Apollinaire, 'Les Fiançailles'/'The Betrothal', *Selected Writings*, p. 69; 'Les Fiançailles', *Alcools*, in *Œuvres poétiques*, p. 132.

12 'Coarse-grained truths', Rimbaud, 'Adieu', *A Season in Hell and Illuminations*, p. 53; 'Adieu', *Une Saison en enfer*, in *Œuvres*, p. 241.

13 Bloom writes: 'For the poet is condemned to learn his profoundest yearning through an awareness of *other selves*. The poem is *within* him, yet he experiences the shame and splendour of *being found by* poems – great poems – *outside* him.' Bloom, *The Anxiety of Influence*, p. 26.

14 Jane Gallop, *Feminism and Psychoanalysis. The Daughter's Seduction* (London: Macmillan, 1982), p. 66; see also Luce Irigaray, *Speculum de l'autre femme* (Paris: Editions de Minuit, 1974), p. 33; and Jacques Lacan, 'L'Amour et le signifiant', in *Encore, Jacques Lacan, le séminaire, xx,* (Paris: Editions du Seuil, 1975), pp. 39–48.

15 Jean Starobinski, *Portrait de l'artiste en saltimbanque* (Paris: Flammarion, 1970).

16 Barbara Johnson, *Défigurations du langage poétique* (Paris: Flammarion, 1979). In particular, see Johnson's account of the final lines of 'La Chevelure' and 'Un hémisphère dans une chevelure', pp. 52–5.

17 Charles Baudelaire, *Le Spleen de Paris (petits poèmes en prose)*, in *Œuvres complètes*, ed. Claude Pichois, vol. 1 (Paris: Gallimard, Editions de la Pléïade, 1975), pp. 295 and 319.

18 'A great surge of people caused by some disturbance, swept me far away from the old performer.' Charles Baudelaire, 'Le Vieux Saltimbanque', *Le Spleen de Paris (petits poèmes en prose)*, in *Œuvres*, vol. 1, p. 296.

19 See Starobinski, *Portrait de l'artiste en saltimbanque*, p. 129.

20 Norman Bryson, *Vision and Painting* (London: Macmillan, 1983), p. 94.

21 Sigmund Freud, *Instincts and their Vicissitudes* (1915), in *On Metapsychology*, Pelican Freud Library 11 (Harmondsworth: Penguin Books, 1984), p. 116.

22 'He is the mortal vehicle of a (possibly) immortal substance – like the inheritor of an entailed property, who is only the temporary holder of an estate which survives him. The separation of the sexual instincts from the ego-instincts would simply reflect this twofold function of the individual.' Sigmund Freud, *On Narcissism: An Introduction* (1914), in *On Metapsychology*, p. 71.

23 Julia Kristeva, 'Le Père, l'amour, l'exil', *Polylogue* (Paris: Editions du Seuil, 1977), pp. 137–47; 'The Father, Love and Banishment', in *Desire in Language: A Semiotic Approach to Literature and Art*, ed. Leon S. Roudiez, trans. Thomas Gosz, Alice Jardine and Leon S. Roudiez (Oxford: Basil Blackwell, 1981), pp. 148–58.

24 Freud, *On Narcissism*, p. 88.

25 Ibid., pp. 88–9.

26 *The Seminar of Jacques Lacan*, book 1, *Freud's Papers on Technique*, ed. Jacques-Alain Miller, trans. with notes by John Forrester (Cambridge: Cambridge University Press, 1988), p. 133.

27 Freud, *On Narcissism*, p. 81.

28 Ibid. p. 90.

29 Ibid. p. 85.

30 Dr Leclaire makes this observation in the course of Lacan's seminar. *The Seminar of Jacques Lacan* 1, p. 136.

31 *The Seminar of Jacques Lacan* 1, pp. 135–6; *On Narcissism*, p. 90.

32 *The Seminar of Jacques Lacan* 1, p. 133.

33 Richard Wollheim, *Painting as an Art* (London: Thames and Hudson, 1987), p. 249.

34 'In creating I would heal. In creating I would get better.' *The Seminar of Jacques Lacan* I, p. 131; see also *On Narcissism*, p. 79.

35 Guillaume Apollinaire, 'Crépuscule', *Alcools*, in *Œuvres poétiques*, p. 64.

36 'These are cripples, they walk on crutches, and charlatans too. They are surprised at having reached their goal which is no longer the horizon.' Guillaume Apollinaire, *Les Peintres cubistes* (Paris: Hermann, 1980 (1913)), p. 73.

37 'brushed by the shadows of the dead', Apollinaire, 'Crépuscule'/'Twilight', *Selected Writings*, p. 61; 'Crépuscule', *Alcools*, in *Œuvres poétiques*, p. 64.

38   'From platform height the harlequin
        Wanly salutes the audience
        Magicians from Bohemia
        Some fairies and some sorcerers'

        Apollinaire, 'Crépuscule'/'Twilight', *Selected Writings* p. 61; 'Crépuscule', *Alcools*, in *Œuvres poétiques*, p. 64.

39   'He brandishes with outstretched arms
        The star he unhooked from the night'

        Apollinaire, 'Crépuscule'/'Twilight', *Selected Writings* p. 61; 'Crépuscule', *Alcools*, in *Œuvres poétiques*, p. 64.

40   'And all the while a hanged man rings
        A cymbal with his hanging feet'

        Apollinaire, 'Crépuscule'/'Twilight', *Selected Writings* p. 61; 'Crépuscule', *Alcools*, in *Œuvres poétiques*, p. 64.

41 See Starobinski's discussion of Apollinaire's reading of these pictures by Picasso in *Portrait de l'artiste en saltimbanque*, pp. 117–27.

42 'Thrice-crowned harlequin.'

43   'The dwarf regards with sad demean
        The magic growth of thrice-crowned harlequin'

        Apollinaire, 'Crépuscule'/'Twilight', *Selected Writings*, p. 61; 'Crépuscule', *Alcools*, in *Œuvres poétiques*, p. 64.

44 'A blind one rocks a lovely child', Apollinaire, 'Crépuscule'/'Twilight', *Selected Writings*, p. 61; 'Crépuscule', *Alcools*, in *Œuvres poétiques*, p. 64.

45 'Looks at her body in the pool'.

46 'The ancient play of verse', Apollinaire, 'Les Fiançailles'/'The Betrothal', *Selected Writings* p. 69; 'Les Fiançailles', *Alcools*, in *Œuvres poétiques*, p. 132.

47 Wollheim, *Painting as an Art*, pp. 244–8.

48 See ibid., chapter 5, 'Painting, omnipotence, and the gaze: Ingres, The Wolf Man, Picasso'.

49 For an extended discussion of the part played by Apollinaire in developing artistic theory in the Parisian avant-garde before the First World War, and of the part such theory plays in the evolution of Apollinaire's own aesthetic, see my *Reading Apollinaire. Theories of Poetic Language* (Manchester: Manchester University Press, 1987).

50 Bryson, *Vision and Painting*, p. 93.

51   'The little saltimbanque turned a cartwheel
       With so much harmony
       That the organ stopped playing
       And the organist hid his face in his hands
       With fingers like descendants of his destiny
       Small foetuses which came out of his beard'

Apollinaire, 'Un Fantôme des nuées'/'Phantom of the Clouds', *Selected Writings*, p. 165; 'Un Fantôme des nuées', *Calligrammes*, in *Œuvres poétiques*, p. 195.

52   'But each spectator looked in himself for the miraculous child
       Century o century of clouds'

Apollinaire, 'Un Fantôme des nuées'/'Phantom of the Clouds', *Selected Writings*, p. 165; 'Un fantôme des nuées', *Calligrammes*, in *Œuvres poétiques*, p. 196.

2 Signs and the imaginary: the pleasures of discontent in Roland Barthes

1 'The image system, total assumption of the image, [. . .] is it not *epistemologically* a coming category?' Roland Barthes, *Roland Barthes*, trans. by Richard Howard (London: Macmillan, 1988 (1977)), p. 105; *Roland Barthes* (Paris: Editions du Seuil, 1975), p. 109.
2 'The semiologist is a man who expresses his future death in the very terms in which he has named and understood the world.' Roland Barthes, *The Fashion System*, trans. by Matthew Ward and Richard Howard (Berkeley and Los Angeles: University of California Press, 1990), p. 294; *Système de la mode* (Paris: Editions du Seuil, 1967), p. 292.
3 'This object in which power is inscribed, for all of human eternity, is language, or to be more precise, its necessary expression: the language we speak and write.' Roland Barthes, 'Inaugural Lecture, Collège de France', trans. by Richard Howard, *Roland Barthes: Selected Writings*, ed. with an introduction by Susan Sontag (London: Fontana/Collins, 1983), p. 460; *Leçon* (Paris: Editions du Seuil, 1978), p. 12.
4 'To speak, and, with even greater reason, to utter a discourse is not, as is too often repeated, to communicate; it is to subjugate'. Barthes, 'Inaugural Lecture, Collège de France', *Selected Writings*, p. 460; *Leçon*, p. 13.
5 'sleeps that monster: the stereotype', Barthes, 'Inaugural Lecture, Collège de France', *Selected Writings*, p. 461; *Leçon*, p. 15.
6 'a speech-system is defined less by what it permits us to say than by what it compels us to say', Barthes, 'Inaugural Lecture, Collège de France', *Selected Writings*, p. 460; *Leçon*, p. 12.
7 'Evidently he [Barthes] dreams of a world which would be *exempt from meaning* (as one is from military service). This began with *Writing Degree Zero*, in which is imagined "the absence of every sign".' Barthes, *Roland Barthes*, trans. Howard, p. 87; *Roland Barthes*, p. 90.
8 Michel Foucault, *Les Mots et les choses* (Paris: Gallimard, 1966), pp. 92–136.
9 See Annette Lavers, *Roland Barthes: Structuralism and After* (London: Methuen, 1982), part I.
10 Homi Bhabha, *The Location of Culture* (Routledge: London, 1994), p. 181.

11 'What happens when an object, whether real or imaginary, is converted into language?' Barthes, *The Fashion System*, p. 12; *Système de la mode*, p. 22.

12 'Clothing "in print" provides the analyst what human languages deny the linguist: a pure synchrony; the synchrony of fashion changes abruptly each year, but during the year it is absolutely stable.' Barthes, *The Fashion System*, p. 8; *Système de la mode*, p. 18.

13 'supervised freedom', Barthes, *The Fashion System*, p. 278; *Système de la mode*, p. 278, n. 1.

14 'Described clothing [. . .] is entirely meaning.' Barthes, *The Fashion System*, p. 18; *Système de la mode*, p. 28.

15 'the past is no longer eliminated, it is put to use', Barthes, *The Fashion System*, p. 291; *Système de la mode*, p. 291.

16 'prints win at the races', Barthes, *The Fashion System*, p. 34; *Système de la mode*, p. 45.

17 'Women will shorten skirts to the knee, adopt pastel checks, and wear two toned pumps.' Barthes, *The Fashion System*, p. 37: *Système de la mode*, p. 48.

18 'Fashion is a connoted value in set A and a denoted value in set B.' Barthes, *The Fashion System*, p. 39; *Système de la mode*, p. 49.

19 'refers to the system of a subject', Roland Barthes, *S/Z*, trans. Richard Miller (Oxford: Blackwell, 1990), p. 8; *S/Z* (Paris: Editions du Seuil, 1970), p. 14.

20 'connotation makes possible a (limited) dissemination of meanings, spread like gold dust on the apparent surface of the text', Barthes, *S/Z*, trans. Miller, pp. 8–9; Barthes, *S/Z*, p. 15.

21 'Such a difference comes down to this: that Fashion is a connoted value in set A and a denoted value in set B.' Barthes, *The Fashion System*, p. 39; *Système de la mode*, p. 49.

22 'At the level of code 2B, the meaning of Fashion does not come from a simple notation (the act of noting), but from vestimentary features themselves; more precisely the notation is immediately absorbed into the detail of the features, it cannot function as a signifier, and Fashion cannot escape its situation as an immediate signified.' Barthes, *The Fashion System*, p. 39; *Système de la mode*, p. 49.

23 'Fashion is an *arbitrary* value; in the case of set B, consequently, the general system turns out to be arbitrary, or, if one prefers, openly cultural.' Barthes, *The Fashion System*, p. 39; *Système de la mode*, p. 49.

24 'To describe "a halter top buttoned down the back", etc, is to establish a sign.' Barthes, *The Fashion System*, p. 39; *Système de la mode*, pp. 49–50.

25 'To describe "a halter top buttoned down the back", etc, is to establish a sign; to declare that "prints win at the races" is to mask the sign beneath the appearance of an affinity between the world and the garment, ie of a nature.' Barthes, *The Fashion System*, p. 39; *Système de la mode*, pp. 49–50.

26 'The mask of an inevitable nature', Barthes, *The Fashion System*, p. 283; *Système de la mode*, p. 283.

27 'The system breaks down when it opens itself up to the world through paths of connotation [set A]. The double system of Fashion (A and B) thus appears as a mirror in which modern man's *ethical* dilemma can be read: every system of signs is forced to load itself down, to convert and corrupt itself as soon as the world "fills" it: in order to open itself to the world, it must become alienated.' (My square brackets, my italics) Barthes, *The Fashion System*, p. 290; *Système de la mode*, p. 289.

28 'To identify accurately language's image-reservoirs, to wit: the word as singular unit, magic monad; speech as instrument or expression of thought', Roland Barthes, *The*

Pleasure of the Text, trans. Richard Miller (Oxford: Basil Blackwell, 1990), p. 33; *Le Plaisir du texte* (Paris: Editions du Seuil, 1973), p. 54.

29 Jacques Lacan, 'L'Agressivité en psychanalyse', *Ecrits* (Paris: Editions du Seuil, 1966), pp. 101–24.

30 'The image-system creeps in stealthily, gently skating over a verb tense, a pronoun, a memory, in short, everything that can be gathered together under the very device of the Mirror and of its Image: *Me, myself, I.'* Barthes, *Roland Barthes,* trans. Howard, p. 105; *Roland Barthes,* p. 109.

31 'The text is language without its image-reservoir, its image-system; it is *what the science of language lacks for its general importance* (and not for its technocratic specialization) *to be manifest.* All that is barely tolerated or bluntly rejected by linguistics (as canonical, positive science), significance, bliss – that is precisely what withdraws the text from the image-systems of language.' Barthes, *The Pleasure of the Text,* p. 33; *Le Plaisir du texte,* p. 55.

32 'With the writer of bliss (and his reader) begins the untenable text, the impossible text. The text is outside pleasure, outside criticism, *unless it is reached through another text of bliss:* you cannot speak "on" such a text, you can only speak "in" it, *in its fashion,* enter into a desperate plagiarism, hysterically affirm the void of bliss (and no longer obsessively repeat the letter of pleasure).' Barthes, *The Pleasure of the Text,* p. 22; *Le Plaisir du texte,* pp. 37–8.

33 For further discussion of the aspirations associated with the notion of play, see chapter 3.

34 An early application of the notion of intransitivity to writing is to be found in Roland Barthes, 'Ecrivains et écrivants', in *Essais critiques* (Paris: Editions du Seuil, 1964), pp. 147–54.

35 'The writerly text is *ourselves writing* [. . .]. The writerly is the novelistic without the novel, poetry without the poem, the essay without the dissertation, writing without style, production without product, structuration without structure.' Barthes, *S/Z,* trans. Miller, p. 5; *S/Z,* p. 11.

36 'Topologically, connotation makes possible a (limited) dissemination of meanings, spread like gold dust on the apparent surface of the text (meaning is golden). Semiologically, each connotation is the starting point of a code which will never be reconstituted, the articulation of a voice which is woven into the text.' Barthes, *S/Z,* trans. Miller, pp. 8–9; *S/Z,* p. 15.

37 'The Voice of Empirics (the proairetisms), the Voice of the Person (the semes), the Voice of Science (the cultural codes), the Voice of Truth (the hermeneutisms), the Voice of Symbol.' Barthes, *S/Z,* trans. Miller, p. 21; *S/Z,* p. 28.

38 'We are, in fact, concerned not to manifest a structure but to produce a structuration.' Barthes, *S/Z,* trans. Miller, p. 20; *S/Z,* p. 27.

39 'Identifying the symbolic and the hermeneutic, making the search for truth (hermeneutic structure) into the search for castration (symbolic structure), making the truth *anecdotally* (and no longer symbolically) the absent phallus.' Barthes, *S/Z,* trans. Miller, p. 164; *S/Z,* pp. 169–70.

40 '"illustrating" castration [symbolic] by being castrated [hermeneutic], like with like, [Sarrasine] mocks the notion of illustration, it abolishes both sides of the equivalence (letter and symbol) without advantage to either one; the latent here occupies the line

of the manifest from the start, *the sign is flattened out: there is no longer any "representa-tion".*'(My square brackets and italics.) Barthes, *S/Z*, trans. Miller, p. 164; *S/Z*, p. 170.

41 See chapter 1.

42 'Ideology: what is repeated and *consistent* (by this last adjective, it is excluded from the order of the signifier). So ideological analysis (or counter ideology) need merely be repeated and consistent (by proclaiming on the spot its validity, by a gesture of pure clearance) in order to become, itself, an ideological object. How to escape this?' Barthes, *Roland Barthes*, trans. Howard, p. 104; *Roland Barthes*, p. 108.

43 'and what if there were, as a second perversion, *a pleasure of ideology?*' Barthes, *Roland Barthes*, trans. Howard, p. 104; *Roland Barthes*, p. 108.

44 'The image-system, total assumption of the image exists in animals (though the sym-bolic does not), since they head straight for the trap, whether sexual or hostile, which is set for them. Does not this zoological horizon give the image-system a preponder-ance of interest? Is it not, *epistemologically,* a coming category?' Barthes, *Roland Barthes*, trans. Howard, p. 105; *Roland Barthes*, p. 109.

45 'Sign his image-system', Barthes, *Roland Barthes,* trans. Howard, p. 105; *Roland Barthes*, p. 109; see also *S/Z*, p. 27.

46 'the great narrative Other', Roland Barthes, *A Lover's Discourse: Fragments,* trans. Richard Howard (Harmondsworth: Penguin Books, 1990), p. 7; *Fragments d'un discours amoureux* (Paris: Editions du Seuil, 1977), p. 11.

47 Marguerite Duras, *La Vie matérielle* (Paris: POL, 1987), pp. 41–2.

48 'Let us begin again', Barthes, *A Lover's Discourse:* p. 24; *Fragments d'un discours*, p. 31.

49 ' "Let us imagine (if we can) a woman covered with an endless garment, itself woven of everything said in a fashion magazine . . . (*The Fashion System*)". This imagination, apparently methodical since it merely sets up an operative notion of semantic analy-sis ("the endless text"), actually (secretly) aims at denouncing the monster of Totality (Totality as monster).' Barthes, *Roland Barthes,* trans. Howard, pp. 179–80; *Roland Barthes*, p. 182.

50 Sigmund Freud, *Civilisation and its Discontents*, trans. from German by Angela Richards, in *Civilisation, Society and Religion,* Pelican Freud Library 12, (Harmondsworth: Penguin Books, 1985), p. 298.

51 Sigmund Freud, *Totem and Taboo* (London: Routledge, 1983).

52 'The vital effort of this book is to stage an image-system. "To stage" means: to arrange the flats one in front of the other, to distribute the roles, to establish levels, and, at the limit: to make the footlights a kind of uncertain barrier.' Barthes, *Roland Barthes,* trans. Howard, p. 105; *Roland Barthes*, p. 109.

53 'The difficulty, however, is that one cannot number these degrees, like the degrees of spirituous liquor or of a torture.' Barthes, *Roland Barthes,* trans. Howard, p. 105; *Roland Barthes*, p. 109.

54 'This is what could be done here for some of the fragments (*quotation marks, paren-theses, dictation, scene,* etc.); the subject, doubled (or *imagining himself* to be doubled), sometimes manages to sign his image-system.' Barthes, *Roland Barthes,* trans. Howard, p. 105; *Roland Barthes*, p. 109.

55 'a text with uncertain quotation marks', Barthes, *Roland Barthes,* trans. by Richard Howard, p. 106; *Roland Barthes*, p. 110.

56 'He is not very good at getting to the heart of things', Barthes, *Roland Barthes,* trans. Howard, p. 127; *Roland Barthes*, p. 131.

57 'Image-system of lucidity', Barthes, *Roland Barthes,* trans. Howard, p. 105; *Roland Barthes,* p. 109.

58 'The image-system creeps in stealthily, gently skating over a verb tense, a pronoun, a memory, in short, everything that can be gathered together under the very device of the Mirror and of its Image: *Me, myself, I.',* Barthes, *Roland Barthes,* trans. Howard, p. 105; *Roland Barthes,* p. 109.

59 'The desire of the other'. Also encompasses the meanings 'the desire for the other', ' the desire coming from the other' and '(the desire for) another's desire'.

60 '"I am nothing of what happens to me. You are nothing of value."' Jacques Lacan, 'Aggressivity in Psychoanalysis', *Ecrits: A Selection,* trans. by Alan Sheridan (London: Tavistock Publications, 1985 (1977)), p. 20; Jacques Lacan, 'L'Agressivité en psychanalyse', *Ecrits* (Paris: Editions du Seuil, 1966), p. 114. For *concurrence/concours,* see Sheridan p. 19; *Ecrits,* p. 113.

61 'Let me take Werther at that fictive moment (in the fiction itself) when he might have renounced suicide. Then the only thing left to him is exile: not to leave Charlotte (he has already done so once, with no result), but to exile himself from her image, or worse still: to cut off that raving energy known as the Image-repertoire. Then begins "a kind of long insomnia". That is the price to be paid: the death of the Image for my own life.' Barthes, *A Lover's Discourse,* p. 106; *Fragments d'un discours,* p. 123.

62 'Each time I unexpectedly glimpsed the other in his "structure" (*sistemato*), I was fascinated: I believed I was contemplating an *essence:* that of conjugality.' Barthes, *A Lover's Discourse,* p. 46; *Fragments d'un discours,* p. 56.

63 'No, what I fantasize in the system is quite modest (fantasy all the more paradoxical in that it has no particular vividness): I want, I desire, quite simply, a *structure* (this word, lately, produced a gritting of teeth: it was regarded as the acme of abstraction). Of course there is not a happiness of structure; but every structure is *habitable.'* Barthes, *A Lover's Discourse,* p. 46. *Fragments d'un discours,* p. 56.

64 'That is the price to be paid: the death of the Image for my own life.' Barthes, *A Lover's Discourse,* p. 106; *Fragments d'un discours,* p. 123.

65 '(Amorous passion is a delirium; but such delirium is not alien; everyone speaks of it, it is henceforth tamed. What is enigmatic is the *loss of delirium;* one returns to . . . what?)' Barthes, *A Lover's Discourse,* p. 106; *Fragments d'un discours,* p. 123.

66 '[. . .] for the Whole cannot be inventoried without being diminished: in *Adorable!* There is no residual quality, but only the *everything* of affect.' Barthes, *A Lover's Discourse,* p. 19; *Fragments d'un discours,* p. 26.

67 'Of this failure of language, there remains only one trace: the word "adorable" (the right translation of "adorable" would be that Latin *ipse:* it is the self, himself, herself, in person).' Barthes, *A Lover's Discourse,* p. 20; *Fragments d'un discours,* p. 27.

68 'What a shame!' Barthes, *A Lover's Discourse,* p. 108; *Fragments d'un discours,* p. 125.

69 '[. . .] in the same way, the loved being – if I sacrifice to that being an Image-repertoire which nonetheless importuned him – the loved being must enter into the melancholy of his own collapse. And concurrently with my own mourning, must anticipate and assume this melancholy on the part of the other, from which I shall suffer, *for I love the other still.'* Barthes, *A Lover's Discourse,* p. 108; *Fragments d'un discours,* p. 125.

70 'panic'. See Barthes, *Fragments d'un discours,* p. 125 and p. 115.

71 'To *destroy* would ultimately come to no more than reconstituting a site of speech whose one characteristic would be exteriority: exterior and motionless: in other

words, dogmatic language.' Barthes, *Roland Barthes*, trans. Howard, p. 63; *Roland Barthes*, p. 68.

72 'Whereas by decomposing, I agree to accompany such a decomposition, to decompose myself as well, in the process: I scrape, catch, and drag.' Barthes, *Roland Barthes*, trans. Howard, p. 63; *Roland Barthes*, p. 68.

3 Dreams, schemes and wordplay: the Surrealism of Robert Desnos

1 André Breton, *Nadja* (Paris: Gallimard, 1964 (1928)).

2 Robert Desnos, 'Confession d'un enfant du siècle', in *Nouvelles Hébrides et autres textes (1922–30)*, édition établie par Marie-Claire Dumas (Paris: Gallimard, 1978), pp. 236–41.

3 'Ultimately the lyrical approach dispenses with literature and signifies through itself alone; a continuity, in any case, is posited between man and work.' Michel Murat, *Robert Desnos: les grands jours du poète* (Paris: Editions José Corti, 1988), p. 109.

4 'Not only this unreserved language which I am attempting to make valid forever, which seems to me to mould itself to all the circumstances of life, not only does this language not deprive me of any of my faculties, but even gives me extraordinary lucidity even in that area where I expected to receive this the least from it.' André Breton, *Manifestes du Surrealisme* (Paris: Gallimard, 1975), p. 47.

5 'In automatic writing, it is not, strictly speaking, the word which becomes free, but the word and my freedom are now one. I slide into the word, it keeps my imprint and it is my imprinted reality; it adheres to my non-adherence.' Maurice Blanchot, *The Work of Fire*, trans. Charlotte Mandell (Stanford: Stanford University Press, 1995), p. 88; *La Part du feu* (Paris: Gallimard, 1949), p. 95.

6 'The signs are countless that this supreme effort by which man tries to turn round on himself and seize a gaze which is no longer his own, has always been the dream and the motivating force of Surrealism.' Blanchot, *The Work of Fire*, p. 93; *La Part du feu*, p. 100.

7 'I've got mine and it's all the same to me.' Arthur Rimbaud, 'Bad Blood', *A Season in Hell and Illuminations,* trans. Mark Treharne (London: J.M. Dent, 1998), p. 5; 'Mauvais Sang', *Une Saison en enfer*, in *Œuvres*, ed. Suzanne Bernard (Paris: Garnier, 1960), pp. 213–19.

8 Walter Benjamin, *One Way Street and Other Writings,* trans. Edmund Jephcott and Kingsley Shorter (London and New York: Verso, 1997 (1979)), p. 236.

9 Murat, *Robert Desnos: les grands jours du poète*, p. 114; Marie Claire Dumas, *Robert Desnos ou l'exploration des limites* (Paris: Klinksieck, 1980), p. 529.

10   *Infinitive*
      To die there oh lovely spark to die there
      to see clouds melting like snow and echo
      origins of the sun of white poor as Job's turkey
      not yet to die and see the shadow lasting still
      to be born with the fire and not to die
      to embrace and kiss fleeting love the unpolished sky
      to attain the heights and abandon ship
      and who knows discover what I love
      omit to transmit my name to future years

to laugh in the stormy hours to sleep at the foot of a pine
thanks to the stars like a spectacle
and to die what I love at the edge of flames.

Mary Ann Caws, *The Surrealist Voice of Robert Desnos* (Amherst, Mass.: University of Massachusetts, 1977), p. 163. This translation gives the sense of the poem and cannot therefore give the acrostic. Robert Desnos, *Corps et biens* (Paris: Gallimard, Collection Poésie, 1968), p. 108.

11 'magic alphabet'.

12 'mysterious hieroglyph'.

13 Gérard de Nerval, *Œuvres complètes*, texte établi par H. Lemaître (Paris: Gallimard, 1986), p. 790.

14 Ibid., p. 407.

15 Samuel Beckett, *Molloy* (Paris: Editions de Minuit, 1951), p. 23.

16 This poem is entirely resistant to translation. Desnos, *Corps et biens*, p. 77.

17 Jean-Paul Sartre, *L'Imaginaire* (Paris: Gallimard, Collection Idées, 1978 (1940) pp. 55–63.

18 'the world strictly intact', Jean-Paul Sartre, *What is Literature?*, trans. Bernard Frechtman (London: Methuen, 1950), p. 139; Jean-Paul Sartre, *Qu'est-ce que la littérature?* (Paris: Gallimard, Collection Folio, 1981 (1948)), p. 229.

19 Benjamin, *One Way Street and Other Writings*, p. 236.

20 'Negritude, triumph of narcissism and the suicide of Narcissus, tension of the soul beyond culture, words and all psychic facts, luminous night of non-knowing [. . .] this expansion of generosity is in its essence, Poetry.' Jean-Paul Sartre 'Orphée noir', in *Anthologie nouvelle de poésie nègre et malgache de la langue française,* ed. Léopold Sédar Senghor (Paris: Presses Universitaires de France, 1948), pp. xliii-iv. Sartre's essay is also reproduced in *Situations III* (Paris: Gallimard, 1949).

21 'Loser takes all', Sartre, *Qu'est-ce que la littérature?*, p. 47.

22 'The writer is a speaker; he designates, demonstrates, orders, refuses, interpolates, begs, insults, persuades, insinuates.' Sartre, *What is Literature?*, p. 10; *Qu'est-ce que la littérature?*, p. 47.

23 'the infinite disorder of matter'.

24 Jean-Paul Sartre, *L'Engagement de Mallarmé* (Paris: Gallimard, Collection Arcades, 1986), p. 91.

25 'the gurgling of Being', ibid., p. 95, p. 153.

26 'Futile effort to limit Being by Nothingness', ibid., p. 101.

27 Ibid., p. 96.

28 'without reality'.

29 'inactive'.

30 Sartre, *L'Imaginaire*, pp. 240–1.

31 Rhiannon Goldthorpe, *Sartre: Literature and Theory* (Cambridge: Cambridge University Press, 1984), pp. 139–42.

32 Sartre, *L'Engagement de Mallarmé*, p. 21.

33 'language is, in essence, prose and prose, in essence, failure', Sartre 'Orphée noir', p. xix.

34 'the present is what is, and its weight crushes us', Jean-Paul Sartre, *L'Etre et le néant,* (Paris: Editions Gallimard, 1943), p. 156.

35 'a remorse of the world', Sartre, *What is Literature?*, p. 24; *Qu'est-ce que la littérature?*, pp. 46–7.

36 'the doughy stuff of things', Sartre, *Qu'est-ce que la littérature?*, p. 72.

37 Sartre, *Qu'est-ce que la littérature?*, pp. 62–6.

38 'Poetry is a case of the loser winning [. . .] the poet [. . .] arranges to [. . .] bear witness, by his individual defeat, to human defeat in general.' Sartre, *What is Literature?*, pp. 47–8; *Qu'est-ce que la littérature?*, p. 47.

39 'we take stock of the mad attempt to name', Sartre 'Orphée noir', p. xix.

40 'incommunicability in its purest form', Sartre, *Qu'est-ce que la littérature?*, pp. 62–5.

41 'the sentence-thing, as inexhaustible as things', Sartre, *Qu'est-ce que la littérature?*, pp. 62–5.

42 'a destruction, an auto-da-fe of language', Sartre 'Orphée noir', p. xx.

43 'a tranquil fusion of oppositions', ibid., p. xx.

44 'to make silence out of language', ibid., p. xx.

45 'It is a matter of arousing *one* of the poles in the couple "black-white" like a sexual organ in its opposition to the other.' Ibid., pp. xxvi–vii.

46   *Sky Song*
     The flower of the Alps told the seashell: 'You're shining'
     The seashell told the sea: 'You echo'
     The sea told the boat: 'You're shuddering'
     The boat told the fire: 'You're glowing brightly'
     The fire told me: 'I glow less brightly than her eyes'
     The boat told me: 'I shudder less than your heart does when she appears'
     The sea told me: 'I echo less than her name in your love-making'
     The seashell told me: 'I shine less brightly than the phosphorous of desire in your
        hollow dream'
     The flower of the Alps told me: 'She's beautiful'
     I said: 'She's beautiful, so beautiful, she moves me.'

The Selected Poems of Robert Desnos, trans. Carolyn Forché and William Kulik (New York: The Echo Press, 1991). p. 26; Desnos, *Corps et biens*, p. 115.

47 'a narcissistic paste', Murat, *Robert Desnos: les grands jours du poète*, pp. 117–18.

48 'I who am Robert Desnos', Caws, *The Surrealist Voice of Robert Desnos*, p. 159.

49 'O form and name of my love', ibid. p. 159.

50 Murat, *Robert Desnos: les grands jours du poète*, p. 137.

51 'The Negro embitters, the Negresses become embittered or emaciated'. Translation is futile with this homonymic play of signifiers; signifieds include the negro, the negress, embitterdness, emaciatedness but all word-play is lost in translation. Jean-François Lyotard, *Les TRANSformateurs DUchamp* (Paris: Editions Galilée, 1977), pp. 13–30, p. 36, p. 37.

52 'dischronic' and 'auto-chronic' moments.

53 'by harnessing natural forces'.

54 'tricks this force and gives birth to a monstrosity: the least strong is stronger than the strongest', Lyotard, *Les TRANSformateurs DUchamp*, pp. 43–4.

55 'the "if . . . then" of implication which produces a link-up between different moments of thought', ibid., pp. 65–70.

56 'a habitable structure', Roland Barthes, *A Lover's Discourse: Fragments,* trans. Richard Howard (Harmondsworth: Penguin Books, 1990), pp. 45–7; *Fragments d'un discours amoureux* (Paris: Editions du Seuil, 1977), pp. 55–7.

57 Marie-Claire Dumas perceives a 'deceptive narrative' buried within 'Identités des images' as well as in other texts in 'Ténèbres'. Marie-Claire Dumas, *Robert Desnos ou l'exploration des limites* (Paris: Klinksieck, 1980), p. 527; Murat, *Robert Desnos: les grands jours du poète*, p. 39; André Breton, 'L'Entrée des médiums', *Les Pas perdus* (Paris: Gallimard, Collection Idées, 1979 (1924)), pp. 92–131.

58 'the temporal is an agile eagle in a temple', Desnos, 'Rrose Sélavy', *Corps et biens*, p. 35; see Dumas, *Robert Desnos ou l'exploration des limites*, p. 308.

59 Roland Barthes, *La Chambre claire* (Paris: Editions Gallimard/Seuil, 1980), p. 59.

60 'the entanglement of language and body', Roland Barthes, *Roland Barthes*, trans. Richard Howard (London: Macmillan, 1977), p. 91; *Roland Barthes* (Paris: Editions du Seuil, 1975), p. 95.

61 Guy Rosolato, *Essais sur le symbolique* (Paris: Gallimard, Collection Tel, 1969), pp. 31–5.

62 'What is utopia for?', Barthes, *Roland Barthes*, trans. Howard, pp. 76–7; *Roland Barthes*, pp. 80–1.

63 See the many references to 'affolement' and panic in Barthes *Fragments d'un discours* e.g. pp. 35, 97, 115, 125.

64 'structuring without structure', Roland Barthes, *S/Z* (Paris: Editions du Seuil, Points, 1970), p. 11.

65 'Every amorous episode can be, of course, endowed with a meaning: it is generated, develops and dies; it follows a path which it is always possible to interpret according to a causality or a finality . . .' Barthes, *A Lover's Discourse*, p. 7; *Fragments d'un discours*, p. 11.

66 This word cannot be directly translated but covers the qualities of fulfilment, of being overwhelmed, of orgasm etc. Barthes, *Fragments d'un discours*, pp. 65–7.

67 'the realm, the system of the Image-repertoire', Barthes, *A Lover's Discourse*, p. 54; Barthes, *Fragments d'un discours*, p. 65.

68 'too much'.

69 Arthur Rimbaud, *Une Saison en enfer*, in *Œuvres*, ed. Suzanne Bernard (Paris: Garnier, 1960).

70 'writerly'.

71 'readerly'.

72 'excess'.

73 'proportion'. The wordplay is lost in translation.

74 Barthes, *Fragments d'un discours*, pp. 65–7.

75 'the transport is the joy of which one cannot speak', Barthes, *A Lover's Discourse*, p. 55; *Fragments d'un discours*, p. 66

76 'I'm stuck on the Image', Barthes, *Fragments d'un discours*, p. 66.

77 'out-of-language'.

78 'extra-textual'.

79 Barthes, *Fragments d'un discours*, pp. 87–8.

80 Judith Butler, *Bodies That Matter: On the Discursive Limits of 'Sex'*, (New York: Routledge, 1993).

81 'I mauve, I chair down, already I'. Desnos, 'Idéal maîtresse', *Corps et biens*, p. 75.

82 'What, already I mirror. Mistress you black square and if the clouds of just now forget-me-not, they windmill in an eternity always present.' Caws, *The Surrealist Voice of Robert Desnos*, p. 67; Desnos, 'Idéal maîtresse', *Corps et biens*, p. 75.

4 Sterility and power: on some paintings by René Magritte

1   'the subject supposed to know'. See for example, Jacques Lacan, *Le Séminaire de Jacques Lacan,* book XI, *Les Quatres Concepts fondamentaux de la psychanalyse* (Paris: Editions du Seuil, 1973), chapter 18.

2   Magritte's titles in the 1940s were often arrived at in collaboration with Marcel Mariën. See Sarah Whitfield, *Magritte* (London: South Bank Centre, 1992), p. 32.

3   See ibid., p. 47.

4   'Magritte especially, I really hate that.' Robert Desnos, *Ecrits sur l'art*, préface de Marie-Claire Dumas (Paris: Flammarion, 1984), p. 181.

5   'an unbearable mystery of the world', Bernard Noël, *Magritte* (Paris: Flammarion, 1977), p. 91.

6   'And the unthought, once again, seeks the light of an image, and will yield to its opposite, only to escape it mysteriously. Everything which exists finds its form in the possibility of form itself, and is constituted by that. But for everything which exists to appear and to materialize, it must meet its resemblance in visible thought.' Ibid., p. 91.

7   'Having wanted to understand non-traditional painting, it is now acknowledged that it is not meant to be understood . . . the poetic image was imagined in response to the natural interest we feel towards the unknown, it directly evokes mystery which is a reality made in the irrational. Poetic images can be taken as such, as a whole, without diminishing the unknown they carry within them, for their reality is of the same kind as the reality of the universe.' René Magritte, *Ecrits complets*, édition établie et annotée par André Blavier (Paris: Flammarion, 1979), p. 674.

8   'Visible thought changes into itself the text of the world, and having done so is lost there.' Noël, *Magritte*, pp. 90–1.

9   Whitfield, *Magritte*, p. 136.

10   Ibid., comments to plate 72.

11   'a chance encounter'.

12   'chance'.

13   'objective'.

14   Whitfield, *Magritte*, comments to plate 148.

15   Ibid., comments to plate 36.

16   'the desire of the other'.

17   'fear'.

18   Whitfield, *Magritte*, comments to plate 36.

19   David Sylvester, *Magritte* (London: Thames and Hudson in association with Menil Foundation, 1992), p. 136.

20   Whitfield *Magritte*, note to plate 39.

21   The earlier version is reproduced in Sylvester, *Magritte*, p. 115.

22   Whitfield, *Magritte*, note to plate 41 and Sylvester, *Magritte*, pp. 19–20.

23   André Breton, *Les Vases communicants* (Paris: Gallimard, Collection Idées, 1981), pp. 148 52.

24   Michel Foucault, *Ceci n'est pas une pipe* (Montpelier: Fata Morgana, 1973).

25   Whitfield, *Magritte*, note to plate 39.

26   Ibid., note to plate 58.

27   Foucault, *Ceci n'est pas une pipe*, chapter 2.

28 'the sky is a form of curtain because it hides something from us. We are surrounded by curtains'. Whitfield, *Magritte*, comment to plate 120 and Magritte, *Ecrits complets*, Ecrit No. 185, p. 599.

29 Magritte, *Ecrits complets*, p. 596.

30 Roland Barthes, *Le Degré zéro de l'écriture* (Paris: Collection Points, Editions du Seuil, 1972 (1953)), p. 55.

31 Whitfield, *Magritte*, comments to plate 28.

32 Ibid., comments to plate 31.

33 'elective affinities', Sylvester, *Magritte*, p. 221.

34 'How can painting which is visible, possibly represent the invisible?' Magritte, *Ecrits complets*, p. 599.

35 Whitfield, *Magritte*, plate 167, fig. a.

36 Sylvester, *Magritte*, p. 288.

5 The offerings of decay: Jean Fautrier, *Les Otages*

1 'I'm not asking you whether you like it, or whether you think it's painting. You simply have to take note that painting has gone into an "abstract" stage, "without form", "non-figurative", call it what you will. And that's a solid piece of good fortune, because since Uccello gave painting its implements of visual illusion and since oil painting has bored us sightless with its many orchestrations, you must admit that painting would really be in a bad way since Ingres and Delacroix if Manet and photography had not come and saved us.

   But to approve of Manet, these days, is to subscribe to *l'informel*.'
   Jean Fautrier, *Ecrits publics*, préface de Castor Seibel (Paris: L'echoppe, 1995), p. 15.

2 Jacques Lacan, 'Tuché et Automaton', *Le Séminaire de Jacques Lacan*, book XI, *Les Quatre Concepts fondamentaux de la psychanalyse* (Paris: Editions de Seuil, 1973), pp. 53–65.

3 Lionel Trilling, *The Liberal Imagination: Essays on Literature and Society* (Oxford University Press: 1981 (1940)), pp. 85–6.

4 Ibid., p. 446.

5 Ibid., p. 435.

6 'How should we react when faced with the idea of the *Otages [Hostages]*. It could be said that this is one of the fundamental questions of our time.' Francis Ponge, 'Le Peintre à l'étude', in *Œuvres*, vol. 1 (Paris: Gallimard, 1965), p. 446.

7 'He transforms current human horror into beauty.' Ibid., p. 435.

8 See D. Hollier in Jacqueline Chénieux-Gendron (ed.), *Lire le regard: André Breton et la peinture* (Arles: Lachenal et Ritter, 1993), pp. 29–57.

9 'The doughy stuff of things', Jean-Paul Sartre, *Qu'est-ce que la littérature?* (Paris: Gallimard, Collection Folio, 1981 (1948)), p. 72.

10 Jacques Lacan, 'L'agressivité en psychanalyse', *Ecrits* (Paris: Editions du Seuil, 1966), pp. 101–25.

11 Sartre investigates both trajectories, seeking also to reconcile the Marxist narration of history with the existential collapse of narrative in *Critique de la raison dialectique*, vol. 1: *Théorie des ensembles pratiques* (Paris: Gallimard, 1960); vol. 2: *L'Intelligibilité de l'histoire* (Paris: Gallimard, 1985).

12 'to look at an object is to come and inhabit it and from there grasp everything

according to the side which faces us', Jean Paris in Bernard Ceysson, 'L'Ecriture griffée ou peindre le réel réalisé' in *L'Ecriture griffée,* ed. Jacques Dessagne, Catalogue de l'exposition du Musée d'art Moderne de Saint Etienne (1993), p. 16.

13 'a becoming-mask of a paternal portrait', Georges Didi-Huberman in ibid., p. 16.

14 'Derealising', Jean-Paul Sartre, *L'Imaginaire* (Paris: Gallimard, 1940).

15 Jean-Paul Sartre, '*La Recherche de l'absolu',* *Situations III* (Paris: Gallimard, 1949).

16 In *L'Engagement de Mallarmé,* much later in the development of his thought on poetry, Sartre carries forward the remnants of this heroic account of Poetry as Passion from within a luxuriant, quasi-Marxist critique of French poetic anxiety from Musset through to the Parnasse and on to Mallarmé.

17 'to make silence out of language', Jean-Paul Sartre, 'Orphée noir', in Léopold Sédar Senghor, *Anthologie nouvelle de poésie nègre et malgache de la langue française* (Paris: Presses Universitaires de France, 1969), p. xx.

18 Paulhan's description of the process. Jean Paulhan, *Fautrier l'enragé* (Paris: Gallimard, 1989 (1962)).

19 'There is no individual who is not a transitory particle of the biological universe and yet an entire world to himself and herself. There is no carnal presence which does not appear as already eaten away by future absence. There is no man or woman whose future is not, whether or not they are clearly aware of it, a marriage between heaven and hell. For those who apply it to human beings and take it to the extreme, can realism lead to anything but tragedy?' Michel Leiris, *Au verso des images* (Montpelier: Fata Morgana, 1980), p. 21.

20 Yves Peyré, *Fautrier, ou les outrages de l'impossible* (Paris: Editions du Regard, 1990), p. 190.

21 For colour reproduction, see ibid., p. 235.

22 Ponge suggests that photographic images would better suit sado-masochistic intentions in relation to this subject-matter. Ponge, 'Le Peintre à l'étude', p. 434.

23 Peyré, *Fautrier, ou les outrages de l'impossible.*

24 'It has been said, rightly, that each colour carries its own tonality and its own feeling. But Fautrier knows how to change the meaning of colours. He uses them as he pleases and from the first stroke astounds us.' Paulhan, *Fautrier l'enragé*, p. 17.

25 'Perhaps it was possible, earlier, to recognise, here and there, traces of the passage of mystery into a duplicity slipping imperceptibly from the subject of the painting to the painting itself; in those colours, perhaps the meaning of which is transformed in our eyes; in discrepancies between drawing and nuance, and between the material and the object, at times rapid ones, at times ones that remain suspended; and right into the ambiguous emotion with which a strange yet brilliant work leaves us; beautiful, not without horror.' Ibid., pp. 50–1.

26 'But here it is important to think of what I mean by colour (and which drawing is not): of what is more intimate about it – more strictly human – than lines, angles and spirals.' Ibid., p. 51.

27 'Inscribing in stone is like inscribing on [a] memory.' Ponge, 'Matière et mémoire', in *Œuvres*, vol. 1, p. 473.

28 'It would be an understatement to say that I am unsure of the pages which follow: these are some strange texts, violent and clumsy. Confident words will miss the mark.' Ponge, 'Le Peintre à l'étude', p. 427.

29 'But suppose that *atrocity itself* were the subject . . .', ibid., p. 427.

30 Ibid., p. 453.

31 'Their bodies will grow old in their chains, turn to ruin, then decompose.' Ibid., p. 430.

32 'the rage of expression (from a tube of colour)', ibid., p. 455.

33 'a soul which we don't need to bother about, which goes without saying', ibid., p. 454.

34 See chapter 2, pp. 58–9.

35 'The relation between imaginary and symbolic identification – between the ideal ego [*Idealich*] and the ego-ideal [*Ich-Ideal*] – is [. . .] that between "constituted" and "constitutive" identification. To put it simply, imaginary identification is the identification with the image in which we appear likeable to ourselves, with the image representing "what we would like to be", and symbolic identification, identification with the very place from where we are being observed, from where we look at ourselves so that we appear to ourselves likeable, worthy of love.' Slavoj Žižek, *The Sublime Object of Ideology* (London: Verso, 1989), p. 105; quoted in Adam Bresnick, 'Absolute fetishism: genius and identification in Balzac's "Unknown Masterpiece"', *Paragraph*, 17, 2 (July 1994), 134–52 (p. 147), a fascinating article in which the author deconstructs the dialogue of imaginary and symbolic identification in the context of Balzac's story, and describes the 'dénouement' as an 'unravelling of the plot's complications and of the artistic subject itself'.

36 Roland Barthes, *Roland Barthes* (Paris: Editions du Seuil, 1975), p. 68; see chapter 2, p. 64.

37 Rifatterre, in *Lire le regard*, argues provocatively that in the case of Breton's writing, intertextuality favours, rather than undermines, the privileging of subjectivity. Chénieux-Gendron, ed., *Lire le regard: André Breton et la peinture*.

38 'It is as though Fautrier had arrived at the side of himself that deals with excrement, and had remained there, handling small or large piles of whitish mortar (as a result of manic attachment to expression from a tube of colour, to an expulsion of colour from the tube) – with the need to cover over, to hide, to bless these excrements with a few quick strokes of ash or of dust. To cover over colour, and matter with a kind of drawing that conceals this trace. To bury the trace. So that we lose the trail. So that we do not pick up the scent too easily. And so sometimes it is knives or fish or faces. According to what he ate? Or according to his drawing, according to the sign whose excrement he re-covers manically, always the same excrement (the thickness and presence of which has to remain palpable).' Ponge, 'Le Peintre à l'étude', pp. 462–3.

39 'The reader will have concluded [. . .] that I have spoken for too long and said nothing', Jacques Derrida, *Signéponge* (Paris: Editions du Seuil, 1988), p. 115.

40 'paint anything'.

41 For colour reproduction, see Peyré, *Fautrier ou les outrages de l'impossible*, p. 164.

42 For colour reproduction, see ibid., p. 176.

43 For colour reproduction, see ibid., p. 179.

44 Not reproduced here. For colour reproduction, see ibid., p. 177.

45 See chapter 2.

46 For colour reproduction, see Peyré, *Fautrier ou les outrages de l'impossible*, p. 175.

47 For colour reproduction, see ibid., p. 49. Also known as *Le Canard*.

48 For colour reproduction, see ibid., p. 309.

49 For colour reproduction, see ibid., p. 191.

6 Clothed intimacy: theatre and sex in Marguerite Duras, *Les Yeux bleus cheveux noirs*

1 'says the actor', Marguerite Duras, *Blue Eyes, Black Hair*, trans. Barbara Bray (London: HarperCollins, 1988), p. 1; *Les Yeux bleus cheveux noirs* (Paris: Editions de Minuit, 1986), p. 9.

2 'A summer evening, says the actor, seems to be at the heart of the affair.' Duras, *Blue Eyes, Black Hair*, p. 1; *Les Yeux bleus cheveux noirs*, p. 9.

3 'is not forthcoming', Duras, *Blue Eyes, Black Hair*, p. 3; *Les Yeux bleus cheveux noirs*, p. 11.

4 *Les Yeux bleus cheveux noirs*, pp. 50–3.

5 'It's in my contract: stay or go it's all the same', Duras, *Blue Eyes, Black Hair*, p. 35; *Les Yeux bleus cheveux noirs*, p. 50.

6 'harsh and steady light', Duras, *Blue Eyes, Black Hair*, p. 35; *Les Yeux bleus cheveux noirs*, p. 50.

7 'a common place', Duras, *Blue Eyes, Black Hair*, p. 36; *Les Yeux bleus cheveux noirs*, p. 51.

8 'She tells him to come to her. "Come." She says it's velvet, vertiginous, but also, make no mistake, a wilderness, something bad that also leads to murder and madness.' Duras, *Blue Eyes, Black Hair*, pp. 35–6; *Les Yeux bleus cheveux noirs*, p. 51.

9 'She asks him to come and see, says it's something horrible, criminal, like murky water, dirty, bloody. She says that one day he'll have to, even if only once, have to rummage in that common place; he won't be able to avoid it all his life. Sooner or later – what's the difference?' Duras, *Blue Eyes, Black Hair*, p. 36; *Les Yeux bleus cheveux noirs*, p. 51.

10 'the black silk', Duras, *Blue Eyes, Black Hair*, p. 36; *Les Yeux bleus cheveux noirs*, p. 51.

11 'He weeps. She goes back by the wall. She leaves him to himself. Puts the black silk on and looks at him through it.' Duras, *Blue Eyes, Black Hair*, p. 36; *Les Yeux bleus cheveux noirs*, p. 51.

12 'He watches her depart, drift off into the forgetfulness of the room, of himself, the story. Of all stories.' Duras, *Les Yeux bleus cheveux noirs*, p. 52.

13 'That night she calls out again, again that same word; wounded, hurt, what does it mean, perhaps a name belonging to someone she never mentions. A name like a sound at once somber and frail, a sort of moan.' Duras, *Blue Eyes, Black Hair*, p. 37; *Les Yeux bleus cheveux noirs*, p. 52.

14 'sound, name'.

15 '"I must tell you, it's as if you were responsible for the thing inside you, that you know nothing of and that appalls me because it seizes other things and changes them within itself without showing signs of doing it."

   She wasn't asleep.

   She says: "It's true I'm responsible for the astral nature of my sex, its lunar and bloody rhythm. In relation to you as to the sea."' Duras, *Blue Eyes, Black Hair*, p. 37; *Les Yeux bleus cheveux noirs*, p. 52.

16 'They draw close, almost close enough to touch. They go back to sleep.' Duras, *Blue Eyes, Black Hair*, p. 37; *Les Yeux bleus cheveux noirs*, p. 53.

17 Julia Kristeva, *Soleil noir* (Paris: Gallimard, 1987).

18 'responsible'.

19 'grief'.

20 'suffering'.

21 'madness'.

22 'sickness'.

23 '[Duras] leads us to X-ray our madnesses, the dangerous edges where the confluence of meaning, personality and life collapses.' Julia Kristeva, 'The Malady of Grief', in *Black Sun*, trans. Leon S. Roudiez (New York: Columbia University Press, 1989), p. 228; Julia Kristeva, *Soleil noir*, p. 236.

24 'We now understand why Duras's books should not be put into the hands of over-sensitive readers. [. . .] Her books [. . .] bring us to the verge of madness. They do not point to it from afar, they neither observe it nor analyse it so as to suffer from it at a distance in the hope of a solution, like it or not, some day or other. Quite the reverse, the texts domesticate the malady of death. [. . .] There is no purification in store for us at the conclusion of these novels [. . .].';'[. . .] identities, bonds and feelings are ruined.' Kristeva, 'The Malady of Grief', in *Black Sun*, pp. 227–8 and p. 257; *Soleil noir*, p. 235 and p. 263.

25 'Would suffering enamoured of death be the supreme individuation?' Kristeva, 'The Malady of Grief', in *Black Sun*, p. 237; *Soleil noir*, p. 245.

26 Marguerite Duras, *La Douleur* (Paris: Gallimard, Collection Folio, 1992).

27 Marguerite Duras, *Hiroshima mon amour* (Paris: Gallimard, Collection Folio, 1972).

28 Kristeva, *Soleil noir*, p. 241.

29 'sovereignty'.

30 'Politics is not, as it is for Hannah Arendt, the field where human freedom is developed. The modern world, the world of wars, the Third World, the underground world of death that acts upon us, do not have the splendid polis of the Greek city state. The modern political domain is massively and, in totalitarian fashion, social, leveling, killing.' Kristeva, 'The Malady of Grief', in *Black Sun*, p. 235; *Soleil noir*, p. 242.

31 Marguerite Duras, *L'Amant* (Paris: Editions de Minuit, 1984).

32 *Duras by Duras* (San Francisco: City Lights Books, 1987), p. 131 (originally published Paris: Albatros, 1976).

33 'Hiroshima happened. It cannot be approached with artifice. Neither tragic nor pacifist artifice to face the atomic explosion nor rhetorical artifice to face the mutilation of our feelings. "The only thing to do is speak of the impossibility of speaking of Hiroshima. The knowledge of Hiroshima is set, a priori, an exemplary delusion of the mind.' Kristeva, 'The Malady of Grief', in *Black Sun*, p. 231; *Soleil noir*, p. 238.

34 'Such a madness, bruised and deadly, might be no more than Her absorption of His death.' Kristeva, 'The Malady of Grief', in *Black Sun*, p. 233; *Soleil noir*, p. 241.

35 'make silence out of language', Jean-Paul Sartre, 'Orphée noir', in Léopold Sédar Senghor, *Anthologie nouvelle de poésie nègre et malgache de la langue française* (Paris: Presses Universitaires de France, 1969), p. xx.

36 'stylistic awkwardness', Kristeva, 'The Malady of Grief', in *Black Sun*, p. 226; *Soleil noir*, p. 234.

37 'a collapsing speech'.

38 'as without make-up or undressed without being disheveled', Kristeva, *Soleil noir*, p. 234.

39 Roland Barthes, *Fragments d'un discours amoureux* (Paris: Editions du Seuil, 1977), pp. 29–31.

40 'I've got mine', Arthur Rimbaud, 'Bad Blood', *A Season in Hell and Illuminations*, trans. Mark Treharne (London: J. M. Dent, 1998), p. 5; 'Mauvais Sang', *Une saison en enfer*, in *Œuvres*, ed. Suzanne Bernard (Paris: Editions Garnier, 1960), pp. 213–19.

41 'Blackout in the auditorium. The play would begin.' Duras, *Les Yeux bleus cheveux noirs*, p. 21.

42 'smell of sex'.

7 'Des milliers de Parisiens': conflict, community and collapse in Jean Genet, *Les Paravents*

1 'Not all the living, nor all the dead, nor the generations yet unborn will be able to see *The Screens.* Humanity as a whole will be deprived of it: there you have something which comes close to being an absolute. The world has managed to get along without them; it will continue to do so. Political nonchalance will allow a chance set of meetings between a few thousand Parisians and the play. In order for this event – the performance, or performances – without disturbing the order of the world, to impose thereon a poetic combustion, acting on a few thousand Parisians, I should like it to be so strong and so dense that it will, by its implications and ramifications, illuminate the world of the dead (or, more properly, of death) – billions and billions – and that of generations yet unborn (but this is less important?).' Jean Genet, *Reflections on the Theatre and Other Writings*, trans. Richard Seaver (London: Faber and Faber, 1972), p.11; Jean Genet, 'Lettres à Roger Blin', in *Oeuvres complètes,* vol. 4 (Paris: Gallimard, 1968), p. 221.

2 Jean-Paul Sartre, *Qu'est-ce que la littérature?* (Paris: Gallimard, 1981 (1948)).

3 Jacques Derrida, *Donner le temps 1, La Fausse Monnaie* (Paris: Galilée, 1991).

4 'Flights or thefts of language', Roland Barthes, *Roland Barthes* (Paris: Editions du Seuil, 1975), p. 142.

5 'death' turned into 'the dead'.

6 'You gave me mud and I turned it into gold', Charles Baudelaire, *Les Fleurs du mal*, 'Projets d'un épilogue pour l'édition de 1861', *Œuvres complètes*, ed. Claude Pichois (Paris: Gallimard, Editions de la Pléïade, 1975), p. 192.

7 Guy Rosolato, *Essais sur le symbolique* (Paris: Gallimard, Collection Tel, 1969), pp. 11–36.

8 'Since I is Other', Arthur Rimbaud, 'Lettre à Paul Demeny 1871', *Œuvres*, ed. Suzanne Bernard (Paris: Editions Garnier, 1960), p. 345.

9 'Coarse-grained truths', Arthur Rimbaud, 'Adieu', *A Season in Hell and Illuminations,* trans. by Mark Treharne (London: J.M. Dent, 1998), p. 53; 'Adieu', *Une Saison en enfer*, in *Œuvres*, p. 241.

10 'Let us learn [. . .] to hail him and to see him, and to dismiss him, and, beneath the tides and high in the deserts of snow, to follow his vision, his breathing, his body, his light.' Rimbaud, 'Génie', *A Season in Hell and Illuminations*, p. 155; 'Génie', *Illuminations*, in *Œuvres*, p. 309.

11 Julia Kristeva, 'Approche de l'abjection', in *Pouvoirs de l'horreur, essais sur l'abjection* (Paris: Editions du Seuil, 1980), pp. 7–40.

12 'As a result of what developments have the words tradition and treason, if they do have the same origin, come to signify such different or such fundamentally – I mean

radically – similar ideas? [. . .] This is what the director should be keeping in mind.'
Jean Genet, *Les Paravents* (Paris: Folio, Marc Barbezat, L'Arbalète, 1985 (1961)), p. 192.

13 'tradition/treason'.

14 'was written to show the degradation of this family', Genet, *Les Paravents*, p. 104.

15 'If I'd asked the dogs – you hear me – the dogs in your belly that are ready to bite us, they'd have answered no! The dogs, the mares, the chickens, the ducks, the broom, the ball of wool would have said no!' Jean Genet, *The Screens*, trans. Bernard Frechtman (London: Faber and Faber, 1963), p. 39; *Les Paravents*, p. 67.

16 'The dead, to be sure, are the last resort. The living spit in your face, but the dead envelop you in their big black or white wings. And protected by the wings, you could flout those who go afoot? But those who walk the earth will be in it before long. They're the same . . .' Genet, *The Screens*, p. 52; *Les Paravents*, p. 89.

17 'Whatever the dramatic intensity one wishes to give to this scene, the actresses should play it in a farcical manner: I mean that despite the seriousness of the curses pronounced by the women or by the Mother, the public should know that it is some kind of game.' Genet, *Les Paravents*, p. 71.

18 'game', but also 'style of feeling'.

19 'But the reader of these notes should not forget that the theatre where this play is being performed is built in a cemetery, that at this moment it is night-time and that, somewhere, perhaps a body is being dug up and buried elsewhere.' Genet, *Les Paravents*, p. 94.

20 'WARDA: (*haughtily, same drawling, disillusioned voice*): Twenty-four years! A whore is not something you can improvise. She has to ripen. It took me twenty-four years. And I'm gifted! A man, what's that? A man remains a man. In our presence, it is the man who strips like a whore from Toul or Nancy.' Genet, *The Screens*, p. 18; *Les Paravents*, p. 30.

21 'WARDA: (*irritated and in a sharper tone):* What she says is for the joy of saying it, the delights of conversation, because if we had the misfortune to take the country's misfortunes seriously, then farewell to our misfortune and farewell to your pleasures.' Genet, *The Screens*, p. 19; *Les Paravents*, p. 31.

22 'A real whore should be able to attract by what she's reduced to being. I worked for years making my hat-pin into a toothpick. My style!!' Genet, *The Screens*, p. 19; *Les Paravents*, p. 33.

23 'Attention!'.

24 'the desire of the other'. Also encompasses the meanings 'desire for the other', 'desire coming from the other' and '(the desire for) another's desire'.

25 See chapter 1.

26 'There are no waiters in the army. (*He turns towards the wing.*) Let every man be a mirror to every other man. Two legs must look at themselves and see themselves in the pair opposite, a torso in the torso opposite, the mouth in another mouth, the eyes in the eyes, the nose in the nose, the teeth in the teeth, the knees in the knees, a curl in . . . another curl, or, if the hair opposite is stiff, in a spit-curl . . . (*Very lyrically*) Look at oneself there and see oneself there supremely handsome . . . (*He about-faces in military fashion and speaks, facing the audience*) . . . utterly seductive.' Genet, *The Screens*, p. 107; *Les Paravents*, p. 182.

27 'It is not a matter of intelligence, but of perpetuating an image that is more than six

centuries old, that grows stronger as what it is supposed to represent crumbles, that leads you all, as you know, to your deaths.' Genet, *The Screens*, p. 106; *Les Paravents*, p. 181.

28 See chapter 1.

29 'Comb your hair *(Felton takes a comb from his inside pocket and combs his hair)* It's not a matter of returning victoriously. What would be the point? *(While he talks, the others all busy themselves, so that* THE LIEUTENANT *seems to be speaking in a void, with a fixed gaze.* PIERRE *ties his boot laces,* MORALES *shaves,* FELTON *combs his hair,* HELMUT *cleans his bayonet,* THE SERGEANT *files his nails)* . . . France has dread, war, she has offered an indelible image. Therefore, not conquer but die. Or half-die, that is, return with a limp, armless, legless, broken and bent, balls torn off, noses eaten away, faces blasted . . . That's very fine too. Painful, but very fine. In the image of its rotting warriors France will be able to watch itself rot . . . But conquer? . . . And conquer what? Or whom? You've seen them dragging themselves through the mud, living on peelings . . . conquer that! *(Shrugging his shoulders and palms outstretched, the gesture of a Levantine merchant.)* Conquer, that's all right for them. *(In the direction of* THE SERGEANT.) Isn't that so? *(to Felton:)* Kepi further over your eye.' Genet, *The Screens*, p. 105; *Les Paravents*, pp. 179–80.

30 Sigmund Freud, *Civilisation and its Discontents*, trans. from German by Angela Richards, in *Civilisation, Society and Religion*, Pelican Freud Library 12 (Harmondsworth: Penguin Books, 1985).

31 'I'll have talked a lot of crap.'

32 Genet, *Les Paravents*, tenth tableau.

33 Albert Camus, *L'Etranger* (Paris: Gallimard, Collection Folio, 1972 (1942)).

34 'She is right, Warda: to whom should we offer our lives and our progress in our art, if not to God? Just like the cops, in the end. We perfect ourselves for God.' Genet, *Les Paravents*, p. 35.

35 Arthur Rimbaud, 'Alchimie du verbe', *Une Saison en enfer*, in *Œuvres*, pp. 228–34.

36 Leo Bersani, *The Culture of Redemption* (Cambridge, Mass.: Harvard University Press, 1992).

37 Rhiannon Goldthorpe, *Sartre: Literature and Theory* (Cambridge: Cambridge University Press, 1984).

38 Jean-Paul Sartre, *L'Engagement de Mallarmé* (Paris: Gallimard, Collection Arcades, 1986).

39 'Without woman what would you be? A spot of sperm on your father's trousers that three flies would have drunk up . . . This is my day! They accuse us and threaten us, and you want us to be prudent. And docile. And humble. And submissive. And ladylike. And honey-tongued. And sweet as pie. And silk-veil. And fine-cigarette. And nice kiss and soft-spoken. And gentle dust on their red pumps!' Genet, *The Screens*, p. 81; *Les Paravents* pp. 143–4.

40 'the first-communion girl'.

41 'I, too, have a word to say. I've kept a piece of holy bread in my alms-purse. I want to feed it to the birds of the desert, the poor dears.' Genet, *The Screens*, p. 84; *Les Paravents*, p. 148.

42 André Breton, *L'Amour fou* (Paris: Gallimard, Collection Folio, 1997 (1937)), p. 26.

43 'a little terrifying'.

44 'the medals are highly visible'.

45 'The actors, to play, – but what I am writing applies to the whole play – should try to go into themselves, to be "absent from the theatre" just as one is absent from the world. I think, finally, that it is the absence of brightness in their looks which will make the audience aware of this concentration within themselves and which I'm relying on. More than anywhere else, in this scene [scene nine], the actors should not play with the public. But throughout the play "their absence from the theatre" should be palpable to the audience, almost offensive.' Genet, *Les Paravents*, pp. 104–5.

46 'I am dead? So I am. Well, not yet! I haven't finished my job. So, Death, It's you and me now! Saïd, Leila, my loved ones! You, too, of an evening would chat about the evil of the day. You realised that in evil lies the only hope. Evil, wonderful evil, that remains when everything buggers off, miraculous evil, you're going to help us now. I beg of you, evil, and I beg you standing on my two feet, impregnate my people. And let them not be idle!' Genet, *The Screens*, p. 86; *Les Paravents*, p. 154.

47 'Lay me out and wash me properly. Without any silly chatter. No, don't chase the flies away. I already know them all by name.' Genet, *The Screens*, p. 94; *Les Paravents*, p. 161.

48 'KADIDJA: Kaddur! What have you done for evil to prevail? *(In the scene that follows, dialogue and gestures will be very rapid: almost like an organised scramble.)*

KADDUR: *(in a hollow but proud tone)*: Their muzzles are still hot – put your hand on them – look: I picked up two revolvers.

KADIDJA: *(curtly)* Set them down there! . . . Smoking barrels. Fierce and grinning . . . *Kaddur very quickly draws the revolvers on the screen with a charcoal pencil. Then he goes to the* LEFT *side of the stage. The drawings should represent the objects in monstrously enlarged forms.*' Genet, *The Screens*, p. 87; *Les Paravents*, p. 154.

49 'Two blue eyes for the young lady. Under the orange trees, raped one of their girls, I bring you the bloodstain.

(He draws the bloodstain, in red, on the screen and exits. The Arabs now enter at a more rapid rate. They wait at the RIGHT, *eager to appear.)*

KADIDJA: *(severely)*: That's your pleasure and hers. But what about the crime that serves us?' Genet, *The Screens*, p. 87; *Les Paravents*, p. 154.

50 'sign the imaginary/to put one's name to one's imaginary', Barthes, *Roland Barthes*, p. 109. See chapter 2.

51 'to go to the limit', Genet, *The Screens*, p. 101; *Les Paravents*, p. 174.

52 'your jitters', Genet, *The Screens*, p. 89; *Les Paravents*, p. 157.

53 'My cruelty, my hypocritical nastiness that I have kept, hidden in the hand behind my back, to wound the whole world.' Genet, *The Screens*, p. 100; *Les Paravents*, pp. 173–4.

54 'Luckily we've got *you*, so that there are smaller people than us, but if they make us call you miss and madame, we'll soon be smaller than you.' Genet, *The Screens*, p. 58; *Les Paravents*, p. 99.

55 'From time to time you can forget the miss and madame and just call us "you there".' Genet, *The Screens*, p. 58; *Les Paravents*, p. 99.

56 'THE GENDARME: And you prefer that don't you? "You there" is more intimate than miss and madame, it protects you better than miss and madame. Though "you there" protects you, you like miss and madame from time to time, I can see that.

THE MOTHER: A little miss and madame, say one day out of four, and "you there" the rest of the time.

THE GENDARME: That's my view. "You there" as a basis, and the miss and madame coming in bit by bit. To get you used to it. We both gain by that. But if I suddenly say madame, who do I say "you there" to? Between us, "you there" is friendly, the "you there" that comes from us to all of you is more limp.

THE MOTHER: Right. Madame's too-too. "You there"'s woo-woo.'

Genet, *The Screens*, p. 58. The wordplay in this interchange is rendered differently in translation; *Les Paravents*, p. 99.

57 'Moslem women! I know your tricks all right! One day – ah! Brittany, the fun you can have there! – one carnival day with a sheet and a rag I disguised myself as an Arab woman, a Fatima. All at once, and straight off, I grasped your mentality. Caught it all in a sudden vision. And if circumstances force me, in spite of my wound and my two daughters, I'll take the veil again.' Genet, *The Screens*, p. 58; *Les Paravents*, p. 103.

58 'He rolls himself up in the blanket [. . .] walking backwards he crosses the stage diagonally and exits far right.' Genet, *The Screens*, p. 61; *Les Paravents*, p. 103.

59 Stendhal, *La Chartreuse de Parme* (Paris: Gallimard, 1972 (1839)).

60 'LEILA *(in a very gentle voice)* . . . . if you had walked fast, and bent forward, and especially if your jacket had been unbuttoned, nobody would have noticed the cans of food bulging under your shirt.

SAÏD: (Same tone): If you're right, it's even worse, you're showing me how to escape now that it's too late. You should have told me before . . .

LEILA: I was already in jail. Locked up in this cell. I couldn't advise you any more.

SAÏD: I don't want advice, but you can guide, you are invisible and far away, behind walls . . . walls that are thick . . . and white . . . *(A pause)* [. . .] Where do *you* stink most?

LEILA *(in ecstasy)*: Oh me! Who isn't thunderstruck at my approach? When I'm there, the night falls back.

SAÏD: In confusion?

LEILA: It gets smaller . . . smaller . . . smaller.'

Genet, *The Screens*, pp. 70–1; *Les Paravents*, pp. 121–2.

61 'A VOICE: *(very loudly, off stage)*: As soon as the hosts and the Latin have been gulped down . . . have coffee served, piping hot.' Genet, *The Screens*, p. 71; *Les Paravents*, p. 122.

62 'THE VOICE [OF THE CONDEMNED MAN] *(very manly and decided)*: No. If it were to do over again, I'd approach from the front, smiling, and I'd offer her an artificial flower, the kind she liked. A violet satin iris. She used to thank me for them. Not even the blond dolls, like those in the movies, would have listened to the kind of crap I dished out, and with a winning smile. Only . . . after my speech, and when she had smelled the rose and stuck it in her grey hair, I'd have . . . *(The Voice gradually becomes exultant; towards the end it chants and sings.)* . . . delicately opened her belly, I'd have lifted up the curtains of her petticoats to watch the guts flow and I'd have toyed with them as fingers toy with jewels. And my look would have conveyed my joy to the horrified eyes of my mother.' Genet, *The Screens*, pp. 75–6; *Les Paravents*, pp. 129–30.

63 *Sleeping Beauty*.

64 'THE GUARD *(roughly)*: To the point where he *must* sing. And you beginners, shut up!' Genet, *The Screens*, p. 76; *Les Paravents*, p. 130.

65 'The cadi' – Moslem judge dealing with judicial, civil and religious affairs.

66 'God has buggered off. If you want to be judged by him – with a remnant of kindness – help me. Tell me what judgement you want, but tell me fast. [. . .] God has taken a

hike, skedaddled, scrammed. God has gone. [. . .] He comes, he goes, I wonder where? Into another head? Into a wasp in the sun? Into the bend in a path?' Genet, *The Screens*, p. 45; *Les Paravents*, p. 79.

67 'LEILA (*in a guttural tone, and talking as though trying to gather a crowd at a fair*): Who? . . . Who? And who still hasn't seen Saïd boned and dislocated when the cops get to work on him! And drooling blood and bleeding snot and oozing from every hole . . . who hasn't seen? [. . .] my man hanging around the jackets [. . .] prowling, crawling on all fours in the grass, his belly scraping up everything . . . [. . .] so cautious, so brisk, so green that he's a patch of leeks, so grey that he's my dry skin . . .' Genet, *The Screens*, p. 78; *Les Paravents*, pp. 133–4.

68 Claude Lévi-Strauss, *La Pensée sauvage* (Paris: Plon, 1962).

69 'We're the lords of language. To tamper with things is to tamper with language', Genet, *The Screens*, p. 78; *Les Paravents*, p. 114.

70 'That's what I deserve. That's what I want.' Genet, *The Screens*, p. 59; *Les Paravents*, p. 101.

71 'We come to you with civilisation and you go on living like tramps.' Genet, *The Screens*, p. 60; *Les Paravents*, p. 102.

72 'So, my fair Kadidja, you're dead! Kicked the bucket! Kicked it heroically. And if I wanted to talk to you, would I have to use the old Mouth of the dead again? But . . . you died doing what? Rousing the men and women to go to the limit? They'll go to the limit of what they are doing anyway, and of what they are becoming!' Genet, *The Screens*, p. 101; *Les Paravents*, p. 174.

73 Hélène Cixous, 'Dédicace à l'autruche', *Manne, aux Mandelstams aux Mandelas* (Paris: Editions des Femmes Antoinette Fouque, 1988).

74 'And they make such a fuss about it', Genet, *The Screens*, p. 126; *Les Paravents*, p. 209.

75 'NEDJMA: Nothing. Nothing to do. Usually time passes, like coffee through a strainer and in the strainer it filters out the incidental. Now time no longer passes.' Genet, *The Screens*, p. 126; *Les Paravents*, p. 210.

76 '. . . You drag a load of refuse beneath your crowns of rubies . . .' Jean Genet, *The Screens*, p. 128; *Les Paravents*, p. 211.

77 'KADIDJA (*smiling*): I died first.
THE MOTHER: Where does it get you? I died of exhaustion.' Genet, *The Screens*, pp. 129–30; *Les Paravents*, p. 213.

78 'KADIDJA: The image of me that I left behind . . . Can I see it?
SI SLIMANE: You want to know whether they've discovered that for twenty years you sold yourself to the soldiers? Everyone knew it by the end of the first month.' Genet, *The Screens*, pp. 127–8; *Les Paravents*, p. 211.

79 'THE CADI (*laughing*): No longer mine. Things cease to belong to those who have been able to make them more beautiful. Once they've been freed, let out, they become agile and scoot off and go and live elsewhere, on whom, on what, how they live, I don't give a shit, I don't give a toss. (*The women burst out laughing.*) . . . better and more beautiful, lightfooted, winged, they gratefully abandon the one who made them better. When they've gone, nothing left, not a particle, zero, fuck all!' Genet, *The Screens*, p. 124; *Les Paravents*, p. 207.

80 'You see . . . I'm rising . . . a lurch . . . Oh, nothing more. Is it the bottom? . . . I'm rising . . . and I'm floating to the surf . . . No? No. All right, if you say so that means it's true since everything's starting to be true . . . all right . . . There. Let's sink again with both

shoulders . . . (*She sinks finally into her dress which is made in such a way – from a sort of crinoline – that she can, towards the end, be swallowed up in it. Light returns to the stage.*)' Genet, *The Screens*, p. 138; *Les Paravents*, p. 223.

81 'WARDA (*to herself*): A whore! I, Warda, who was to fade away and leave in my place only a perfect whore, a simple skeleton, draped in gilded gowns, here am I becoming Warda again at top speed. (*Uttering a long wail, she starts tearing her dress. By the time* MALIKA *arrives she will be in rags.*)' Genet, *The Screens*, p. 116; *Les Paravents*, p. 199.

82 'a real monster of hatred and sadness', Genet, *Les Paravents*, p. 224.

83 Genet, *Les Paravents*, p. 230.

84 'France has already conquered, that is, she has offered an indelible image.' Genet, *The Screens*, p. 105; *Les Paravents*, p. 180.

85 '*The stage is empty. It's all over.*'

86 'THE MOTHER: Saïd! . . . I'll simply have to wait for him . . .
   KADIDJA (*laughing*): Don't bother. He won't be back any more than Leila will.
   THE MOTHER: Then where is he? In a song?
   (KADIDJA *gestures doubt.*)'
   Genet, *The Screens*, p.176; *Les Paravents*, p. 276.

87 'The Prussian Eagle. The emblem aims to impose – and succeeds in imposing – the idea of irrepressible force, and also the idea of violence and cruelty.' Genet, 'Commentaire du treizième tableau', *Les Paravents*, p. 194.

88 'Mme BLANKENSEE: [. . .] That love should begin with an act of betrayal perpetuated like the secret wound of an order one still respects.' Genet, *The Screens*, pp. 77–8; *Les Paravents*, p. 133.

89 'It's putting it badly to say that around an invisible wound a man piles up what hides that wound and at the same time he points his finger at it. So it seems to me that each character is simply a wound disappearing under ornaments and appearing through them.' Genet, *Les Paravents*, p. 141.

Bibliography

This is a list of works consulted or that have been especially helpful in the writing of this book.

Anderson, Stéphanie, *Le Discours féminin de Marguerite Duras, un désir pervers et ses métamorphoses*, Geneva: Droz, 1995

Anzieu, Didier, *Le Moi-peau*, Paris: Bordas, 1985

   Les Peintres cubistes, Paris: Hermann, 1980 (1913)

   Œuvres poétiques, ed. Marcel Adéma and Michel Décaudin, Paris: Gallimard, Editions de la Pléïade, 1965

Apollinaire, Guillaume, *Selected Writings*, trans. Roger Shattuck, New York: New Directions, 1971

Barthes, Roland, *Le Degré zéro de l'écriture*, Paris: Editions du Seuil, Collection Points, 1972 (1953)

   Essais critiques, Paris: Editions du Seuil, 1964

   Système de la mode, Paris: Editions du Seuil, 1967

   S/Z, Paris: Editions du Seuil, Points, 1970

   Le Plaisir du texte, Paris: Editions du Seuil, 1973

   Roland Barthes, Paris: Editions du Seuil, 1975

   Roland Barthes, trans. Richard Howard, London: Macmillan, 1988 (1977)

   Fragments d'un discours amoureux, Paris: Editions du Seuil, 1977

   Leçon, Paris: Editions du Seuil, 1978

   La Chambre claire, Paris: Editions Gallimard/Seuil, 1980

   Selected Writings, ed. with an introduction by Susan Sontag, London: Fontana/Collins, 1983

   The Fashion System, trans. Matthew Ward and Richard Howard, Berkeley and Los Angeles: University of California Press, 1990

   S/Z, trans. Richard Miller, Oxford: Blackwell Ltd, 1990

   The Pleasure of the Text, trans. Richard Miller, Oxford: Blackwell, 1990

   A Lover's Discourse: Fragments, trans. Richard Howard, Harmondsworth: Penguin Books, 1990

Bataille, Georges, 'Informe', *Documents* 7, Paris: 1929

    Le Bleu du ciel, Paris: Gallimard, Collection Imaginaire, 1991 (1957)

Baudelaire, Charles, *Œuvres complètes*, ed. Claude Pichois, vol. 1, Paris: Gallimard, Editions de la Pléïade, 1975

Beckett, Samuel, *Molloy*, Paris: Editions de Minuit, 1951

Benjamin, Walter, *One Way Street and Other Writings,* trans. Edmund Jephcott and Kingsley Shorter, London and New York: Verso, 1997 (1979)

Bersani, Leo, *The Freudian Body*, New York: Columbia University Press, 1990

    The Culture of Redemption, Cambridge, Mass.: Harvard University Press, 1992

    Homos, Cambridge, Mass. and London: Harvard University Press, 1995

Bhabha, Homi, *The Location of Culture*, London: Routledge, 1994

Blanchot, Maurice, *La Part du feu*, Paris: Gallimard, 1949

    La Communauté inavouable, Paris: Editions de Minuit, 1983

    The Work of Fire, trans. Charlotte Mandell, Stanford: Stanford University Press, 1995

Bloom, Harold, *The Anxiety of Influence*, Oxford: Oxford University Press, 1973

Booth, Wayne, *The Company We Keep: An Ethics of Fiction*, Berkeley and Los Angeles: University of California Press, 1986

Bowie, Malcolm, *Psychoanalysis and the Future of Theory,* Oxford: Blackwell, 1993

Bresnick, Adam, 'Absolute fetishism: genius and identification in Balzac's "Unknown Masterpiece"', *Paragraph* 17, 2 (July 1994), 134–52

Breton, André, *Les Pas perdus,* Paris: Gallimard, Collection Idées, 1979 (1924)

    Manifestes du Surrealisme, Paris: Gallimard, 1975 (1924, 1930)

    Nadja, Paris: Gallimard, 1928

    Les Vases communicants, Paris: Gallimard, Collection Idées, 1981 (1932)

    L'Amour fou, Paris: Gallimard, Collection Folio, 1997 (1937)

Brooks, Peter, and Joseph Halpern, eds., *Genet: A Collection of Critical Essays,* London: Prentice Hall, 1979

Brown, Andrew, *Roland Barthes: The Figures of Writing,* Oxford: Clarendon Press, 1992

Bryson, Norman, *Vision and Painting*, London: Macmillan, 1983

Butler, Judith, *Bodies That Matter: On the Discursive Limits of 'Sex',* New York: Routledge, 1993

Camus, Albert, *L'Etranger*, Paris: Gallimard, Collection Folio, 1972 (1942)

    Lettres à un ami allemand, Paris: Gallimard, Collection Blanche, 1984 (1948)

    La Chute, Paris: Gallimard, Collection Folio, 1972 (1956)

Cave, Terence, *Recognitions,* Oxford: Oxford University Press, 1990

Caws, Mary Ann, *The Surrealist Voice of Robert Desnos*, Amherst, Mass.: University of Massachusetts, 1977

Chénieux-Gendron, Jacqueline, ed., *Lire le regard: André Breton et la peinture,* Arles: Lachenal et Ritter, 1993

Cixous, Hélène, *Manne, aux Mandelstams aux Mandelas,* Paris: Editions des Femmes Antoinette Fouque, 1988

Cohen, Susan D., *Women and Discourse in the Fiction of Marguerite Duras: love legends and language*, London: Macmillan, 1993

Connor, Steven, *Theory and Cultural Value,* Oxford and Cambridge, Mass.: Blackwell, 1992

Critchley, Simon, *The Ethics of Deconstruction: Derrida and Levinas*, Oxford and
    Cambridge, Mass.: Blackwell, 1992
Derrida, Jacques, *Marges de la philosophie*, Paris: Editions de Minuit, 1972
    Glas, Paris: Denoël/Gauthier, 1981
    Signéponge, Paris: Editions du Seuil, 1988
    Donner le temps 1, La Fausse Monnaie, Paris: Galilée, 1991
Desnos, Robert, *Corps et biens*, Paris: Gallimard, Collection Poésie, 1968
    Nouvelles Hébrides et autres textes (1922–30), édition établie par Marie-Claire Dumas,
        Paris: Gallimard, 1978
    Ecrits sur l'art, préface de Marie-Claire Dumas, Paris: Flammarion, 1984
    The Selected Poems of Robert Desnos, trans. Carolyn Forché and William Kulik, New
        York: The Echo Press, 1991
Dessagne, Jacques, ed., *L'Ecriture griffée*, Catalogue de l'exposition du Musée d'Art
    Moderne de Saint Etienne, 1993
Didi-Huberman, Georges, *Le Cube et le visage autour d'un sculpteur: Alberto Giacometti*,
    Paris: Editions Macula, 1993
Dumas, Marie-Claire, *Robert Desnos ou l'exploration des limites*, Paris: Klinksieck, 1980
Duras, Marguerite, *Hiroshima mon amour*, Paris: Gallimard, Collection Folio, 1972
    L'Amant, Paris: Editions de Minuit, 1984
    Les Yeux bleus cheveux noirs, Paris: Editions de Minuit, 1986
    Duras by Duras, San Francisco: City Lights Books, 1987 (1976)
    La Vie matérielle, Paris: POL, 1987
    Blue Eyes, Black Hair, trans. Barbara Bray, London: HarperCollins, 1988
    La Douleur, Paris: Gallimard, Collection Folio, 1992
Felman, Shoshana, and Dori Laub, *Testimony: crises of witnessing in literature, psycho-
    analysis and history*, New York and London: Routledge, 1992
Flaubert, Gustave, *Madame Bovary*, Paris: Gallimard, Collection Folio, 1976 (1856)
    L'Education sentimentale, Paris: Gallimard, Collection Folio, 1972 (1869)
Foucault, Michel, *Les Mots et les choses*, Paris: Gallimard, 1966
    Ceci n'est pas une pipe, Montpelier: Fata Morgana, 1973
Freud, Sigmund, *New Introductory Lectures*, Pelican Freud Library 2, Harmondsworth:
    Penguin Books, 1973
    Totem and Taboo, London: Routledge, 1983
    Jokes and Their Relation to the Unconscious, Pelican Freud Library 6, Harmondsworth:
        Penguin Books, 1986 (1905)
    On Metapsychology, Pelican Freud Library 11, Harmondsworth: Penguin Books,
        1984
    Civilisation, Society and Religion, Pelican Freud Library 12, Harmondsworth:
        Penguin Books, 1985
Gallop, Jane, *Feminism and Psychoanalysis. The Daughter's Seduction*, London:
    Macmillan, 1982
Genet, Jean, *Les Bonnes*, Paris: Folio, Marc Barbezat–L'Arbalète, 1976 (1947)
    Haute surveillance, Paris: Gallimard, 1949
    Le Balcon, Paris: Gallimard, 1956
    Les Paravents, Paris: Folio, Marc Barbezat, L'Arbalète, 1985 (1961)

The Screens, trans. Bernard Frechtman, London: Faber and Faber, 1963

Œuvres complètes, vol. 4, Paris: Gallimard, 1968

Reflections on the Theatre and Other Writings, trans. Richard Seaver, London: Faber and Faber, 1972

Gide, André, *Paludes,* Paris: Gallimard, Collection Folio, 1983 (1920)

   Les Faux-Monnayeurs, Paris: Gallimard, Collection Folio, 1972 (1925)

Goldthorpe, Rhiannon, *Sartre: Literature and Theory,* Cambridge: Cambridge University Press, 1984

Green, André, *Narcissisme de vie, narcissisme de mort,* Paris: Editions de Minuit, 1983

Hill, Leslie, *Marguerite Duras: Apocalyptic Desires,* London: Routledge, 1993

Hugo, Victor, *Les Contemplations,* in *Œuvres poétiques*, edition établie et annotée par Pierre Albouy, Gallimard, Editions de la Pléïade, 1967 (1856)

Irigaray, Luce, *Speculum de l'autre femme,* Paris: Editions de Minuit, 1974

   Ethique de la différence sexuelle, Paris: Editions de Minuit, 1984

   Etre Deux, Paris: Editions Grasset et Fasquelle, 1997

Jameson, Fredric, *The Ideologies of Theory: Essays 1971–1986,* London: Routledge, 1988

Johnson, Barbara *Défigurations du langage poétique,* Paris: Flammarion, 1979

Kafka, Franz, *The Trial,* London: Penguin, 1994 (1925)

   The Castle, London: Penguin, 1997 (1926)

Krauss, Rosalind, E., *The Optical Unconscious,* Cambridge, Mass.: MIT Press, 1993

Kristeva, Julia, *Polylogue,* Paris: Editions du Seuil, 1972

   Pouvoirs de l'horreur, Essais sur l'abjection, Paris: Editions du Seuil, 1980

   Desire in Language: *A Semiotic Approach to Literature and Art,* ed. Leon S. Roudiez, trans. Thomas Gosz, Alice Jardine and Leon S. Roudiez, Oxford: Blackwell, 1981

   Soleil noir, Paris: Gallimard, 1987

   Black Sun, trans. Leon S. Roudiez, New York: Columbia University Press, 1989

Lacan, Jacques, *Ecrits,* Paris: Editions du Seuil, 1966

   Le Séminaire de Jacques Lacan, book XI, *Les Quatre Concepts fondamentaux de la psychanalyse,* Paris: Editions de Seuil, 1973

   Encore, Jacques Lacan, le séminaire, book XX, Paris: Editions du Seuil, 1975

   Ecrits: A Selection, trans. Alan Sheridan, London: Tavistock Publications, 1985 (1977)

   The Seminar of Jacques Lacan, book I, *Freud's Papers on Technique,* ed. Jacques-Alain Miller, trans. with notes by John Forrester, Cambridge: Cambridge University Press, 1988

Lavers, Annette, *Roland Barthes: Structuralism and After,* London: Methuen, 1982

Leiris, Michel, *Au verso des images,* Montpelier: Fata Morgana, 1980

Lévi-Strauss, Claude, *La Pensée sauvage,* Paris: Plon, 1962

   Anthropologie structurelle deux, Paris: Plon, 1973

Lyotard, Jean-François, *Les* TRANS*formateurs* DU*champ,* Paris: Editions Galilée, 1977

Lyotard, Jean-Francois and Jean Loup Thébaud, *Au Juste,* trans. Wlad Godzick as *Just Gaming,* with an afterword by Samuel Weber, trans. Brian Massumi, Manchester: Manchester University Press, 1985

Magritte, René, *Ecrits complets,* edition établie et annotée par André Blavier, Paris: Flammarion, 1979

Mathews, Timothy, *Reading Apollinaire. Theories of Poetic Language,* Manchester: Manchester University Press, 1987

Miller, J. Hillis, *The Ethics of Reading: Kant, De Man, Eliot, Trollope, James and Benjamin,* New York: Columbia University Press, 1987

Moriarty, Michael, *Roland Barthes,* Cambridge: Polity Press, 1991

Murat, Michel, *Robert Desnos: les grands jours du poète,* Paris: Editions José Corti, 1988

Nerval, Gerard de, *Œuvres complètes,* texte établi par H. Lemaître, Paris: Gallimard, 1986

Nietzsche, Friedrich, *Beyond Good and Evil,* Harmondsworth: Penguin Books, 1990

Noël, Bernard, *Magritte,* Paris: Flammarion, 1977

Nussbaum, Martha, *Love's Knowledge: Essays on Philosophy and Literature,* New York and Oxford: Oxford University Press, 1990

Oswald, Laura, *Jean Genet and the Semiotics of Performance,* Bloomington: Indiana University Press, 1989

Paris, Jean, *L'Espace et le regard,* Paris: 1965

Paulhan, Jean, *Fautrier l'enragé,* Paris: Gallimard, 1989 (1962)

Peyré, Yves, *Fautrier, ou les outrages de l'impossible,* Paris: Editions du Regard, 1990

Ponge, Francis, *Œuvres,* vol. 1, Paris: Gallimard, 1965

Proust, Marcel, *Le Temps retrouvé,* Paris: Gallimard, 1990 (1927)

Read, Barbara and Ian Birchall, eds., *Flowers and Revolution: a Collection of Writings on Jean Genet,* London: Middlesex University Press, 1997

Rimbaud, Arthur, *Œuvres,* ed. Suzanne Bernard, Paris: Garnier, 1960

  A Season in Hell and Illuminations, trans. Mark Treharne, London: J.M. Dent, 1998

Rorty, Richard, *Contingency, Irony and Solidarity,* Cambridge and New York: Cambridge University Press, 1986

Rosolato, Guy, *Essais sur le symbolique,* Paris: Gallimard, Collection Tel, 1969

Sartre, Jean-Paul, *L'Imaginaire,* Paris: Gallimard, Collection Idées, 1978 (1940)

  L'Etre et le néant, Paris: Gallimard, 1943

  Huis clos, Les Mouches, Paris: Gallimard, Collection Folio, 1976 (1947)

  Qu'est-ce que la littérature?, Paris: Editions Gallimard, Collection Idées, 1981 (1948)

  Situations III, Paris: Gallimard, 1949

  What is Literature?, trans. Bernard Frechtman, London: Methuen, 1950

  Saint Genet, comédien et martyre, in Jean Genet, *Œuvres complètes* vol. 1, Paris: Gallimard, 1952

  Les Séquestrés d'Altona, Paris: Gallimard, 1960

  Critique de la raison dialectique, vol. 1: *Théorie des ensembles pratiques,* Paris: Gallimard, 1960

  Critique de la raison dialectique, vol. 2: *L'Intelligibilité de l'histoire,* Paris: Gallimard, 1985

  L'Engagement de Mallarmé, Paris: Gallimard, Collection Arcades, 1986

Senghor, Léopold Sédar, ed., *Anthologie nouvelle de poésie nègre et malgache de la langue française,* Paris: Presses Universitaires de France, 1948

Starobinski, Jean, *Portrait de l'artiste en saltimbanque,* Paris: Flammarion, 1970

Stendhal, *La Chartreuse de Parme,* Paris: Gallimard, 1972 (1839)

Sylvester, David, *Magritte,* London: Thames and Hudson in association with Menil Foundation, 1992

Trilling, Lionel, *The Liberal Imagination: Essays on Literature and Society,* Oxford: Oxford University Press, 1981 (1940)

Williams, James S., *The Erotics of Passage: Pleasure, Politics and Form in the Later Works of Marguerite Duras,* Liverpool: Liverpool University Press, 1997

Whitfield, Sarah, *Magritte,* London: South Bank Centre, 1992

Wing, Nathaniel, *The Limits of Narrative,* Cambridge: Cambridge University Press, 1986

Wollheim, Richard, *Painting as an Art,* London: Thames and Hudson, 1987

Zizek, Slavoj, *The Sublime Object of Ideology,* London: Verso, 1989

Index

CAMBRIDGE STUDIES IN FRENCH

Gone Forever!
Woolly Mammoth

Rupert Matthews

Heinemann Library
Chicago, Illinois

Customer Service 888-454-2279
Visit our website at www.heinemannlibrary.com

Designed by Ron Kamen and Paul Davies & Associates
Illustrations by Maueen and Gordon Gray, James Field (SGA), and Darren Lingard
Originated by Ambassador Litho Ltd.
Printed and bound in China by South China Printing Company

07 06 05 04
10 9 8 7 6 5 4 3 2

Library of Congress Cataloging-in-Publication Data
Matthews, Rupert.
  Mammoth / Rupert Matthews.
    p. cm. -- (Gone forever)
Includes index.
Summary: Describes what has been learned about the physical appearance,
behavior, and surroundings of the long-extinct woolly mammoth.
  ISBN 1-40340-789-4 (HC), 1-4034-3417-4 (Pbk)
  1. Woolly mammoth--Juvenile literature. [1. Woolly mammoth. 2.
Mammoths. 3. Prehistoric animals.] I. Title. II. Gone forever
(Heinemann Library)
  QE882.P8 M37 2003
  569'.67--dc21

                     2002003699

Acknowledgments
The author and publishers are grateful to the following for permission to reproduce copyright material: p. 4 Roger Tidman/NHPA; p. 6 Francois Gohier/Ardea; p. 8 Corbis; p. 10 Scala Art Resource; p. 12 Masahiro Iijuna/Ardea; pp. 14, 18 Natural History Museum, London; p. 16 Novosti; p. 20 Stephen Kraseman/NHPA; p. 22 Peter Morris/Ardea; p. 24 Museum of Natural History, Vienna; p. 26 Science Photo Library.

Cover photo reproduced with permission of The Natural History Museum, London.

Special thanks to Dr. Peter Mackovicky for his review of this book.

Every effort has been made to contact copyright holders of any material reproduced in this book. Any omissions will be rectified in subsequent printings if notice is given to the publishers.

Some words are shown in bold, **like this.** You can find out what they mean by looking in the glossary.

Contents

Gone Forever!

Many thousands of years ago, the weather was very, very cold. Scientists call this time the **Ice Age.** Several kinds of animals lived during the Ice Age. Scientists know this because they have found **fossils** of these animals.

One of the animals that lived during the Ice Age
was the woolly mammoth. When warmer weather
came, the woolly mammoth became **extinct.**
This means that all the woolly mammoths died.

Woolly Mammoth's Home

Woolly mammoths lived where there were deep **valleys** with very steep sides. The valleys were formed by huge sheets of ice called **glaciers.** The glaciers filled the valleys with thick layers of ice.

6

Much of the land was covered with solid ice, and it was very cold. In places where the woolly mammoth lived, it snowed for most of the year. But some plants grew for part of the year.

Plants

Scientists learn which plants grew many years ago by studying old plant seeds. These plant seeds were trapped in the ground a long time ago. Today, scientists dig them up to learn about them.

At the time of the woolly mammoth, some plants could live in the cold weather. These plants included short trees, like **birch** and **willow,** and bushes, like **heather.** Grasses grew during the short summer.

9

Other Animals

Several other types of animal lived in the
Ice Age besides the woolly mammoth.
Humans also lived at this time. They painted
pictures on cave walls that show some of
these animals.

**cave painting from
Lascaux, France**

The **woolly rhinoceros** lived at the same time as the woolly mammoth. The woolly rhinoceros was covered in fur to keep it warm. It had one long horn and one shorter horn. Like the woolly mammoth, this animal is now **extinct.**

What Was the Woolly Mammoth?

Scientists have found some bodies of woolly mammoths frozen in the ground in Alaska and Siberia. Ice in the ground has **preserved** their bodies. Scientists have studied these frozen woolly mammoths to find out how they lived.

The woolly mammoth was a type of elephant. It had a thick coat of fur to keep it warm. The animal also had thick layers of fat over its shoulders.

Baby Woolly Mammoths

**remains
of a baby
mammoth**

Some scientists think that woolly mammoths spent
the winter in warmer places to the south. Babies
would have been born in the spring, when the
woolly mammoths moved back north again.
The babies took several years to grow into adults.

14

Young woolly mammoths were looked after by their mothers. For several years, each youngster followed its mother. The mother showed it which plants were good to eat and where to go to get away from the wind, rain, and snow.

The Woolly Coat

Scientists have found frozen woolly mammoths that still have their woolly **hides.** These show that the woolly mammoth had two types of hair. The outside hair was long and thick. There was soft fur under this hair.

16

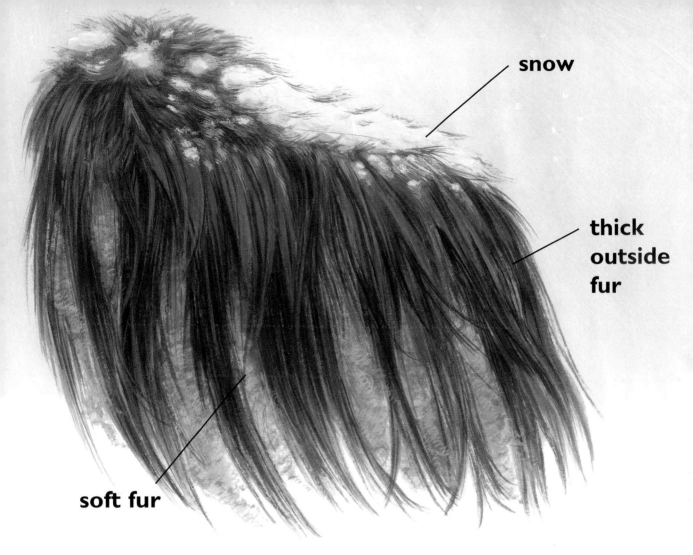

snow

thick outside fur

soft fur

The soft fur next to its skin kept the woolly mammoth warm in the coldest weather. The thick outside hair stopped snow or rain from reaching the soft fur and making it wet and cold.

17

The Mighty Tusks

Woolly mammoths had pointed, curved **tusks.**
Some were as long as 10 feet (3 meters). That is
as long as a car. Each one weighed as much as
you plus two friends.

The tusks had cuts on the bottom sides, because woolly mammoths rubbed their tusks along the ground. They may have used them to push the snow off plants that they wanted to eat.

19

A Herd on the Move

During the winter, the land in the north became very cold. Deep snow covered the ground, and there was nothing for woolly mammoths to eat. The woolly mammoths moved south to warmer areas to find food.

Woolly mammoths may have marched south in small
herds. Each herd was probably led by the oldest
female mammoth. When it got warmer in the spring,
the woolly mammoths moved north again.

Feast for a Woolly Mammoth

The teeth of the woolly mammoth were large and strong. They had a surface made up of many sharp **ridges.** These ridges show that the woolly mammoth ate tough plants like grasses or pine needles.

woolly mammoth tooth

ridges

22

The woolly mammoth used its **trunk** to pull grass from the ground or needles from pine trees. Then the mammoth used its trunk to put the food in its mouth. The teeth chewed and smashed the plants before they were swallowed.

Lion Attack!

The bodies of large lions have been found in the same places as woolly mammoth bodies. These lions had powerful claws and long, sharp teeth. They used these to attack their **prey.**

**fossil of a
lion's skull**

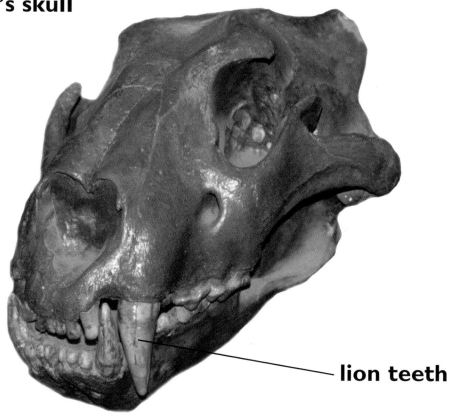

lion teeth

Lions and other animals probably attacked young woolly mammoths. Adult woolly mammoths would try to protect the young ones. If the attacker could not reach the young easily, it would give up and leave.

Hunted by Humans

Scientists have found pieces of human campsites near where woolly mammoths lived. Many mammoth bones have been found at these sites. Woolly mammoths were very useful to humans.

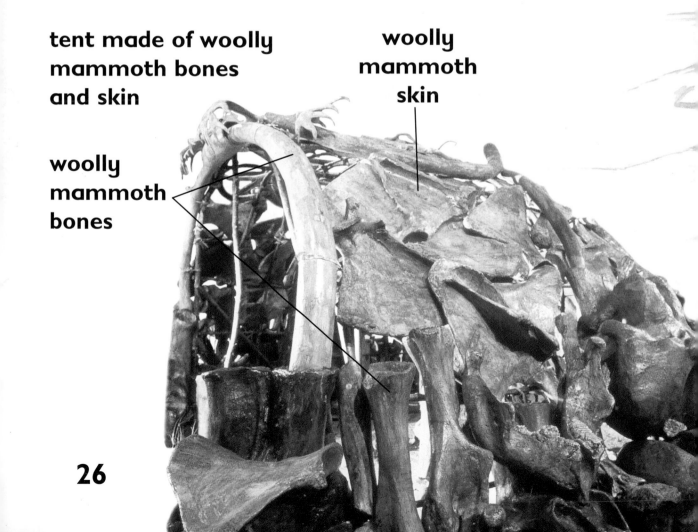

tent made of woolly mammoth bones and skin

woolly mammoth skin

woolly mammoth bones

Humans ate the meat of woolly mammoths. They used the skins of woolly mammoths to make clothes and tents. They built **huts** out of woolly mammoth **tusks** and leg bones.

27

Where Did Woolly Mammoths Live?

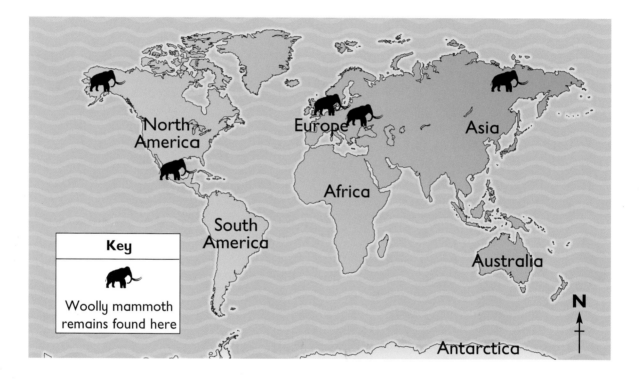

Woolly mammoths lived across the northern lands of the world. Most woolly mammoths lived in northern Asia and Europe, but some lived in North America.

28

When Did Woolly Mammoths Live?

Mammoths lived on Earth from about three million years ago to about 4,500 years ago. We call these years the Age of Mammals. This was during the Pliocene and Pleistocene **Epochs.**

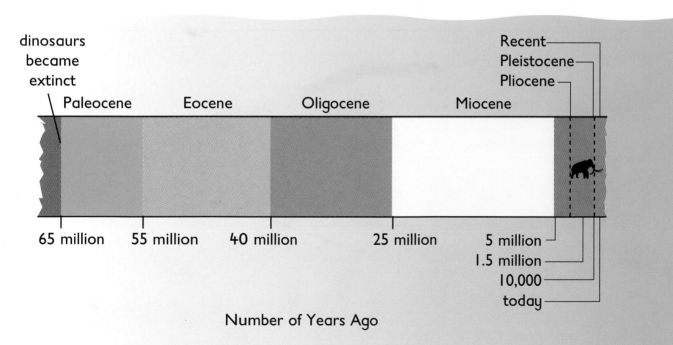

dinosaurs became extinct

| Recent
| Pleistocene
| Pliocene

Paleocene   Eocene   Oligocene   Miocene

65 million   55 million   40 million   25 million   5 million
1.5 million
10,000
today

Number of Years Ago

Fact File

Woolly Mammoth	
Length:	about 10 feet (3 meters)
Weight:	up to 5 tons (4.5 metric tons)
Time:	Pliocene and Pleistocene Epochs, between 3 million and 4,500 years ago
Place:	Asia, Europe and North America

How to Say It

mammoth—maam-uth
Pleistocene—pli-stow-seen
rhinoceros—ri-nah-ser-us

Glossary

birch short tree with white bark that can grow in places where the weather is very cold

epoch a time period of millions of years that happened a very long time ago

extinct no longer living on Earth

fossil remains of a plant or animal, usually found in rocks

glacier huge sheet of ice

heather woody bush with purple flowers

herd group of plant-eating animals that live together

hide animal's skin

hut house built of wood, bones, animals skins, or other things

Ice Age very cold period of time. An Ice Age lasts many years.

preserve make something last a long time

prey animal hunted for food

ridge bumpy edge

trunk long nose used by the woolly mammoth and the modern-day elephant to gather food

tusk very long tooth

valley low area of land found between hills and mountains

willow tree with narrow leaves, often found near water

woolly rhinoceros type of rhinoceros with thick fur. It is now extinct.

31

More Books to Read

Goecke, Michael P. *Woolly Mammoth*. Edina, Minn.: Abdo Publishing Company, 2003.
Miller, Debbie S. *A Woolly Mammoth Journey*. Boston: Little Brown & Co., 2001.

An older person can help you read this book.
Hehner, Barbara. *Ice Age Mammoth: Will This Ancient Giant come Back to Life?* New York: Crown Publishing, 2001.

Index